Literature and the Critic

This timely volume presents a rich and absorbing selection of extracts from over two hundred leading literary critics of the last several decades, writing on many of the most widely studied literary texts in English, from Shakespeare to Toni Morrison.

Structured chronologically, working through familiar literary periods, this book presents illuminating and stimulating examples of critical readings of familiar texts, demonstrating a variety of methods and approaches to critical practice. The range of critical voices represented – from Abrams and Adelman to Zimmerman and Žižek – provides students with eloquent and insightful models of how to read, think and write about texts so that they can form their own critical responses and develop as independent readers. The book also shows how criticism has developed over time and how it has always been intimately involved in wider cultural, social and political debates. Connections between criticism, culture and politics are explored in the book's wide-ranging first chapter.

In his warm, clear and engaging style, Richard Jacobs provides the perfect introduction to literature and criticism. *Literature and the Critics* is a book to which students will want to return throughout their courses as they read more widely and encounter new texts and critical voices.

Richard Jacobs is an Honorary Fellow at the University of Brighton, School of Humanities, UK where he was subject leader for literature and Principal Lecturer for many years and where he received teaching excellence awards. His many publications include *A Beginner's Guide to Critical Reading: An Anthology of Literary Texts* (2001) and *Literature in Our Lives: Talking About Texts from Shakespeare to Philip Pullman* (2020).

Literature and the Critics

Developing Responses to Texts

Richard Jacobs

with Sam Cutting, Sean McEvoy and Joel Roberts

LONDON AND NEW YORK

First published 2022
by Routledge
4 Park Square, Milton Park, Abingdon, Oxon OX14 4RN

and by Routledge
605 Third Avenue, New York, NY 10158

Routledge is an imprint of the Taylor & Francis Group, an informa business

British Library Cataloguing-in-Publication Data
A catalogue record for this book is available from the British Library

Library of Congress Cataloging-in-Publication Data
A catalog record has been requested for this book

ISBN: 978-0-367-65040-7 (hbk)
ISBN: 978-0-367-65038-4 (pbk)
ISBN: 978-1-003-12756-7 (ebk)

DOI: 10.4324/9781003127567

Typeset in Bembo
by Taylor & Francis Books

Contents

Acknowledgements

The first and most obvious debt to acknowledge is to Sam Cutting, Sean McEvoy and Joel Roberts whose contributions to Chapter 2, Chapter 3 and Chapter 9 were indispensable to the project and without which the book would have been a much lesser thing. I'm enormously grateful to them for their work.

Sean contributed much more than words on the page. He was intimately involved in the project from the very start, advising and helping move it forward throughout its evolution, reading and providing feedback on many of the chapters and offering assistance in many ways. I really can't thank Sean enough for his unstinting support and friendship.

Rosanna Wood also read and advised on some of the chapters and I'm very grateful to her, as I am to Kate Aughterson for critical advice on Aphra Behn, and to Will Norman for kind permission to include unpublished material from a forthcoming book.

Warmest thanks to Polly Dodson at Routledge for commissioning the book and supporting it throughout with her help and advice. Thanks also to the editorial team at Routledge.

This book has, in retrospect, turned out to be the third and last of a trilogy of books published by Routledge addressed to and devoted to supporting students of literature. The first was *A Beginner's Guide to Critical Reading: An Anthology of Literary Texts* (2001) and the second was *Literature in Our Lives: Talking About Texts from Shakespeare to Philip Pullman* (2020). The first was a hybrid of primary texts and commentaries; the second was a collection of lectures. This third and last one shares with the others a desire to model what it means to be critically engaged with literature.

All three are personal books coming directly out of 45 years of teaching at university and at post-16 in the UK (and for a year in the US). I want to acknowledge and thank those many thousands of students, some of them now friends, at the University of Brighton, the College of Richard Collyer, and Westminster School, who collectively, over those 45 years, made these books (and more broadly a fulfilling professional life) possible. Thank you to them.

As ever, I'm deeply grateful to Winnie and Rose for their love and forbearance. For this has not been an easy book to write.

Introduction

What this book is, how it is different, and how to use it

What is this book trying to do? The principal objective is to provide you with a rich and varied collection of numerous short literary-critical extracts on a wide range of English and American literary texts that you may well meet in your studies, from about 1600 to the present. The extracts have been selected from over two hundred leading critics (with a large proportion from the US) in the period from the 1930s and 1940s up to the contemporary critical-theoretical scene, with a sprinkling from the 18th and 19th centuries. (As I planned the book it became clear that it would be something of a tribute to what in retrospect looks like a golden age of Anglo-American criticism from about 1940 to about 1980.) A simple way of describing the book might be this: the best critics on the best books.

This book is different from other literary guides or companions principally because it is organized around the literary texts that you study and enjoy. Other books are typically arranged by critical 'school', and anthologies of criticism of that kind assume that it's the story of criticism and theory in the abstract that you want to know about. Such books rarely if ever provide you with easily arranged access to what critics (or theorists) have said about your primary texts. Collections of criticism on primary texts, on the other hand, are almost always based around single texts and the critical materials provided can often be very lengthy and challenging. And that means buying or reading very many books to 'cover' the authors on your course.

So this book is different and using it should be straightforward and, I very much hope, enjoyably friendly. It's just one book (covering, as I say, Shakespeare to today) and the extracts from critics are all short and, in almost all cases, edited for even easier reading (as well as for reasons of space).

Using the Contents page, or the lists of authors in bold (which are in the order in which they appear in the text) at the head of each chapter, or the Index, you will quickly find what you want. If you want, for instance, to sample some critical extracts on the love poetry of John Donne, you'll quickly discover that he's in Chapter 3 and you'll see how I contextualize his poetry and present short critical extracts from leading Donne critics, with my thoughts

DOI: 10.4324/9781003127567-1

running between them. So, in effect, each author dealt with in the book will be there as a kind of narrative: critical materials with a thread of commentary between them. If, to take another example, you want to explore more generally in what we call romanticism, you'll quickly see that the topic is spread over two chapters (Chapters 4 and 5) where, again, you'll find the term discussed in its historical contexts and then a rich variety of authors, each with his or her critical extracts with, again, a thread that aims to link them together in a kind of story.

So each of the chronologically arranged chapters (Chapters 2–9) takes a defined period of literary history in the way that will reflect the organization of many of your literature courses. The importance of the long 19th century, encompassing as it does romanticism, the realist novel and the movement towards modernism, is reflected in the four chapters devoted to it (Chapters 4–7). By the same token Shakespeare has a chapter to himself (Chapter 2). In each case I've tried to contextualize the periods as the book unfolds and explain some key terms as we meet them.

Chapter 1 takes a broader view of literature and the critics. Rather than trace a chronological path through the field, it follows its own narrative which I hope you find stimulating. Starting with Disney's *Beauty and the Beast* and the iconic 1931 film *Frankenstein*, the chapter explores a series of cultural interactions between texts and history.

I'll say here that I've tried to make the book read without the hindrances of too much academic baggage. So the references to almost all the primary texts are restricted to chapter (and act/scene) numbers and are not tied to any particular editions. (The editions used for the older texts are all in the public domain). References to the critical materials (in brackets and in abbreviated form after each quotation in the body of the text) are keyed to the 'Works cited' list (critical works) at the end of each chapter: these are sources that you are likely to find most easily when it comes to things like journal articles or less known books.

A personal book, for your own personal journeys

My aim throughout is to provide you with models of how to read, think and write about literary texts, so that you can help develop and articulate your own literary-critical voices. (That's why my subtitle is 'Developing Responses to Texts'.) The short critical extracts provided have been chosen as ones that are particularly eloquent and inspiring, to give you the confidence to believe in and develop your own critical powers. The aim is also to send you away to read more extensively in the books and articles by the chosen critics. The extracts are there, not to replace or stand in for the whole books, but to entice you into them. I think and hope that this is a book to which you will want to return throughout your courses as you read more and more widely.

Rather than a neutral and uninterrupted presentation of the critical extracts as we move through the primary texts, I've made the book speak with what I hope is a personal voice. I didn't want to come across as a disinterested (or even absent) authority as that is the last thing I feel like. Indeed, I've intervened regularly with my own thoughts and feelings about the books and the critics, in some cases with ideas that have been developed in the course of researching and writing this book. This happened, for instance, with Wordsworth where the critics I chose made me realize how I had things to say myself, very belatedly (as my Wordsworth-loving students would correctly say). So it has been an education for me as well, to write the book. And for the same reason I've made little attempt to ensure that all the mainstream ('canonical') writers have the same space allocated to them. Some big names are missing, again for personal reasons. (I'd better name D.H. Lawrence as one obvious example.)

So it's a personal book. And I want it to be a book to which you too respond personally and with the effect of enlarging and enriching your critical and therefore your personal lives. During its course, I'll have the chance to share with you many of the critics who have spoken most powerfully and eloquently to me over the years, some of whom were directly caught up in the difficult currents of mid-20th century politics and cultural arguments. Critical and cultural writing is never done in a vacuum.

One other thing. I've been inspired, over a long teaching life, by scores of critics from a wide variety of 'schools' of criticism and theory, but I should say now that this book, though certainly giving space to that variety, has not been led by the need to classify and separate such critical schools or to give you a potted history of criticism and theory. The starting point has been the primary texts that you study and enjoy, which, of course, is why the chapters that follow Chapter 1 are arranged in their chronological order. The critical extracts chosen are chosen for their ability to illuminate those texts rather than because of their allegiance to particular schools or approaches. You'll find many key players in 'literary theory' here, but they're here more because of what they say about the primary texts than what they say about theory.

But I'll say this here. Modern criticism and theory have excitingly opened out the discipline to many pressing contemporary concerns, especially in relation to gender and sexuality, race and the environment, as well as the workings of the unconscious, so I'll use this opportunity to share as samples a few very vivid extracts from leading critics (and practitioners) in their fields before we move to the main business of this book. Critics in these fields all share the critique of older notions of the 'essentialist' nature of the self, of the subject or indeed of 'human nature' (more on 'essentialist' criticism in Chapter 1).

A critical sampling

I'll start this very short sampling with Nancy Armstrong's great 1989 book *Desire and Domestic Fiction* (more below and in Chapter 5). She responds here to a classic and, in its emphases, very male account of early fiction in Ian Watt's 1957 *The Rise of the Novel* when, needing to include Jane Austen in the narrative, Watt rather lamely says this.

> The feminine sensibility was in some ways better equipped to reveal the intricacies of personal relationships and was therefore at a real advantage in the realm of the novel.
>
> (Watt 1957: 57)

Armstrong has some questions to ask.

> Why the 'female sensibility'? How 'better equipped'? What 'intricacies'? Whose 'personal relationships'? Why 'an advantage in the realm of the novel'? And, finally, how did all this become commonplace?
>
> (Armstrong 1989: 7)

Criticism asks questions but rarely as pointedly as that. Judith Butler and Eve Sedgwick are equivalently interrogative and they both published in 1993 strong challenges to conventional thinking about gender and sexuality. Butler is best known for her major intervention *Gender Trouble* (1990) in which she says that gender identity 'is performatively constituted by the very "expressions" that are said to be its results' (Butler 1990: 25), and in an essay three years later she said this about sex and gender as performances.

> If heterosexuality is compelled to *repeat itself* in order to establish the illusion of its own uniformity and identity, then this is an identity permanently at risk, for what if it fails to repeat, or if the very exercise of repetition is redeployed for a very different performative purpose? If there is … always a compulsion to repeat, repetition never fully accomplishes identity.
>
> (In Abelove et al. edd. 1993: 315)

And Sedgwick, in her book *Tendencies*, defined 'queer' in this collectively empowering way.

> [It embraces] the open mesh of possibilities, gaps, overlaps, dissonances and resonances, lapses and excesses of meaning when the constituent elements of anyone's gender, of anyone's sexuality aren't made (or *can't* be made) to signify monolithically.
>
> (Sedgwick 1993: 8)

Race and postcoloniality critics draw on the truly startling fact that 'more than three-quarters of the people living in the world today have had their lives shaped by the shared experience of colonialism' (Ashcroft et al. 1989: 1). Colonialism notoriously identifies subjected peoples as 'other', and Andrew Bennett and Nicholas Royle make this powerful point.

> The internationalising of contemporary 'English' literature … has also permanently altered our conception of such 'otherness'. The emphatic multi-culturalism of the postcolonial canon suggests … that the racial,

> linguistic and cultural 'other' may indeed be conceived as the white Anglo-Saxon writer him- or herself. … The heterogeneity of postcolonial discourses itself provokes a questioning of the apparently stable, established values of canonicity, with its assumptions of paternity and inheritance, its homogenizing linearity of influence, and its cultural exclusivity.
>
> (Bennett and Royle 2014: 238)

And they insist that racism is, more than anything, the 'delusion of essentialism'. Ideas about the essential 'nature of humanity' coincide with what Robert Young called 'those particularly violent centuries in the history of the world now known as the era of Western colonialization' (Young 1990: 121).

There is a close connection between the colonial project and the establishment of English Literature as an academic discipline with, notoriously, Shakespeare vigorously deployed in the colonies, especially in India, to 'anglicize' the population (as we'll see in Chapter 2). Gauri Vismanathan says this in her 1989 book *Masks of Conquest.*

> The amazingly young history of the English literature as a subject of study (it is less than a hundred and fifty years old) is frequently noted, but less appreciated is the irony that English literature appeared as a subject in the curriculum of the colonies long before it was institutionalized in the home country.
>
> (Vismanathan 1989: 2–3)

Eco or green theory may be said to start with the great Kenneth Burke who died in 1993. Not long before he died, he wrote a statement of his ideas in the form of a poem (in capitals) and based on an article he'd written decades earlier. (By 'perfection' Burke means the ruinous pride that drives humans to 'perfect' what they have begun, regardless of its effects.)

> BEING BODIES THAT LEARN LANGUAGE
> THEREBY BECOMING WORLDLINGS
> HUMANS ARE THE
> SYMBOL-MAKING, SYMBOL-USING, SYMBOL-MISUSING ANIMAL…
> SEPARATED FROM OUR NATURAL CONDITION
> BY INSTRUMENTS OF OUR OWN MAKING
> GOADED BY THE SPIRIT OF HIERARCHY…
> AND ROTTEN WITH PERFECTION
>
> (In Simons and Melia edd. 1989: 263)

In a wonderful moment in his first book (1931), Burke says that the value of literature and of criticism lies in 'preventing a society from becoming too assertively, too hopelessly itself' (Burke 1968: 105).

In the next chapter we'll meet David Jones whose 1937 masterpiece of the First World War *In Parenthesis* also anticipates the anxiety about progress and the environment. In another wonderful moment, Jones in the Preface says this: 'Even while we watch the boatman mending his sail, the petroleum is hurting the sea' (Jones 1963: ix).

The modern painter Francis Bacon gave a series of extraordinary interviews with the art critic David Sylvester in 1975 and these had a considerable impact on many people of my age when we were students. At one point he gives an account of how, struggling to paint a particular friend's head, and in a state where he 'simply didn't know' what he was doing, it suddenly 'clicked' – but not in any way connected with his 'conscious will' or, even less, with what he calls 'illustration' and its demands for consciously intended accuracy. Bacon says this. (His use here of 'poignant' and 'poignantly' is peculiarly touching.)

> What has never yet been analysed is why this particular way of painting is more poignant than illustration. I suppose because it has a life completely of its own. It lives on its own like the image one's trying to trap; it lives on its own and therefore transfers the … image more poignantly. So that the artist may be able to open up or rather, should I say, unlock the valves of feeling and therefore return the onlooker to life more violently.
>
> (Sylvester 1975: 17)

Returning us to life 'more violently' is strongly (indeed, poignantly) worded and it struck a deep chord with many of us in the 1970s as we tried to work as critical readers of texts. This, we felt, was what the great texts do: and it was the role of criticism to further that process – as critics and as teachers.

As a university teacher towards the end of my career, I think I unintentionally echoed Bacon when, in a book about teaching narrative, I contrasted the ways we can be moved to tears by a text. On the one hand, as part of an audience in the theatre or cinema, the tears can seem (I wonder if you've felt this?) somehow not quite ours and somehow displaced 'out there' on the stage or screen. On the other hand, the tears we shed when finishing a novel are somehow intensified by being shed alone in the presence of just words on the page, and with the inconsolable absence of the community of presences those words had evoked in our heads. After finishing the novel in that painfully solitary way, we are returned to communal life in a more complex, more provisional but also more powerfully lasting way.

I'd like to end this sampling with two of the exemplary figures whom we'll be meeting soon in this book, both French. They are Roland Barthes and Michel Foucault. (Sadly, Barthes and Foucault both died prematurely. Barthes died in his early sixties after being hit by a delivery van in a Paris street; Foucault died in his mid-fifties of AIDS.)

Here's Barthes in his wonderful book, *A Lover's Discourse*, originally published in 1977. This is on jealousy. Vividly personal, it has illuminated most of the texts about love that I've turned to again and again, like Shakespeare's Sonnets, Keats's letters and poems (more on Keats in love at the end of Chapter 4) and Proust's *In Search of Lost Time*. What such texts insist on is that love is constituted in jealousy and loss. Love thrives on obstacles. (The key theorist here is Denis de Rougemont whom we'll meet in Chapter 1 and we'll see more on love's obstacles when we read the Sonnets in Chapter 2.)

> As a jealous man, I suffer four times over: because I am jealous, because I blame myself for being so, because I fear that my jealousy will wound the other, because I allow myself to be subject to a banality. I suffer from being excluded, from being aggressive, from being crazy, from being vulgar.
>
> (Barthes 2002: 146)

And to end with one of the funniest things in the entire critical-cultural field, Foucault, at the start of *The Order of Things* (originally published in 1966), tells how his book arose out of his coming across an almost certainly fictitious Chinese encyclopaedia, as popularized (invented?) by the Argentinian fabulist Jorge Luis Borges. (So we're ending this sampling with Borges as much as Foucault.) Here's the alleged encyclopaedia entry.

> Animals are divided into: (a) belonging to the Emperor, (b) embalmed, (c) tame, (d) sucking pigs, (e) sirens, (f) fabulous, (g) stray dogs, (h) included in the present classification, (i) frenzied, (j) innumerable, (k) drawn with a very fine camelhair brush, (l) *et cetera*, (m) having just broken the water pitcher, (n) that from a long way off look like flies.

And Foucault says this.

> In the wonderment of this taxonomy, the thing we apprehend in one great leap … [about] the exotic charm of another system of thought, is the limitation of our own, the stark impossibility of thinking *that*. But what is it impossible to think, and what kind of impossibility are we faced with here?
>
> (Foucault 1970: xv)

A last word as we move into the chapters that follow. The book is devoted to beliefs I've expressed before: that criticism is the process of making meanings that are socially produced, changing, various and multiple; that texts, creative and critical, are interventions in social processes; that contexts are the conditions of possibility for the production and consumption of texts; contexts are the means whereby the text finds and makes a place in the world, the ways in which it is enabled to speak and the ways in which it makes a difference. Criticism is the act of contextualizing and thereby an opening out that returns us to the text in an adventure that never finishes. Criticism and theory are perhaps best seen as the names for good reading. Good reading is the asking of questions that generate more and better questions.

Good reading advances critical literacy. Good educational policy from an enlightened government would place critical literacy at the heart of the curriculum. But it isn't, for the obvious reason that critical literacy is inherently political. K.M. Newton in 1988 put it clearly enough. The 'crisis' he mentions is one that we always face.

> Ultimately literary criticism is about politics and power, and a sign of crisis is more likely to be a situation in which debate and rational argument are stifled than one in which they are conducted vigorously.
>
> (Newton 1988: 16)

I'll just add that late in the writing of this book I revisited Nancy Armstrong's *Desire and Domestic Fiction* (quoted above and you'll also find her book excerpted in Chapter 5) and was much heartened by what she says at the end of her first chapter.

> I have made no effort to be faithful to any particular theory … Rather than distinguish theory from interpretation, and feminism from Marxism, deconstructionism, or formalism, I care mainly about those scholars and critics who have helped me to discover traces of the history of the present in several [older] texts and to understand my own insights as part of the larger project now going on within those disciplines where individuals have undertaken the work of creating a new political literacy.
>
> (Armstrong 1989: 27)

This book collects, and is dedicated to share with you, examples of the best that critical readings can offer: to stimulate, inspire and help you on your own critical journeys. I wish you the very best as you journey deeper and further.

Works cited

Henry Abelove *et al.* edd., *The Lesbian and Gay Studies Reader* (Routledge: 1993)
Nancy Armstrong, *Desire and Domestic Fiction* (Oxford U.P.: 1989)
Bill Ashcroft *et al.*, *The Empire Writes Back* (Routledge: 1989)
Roland Barthes, *A Lover's Discourse* trs. Richard Howard (Vintage: 2002)
Andrew Bennett and Nicholas Royle, *An Introduction to Literature, Criticism and Theory* (Routledge: 2014)
Kenneth Burke, *Counter-Statement* (California U.P.: 1968)
Judith Butler, *Gender Trouble* (Routledge: 1990)
Michel Foucault, *The Order of Things* trs. Alan Sheridan (Pantheon: 1970)
David Jones, *In Parenthesis* (Faber: 1963)
K.M. Newton, *Twentieth Century Literary Theory* (Macmillan: 1988)
Eve Sedgwick, *Tendencies* (Duke U.P.: 1993)
Herbert Simons and Trevor Melia, *The Legacy of Kenneth Burke* (Wisconsin U.P.: 1989)
David Sylvester, *Interviews with Francis Bacon* (Thames and Hudson: 1975)
Gauri Vismanathan, *Masks of Conquest* (Columbia U.P.: 1989)
Ian Watt, *The Rise of the Novel* (California U.P.: 1957)
Robert Young, *White Mythologies* (Routledge: 1990)

1 Literature, criticism, culture, and why they matter

Disney, *Frankenstein, Hamlet*: adaptations and interventions

Unlike the eight chronologically arranged chapters that follow this one, this first chapter will take a broader view of literature and the critics in the context of culture more generally understood, which means understanding culture in necessarily social and political terms. As a means of leading you into the chapters that follow, we'll explore a series of encounters between texts, criticism, culture and history. This first chapter serves also as a statement about the role that criticism plays or should play in our cultural and therefore our social lives.

So let's start with Disney.

Disney's 1991 *Beauty and the Beast* was affected by criticism Disney had received over *The Little Mermaid* from two years earlier, which, among other things, eroticized its pubescent mermaid in her search for a boyfriend. The studio hired a woman screenwriter for the new film and promised its heroine would be more modern, active and even 'feminist'. Those qualities were presumably meant to be reflected in Belle reading books. But it's what Disney did with their Beast that really stirred things up. It was a striking example of criticism as creative re-reading – in this case of a series of texts in a cultural tradition. Kathi Maio takes up the story, in her vivid 1998 critical response to Disney's critical intervention.

> The original fairy-tale (and all the retellings I've ever read or seen [including] Cocteau's 1946 movie masterpiece) portrayed the 'Beast' of the story as a big teddy bear. He looked fierce and strange, but was really kind, tender – and hopelessly devoted … But Disney admitted that they went out of their way to create a hero with a 'very serious problem'. Their Beast … terrorizes his household staff. And he intimidates his lovely prisoner as well. Although he isn't violent with Belle, that always seems a distinct possibility. It is her poise and exquisite beauty that tame his savagery. The problem? Disney's reworking of the old fable implies that women are responsible for controlling male anger and violence. If a woman is only pretty and sweet enough, she can

DOI: 10.4324/9781003127567-2

> transform an abusive man into a prince – forever. If only it were true. But this is a blame-the-victim scenario waiting to happen.
>
> (Maio 1998: online)

The film was an enormous hit and led to an equally successful stage musical – and, in 1992, the film *Aladdin*, which made little attempt to hide what Maio calls its 'obvious racism and ethnic stereotyping', including the 'most insulting' of the 'fresh-faced American' looking hero's lyrics which ran: 'I come from a land … where they cut off your ears if they don't like your face. It's barbaric, but hey, it's home.' (Those words were later removed from the video version.)

Sometimes it takes something said in person by someone you know for a critical response to hit really hard. Some years ago, a colleague of mine told a hall full of first year undergraduates, during the annual 'Disney debate' that concluded a Narrative module I used to run, what she had learned as a little girl from the films. She said this: 'I knew I would never be happy because I wasn't beautiful'.

A brief word on another fairy-tale, Red Riding Hood. Critical historians have traced the way this story evolved from a medieval oral tale ('The Grandmother'), through Perrault's 18th century and then Grimm's 19th century versions to the composite versions we know today. Here the retellings have enacted a process of gendered critical responses, criticism as re-reading again. The tale first emerges in a matriarchal culture and celebrates female cunning, with an unnamed young girl using her wits to fool and escape from her male sexual aggressor (in the oral version); and it evolves into a micro-novel about a young woman – characterized, in the way novels do, as vain, gullible and disobedient – who is rescued by the forest's patriarchal guardian and who learns to internalize the blame for her own 'rape' (in the Grimm version).

Internalizing the blame is what women do. It's what my colleague did as a child, blaming herself for not being as 'beautiful' as Disney babes. (She is.) The unnamed narrator of 'The Yellow Wallpaper' internalizes the hysteria with which she's labelled but which is actually her husband's (more in Chapter 8). Desdemona, murdered by Othello (smothered: in effect death by rape), dies claiming it's her own fault.

Let's go to another landmark critical intervention into a key cultural text. It's another film adaptation and it led, again, to a fine and strongly argued recent critical response.

When Mary Shelley's *Frankenstein* was turned into the hit 1931 film (with Boris Karloff), many changes to the novel, as is always the case with film adaptations, were made. (For more on the novel and its key role in romanticism, see Chapter 5.) But Paul O'Flinn's important 1983 essay showed how extraordinary some of the changes were, especially to the nature of the Creature, and to the ending, changes that played into the politics and ideology of the early 1930s, and that went far beyond the usual parameters of adaptation. To use the current phrase, the film was a significant intervention in 1930s culture wars. And in so intervening, the radical politics of Shelley's novel, with its (admittedly uneasy) sympathy with and support for the Creature in his deeply human needs for parental recognition, human company and love (systematically denied in the novel), get edited out of existence.

O'Flinn points out that a wholly new scene was created in which Frankenstein's assistant Fritz is ordered to steal a brain to be inserted into the Creature. He sees in the lab two brains in jars labelled 'NORMAL BRAIN' and 'ABNORMAL BRAIN'. The film has already described the abnormal brain as 'degenerate' and therefore responsible for brutality and violence. Fritz, reasonably enough, steals the normal brain in its jar but (these things happen) drops and smashes it, so he takes the abnormal one instead. The consequences of this are very marked. O'Flinn says this.

> A central part of Mary Shelley's thesis is to insist that the [Creature's] eventual life of violence and revenge is the direct product of his [treatment and] social circumstances … 'I was benevolent and good; misery made me a fiend' [Ch. 10] … The film deletes this reading … through its insistence that [his] behaviour is not a reaction to his experience but biologically determined, a result of nature, not nurture … [with] violence as rooted in personal deficiencies, to be viewed with horror and labelled, literally, ABNORMAL and so sub-human.
>
> (In Humm et al. edd. 1986: 210–11)

O'Flinn connects this with other changes, the most momentous of which is depriving the Creature of speech – and therefore simply deleting his long and intensely eloquent autobiographical narrative at the heart of the book. (It's a kind of political emasculation.) One smaller but sharply pointed change is that in the novel, at one point, the Creature saves a child from drowning; in the film he drowns the child. The film's ending is very remarkable. After the child drowns, a mob chases and traps the Creature in a windmill which they burn down (the film then ending with a brief sight of Frankenstein happily reunited with Elizabeth – who, unsurprisingly, hasn't been killed).

> As the blaze engulfs the blades, they form a gigantic fiery cross that deliberately suggests the Ku Klux Klan, virulently active at the time … The response of the community … to eliminate the savage culprit comes across as a kind of ritual cleansing of that community, the prompt removal of an inhuman threat to civilised life which is comfortably justifiable within routine populist politics … If Mary Shelley's [Creature] alludes indirectly to working-class insurrection, one answer to that canvassed in the 1930s was counter-revolutionary mob violence.
>
> (212–13)

I'll just add here that the later 1930s classic *Gone with the Wind* features the Ku Klux Klan unleashing carnage in another ritual cleansing after another savage culprit is identified – when Scarlett is 'raped' by a black man. But Eve

Sedgwick notes that in this 'rape' it apparently 'makes no difference at all that one constituent element of rape is missing'.

> But the missing constituent is simply sex. The attack on Scarlett had been for money ... There is no mention of any other motive, but it does not matter in the least, the absent sexuality leaves no gap in the character's, the novel's, or the society's discourse of rape.
>
> (Sedgwick 1985: 10)

I'll turn now to a text at the very centre of the Western canon, Shakespeare's *Hamlet*. (More on the play in Chapter 2.) This, too, is an adaptation. With one or two possible exceptions, none of the plots of Shakespeare's plays are his invention and, in the case of *Hamlet* (ironically for a play celebrated for its break-through originality), there's a clear debt to an earlier play. One problem is that it hasn't survived.

Three critics, two very famous and one much less so, have approached this 'problem' in strikingly different ways. Easily the most entertaining of them is the great William Empson (a favourite critic of mine whom we'll meet regularly in this book) and, though second of the three in date, I'll turn to him now.

Empson (in his '*Hamlet* When New' of 1953) argues that Shakespeare, who before *Hamlet* was celebrated most in his day as the creator of Falstaff in the *Henry IV* plays, stumbled across his breakthrough into the profundity of the great 'tragic period'. Told by his company to dust off and improve the old revenge tragedy (the so-called Ur-Hamlet which was probably by Thomas Kyd), a play which Empson shows had become a by-word for mockery and calls of 'hurry up!' from the audience exasperated by the hero's repeated and unfulfilled cries for vengeance, Shakespeare (as Empson nicely puts it) said this to himself 'when walking home'.

> 'The only way to shut this hole is to make it big. I shall make Hamlet walk up to the audience and tell them, again and again, "I don't know why I'm delaying any more than you do; the motivation of this play is just as blank to me as it is to you; but I can't help it." What is more, I shall make it impossible for them to blame him. And *then* they daren't laugh.' It turned out, of course, that this method, instead of reducing the old play to farce, made it thrillingly life-like and profound.
>
> (Empson 1986: 84)

This marvellously accounts for what critic after critic have described as the play's fascination with the meta-critical, its highly self-conscious and self-reflective concern with the opacity of the 'self' and its motivations.

The poet-critic T.S. Eliot (we'll meet him regularly in this book as well: I'll admit that 'favourite' is not the word in his case) starts, in a famous essay of 1919, from the same position as Empson, the idea that Shakespeare worked on the old play by Kyd, which was centred merely on revenge. But Eliot's critical angle is that Shakespeare then superimposed on the old material the new matter of the effect on Hamlet of his mother Gertrude's guilt. Crucially for Eliot, this had the effect of making the play full of 'some stuff' that Shakespeare couldn't 'drag' to the light. This was apparently because there is an inadequately realized 'objective correlative' (a phrase Eliot came to regret).

For Eliot *Hamlet* is terminally damaged as a play because Hamlet himself is dominated by emotions that can't be expressed, emotions judged by Eliot as being in 'excess of the facts'. What Hamlet's mother has done, and the impact on her son, was apparently for Eliot inadequately equivalent to Hamlet's disgust as expressed in the play – though expressed powerfully and fully enough, one would have thought, in his very first soliloquy. (And, in the light of Eliot's reading, so much for the Oedipus complex – the son's unconscious wish to kill the father and marry the mother – that Freud and Ernest Jones found exemplified in the play.) For Eliot, the play is 'most certainly an artistic failure' and its failure is not so much the mismatch between the Kyd and the Shakespeare plays as the mismatch between Hamlet's emotional disgust and the 'facts' of his mother's sexual betrayal (in Kermode ed. 1975: 45–49).

In Chapter 8, you'll find material on Eliot's own poetry, and his perhaps not entirely usual attitude toward women and sexuality. It's at least possible that we have more evidence of this in his reading of *Hamlet*. I'll add that on Gertrude you'll find the excellent Janet Adelman in the next chapter.

Francis Barker, in a really stimulating 1984 book (it had a powerful impact on me personally and I very much hope you come across it: we'll meet it again in Chapter 3), reads the issue, like Empson, historically. That is, he reads it in the light of the play's incipient modernity, its stumbling across what I'll call the burden of consciousness that made it so important to romantic poets like Keats and that made the modern critic Harold Bloom talk (with typical extravagance) about Shakespeare as the inventor of our being or feeling human. But what distinguishes Barker's reading from Empson's is that he historicizes the issue in terms of what might be called the modern problem of 'essence'. What Barker shows is that the apparently only 'gestural' interiority and 'essence' of Hamlet is actually a prefiguring of the void at the heart of the 'bourgeois' conception of human 'essence' itself, as if already partly created or intimated in *Hamlet*.

This notion of essence (I'll come back to it) arises in humanism as a kind of replacement for the religious 'soul' and is based on a consoling belief in the unitary 'self' that informs everything we do and is unchangeably 'essential' to us. Barker's reading suggests that in the play not just modernity but even postmodernity is prefigured. (More on those words in Chapters 8 and 9. They refer to the discontinuities and indeterminacy that inform our conceptions of our 'selves' and our actions in an increasingly alienating world which it is more and more difficult to express or interpret.)

Barker quotes Hamlet's early speech distinguishing between 'actions that a man might play' and his own claim to 'have that within that passes show' (1.2).

> Hamlet asserts … an essential interiority … In him a separation has already opened up between the inner reality of the subject … and an inauthentic exterior: and in that opening there begins to insist, however prematurely, the figure that is to dominate and organise bourgeois culture. Seen from the viewpoint of this speech, the narrative of *Hamlet* is nothing but the prince's evasion of a series of potentialities offered to him … Even the central task of revenge provides, in its deferral, no more than a major axis of the play's duration. In dismissing these modes, or 'actions' as he calls them, Hamlet utters … a first demand for the modern subject … But this interiority remains, in *Hamlet*, gestural … The historical prematurity of this subjectivity places it outside the limits of the text-world … The text continually offers to fulfil the claim of that first speech, but whenever it appears that the claimed core of that within which passes the show of the spectacle will be substantially articulated, Hamlet's riddling, antic language shifts its ground and the text slides away from essence … The promise of essential subjectivity remains unfulfilled. [But] from its point of vantage on the threshold of the modern but not yet within it, the text scandalously reveals the emptiness at the heart of that bourgeois trope. Rather than the plenitude of an individual presence, the text dramatizes its impossibility.
>
> (Barker 1984: 35–38)

Hamlet as literary-critical guide

I'll stay for a bit with what Barker says about 'essence' and add that *Hamlet*, of all Shakespeare's plays, is almost obsessively concerned with interpretation and its crises. (After all, there's a play within a play at its centre.) Put another way, *Hamlet* is (to use the word used above) meta-critical, embodying and dramatizing the urge to critique. The play – some would add, like all complex works of art – includes its own critical commentary. (In Chapter 2, Rosalie Colie says exactly that about Shakespeare's Sonnets.)

Let me sample, almost at random, the way this happens in the textures of the play. (In so doing I might be able to shed a little sidelight on some leading critical, and theoretical, approaches to texts over the last century or so.) The search for 'essence' (in effect, Eliot was on that search when he said he couldn't find it and blamed the play) is at the heart of earlier liberal-humanist or essentialist criticism (from the Victorian period to the 1920s and 1930s and the arrival of the 'new criticism') and it's where Barker starts with Hamlet's claim for 'that within that passes show'. But an even clearer example is from Polonius who is predictably old-fashioned in his critical thinking. He tells the king and queen that he has found out the cause of Hamlet's 'lunacy' in Ophelia's rejection (on his advice) of Hamlet's love. He claims he has a track record for such discoveries of hidden essence and adds: 'I will find / Where truth is hid, though it were hid indeed / Within the centre' (2.2).

Any number of confident post-Victorian critics could have made the same claim, based on the same comfortable belief that texts, and characters in texts, have, allegedly like us all, centres that are stable and readable, and – once teased out by the gifted critic – expressed. Behind these ideas is the humanist notion of the unitary self, as critiqued in modernity. Indeed, it goes without saying that all modern varieties of criticism start by questioning those assumptions.

Polonius and the king and queen decide, of course, to test the theory and listen in on the so-called nunnery scene where Hamlet hysterically bullies and abuses Ophelia. (Many critics sentimentalize the scene by arguing, with no evidence from the text, that Hamlet knows he's being listened to.) Claudius's ensuing critical response is one of the funniest things in the play: 'Love! His affections do not that way tend, / Nor what he spake, though it lacked form a little, / Was not like madness' (3.1) – though it lacked form a little! This is Claudius as new critic, a formalist, paying attention closely to the text's form, its internal coherence or lack of it, its inner tensions and ambiguities. This school of criticism, still with us, lies behind 'close reading' as we were all taught in schools.

But where we have decidedly moved on from the basics of new criticism is the way that, unlike its early advocates, we pay close attention to the contexts, especially historical, in which writing and reading take place and the different ways readers read, not all of which are conscious. Those last two notions lie behind the most important of modern critical schools or theories, those loosely defined as reader-response and new-historicist (with its cousin 'cultural-materialist') criticism. (See Chapter 2 for historicist readings of Shakespeare.) The turn to history, as it is sometimes called, would crucially include criticism informed by histories in terms of gender, sexuality, race and the environment. One particularly influential figure behind the varieties of historicism was Michel Foucault whom we'll meet (again) below.

As it happens, we can look again at *Hamlet* for a nice example of early reader-response criticism in practice. When Hamlet is quizzing Rosencrantz and Guildenstern, he asks them why they've come to Denmark, which is, after all, a prison, 'one of the worst'. Uncomfortably, they say they don't think that about Denmark. Hamlet replies: 'Then 'tis none to you; for there is nothing either good or bad but thinking makes it so' (2.2). So the meaning of Denmark as text is up to the reader whose interpretation of the text completes it as text. (Hamlet is also there coming over as a moral relativist, a position that usually displeases more conventional critics.)

And we can even, at a stretch, see Hamlet as an early 'new historicist' – critics who deploy together the notions that history is always textualized and texts always historicized – when, still questioning his once school friends, he brings together what, on the face of it, is a random-sounding digression about the new fashion for theatre companies made up exclusively of boys, and the popularity of the current king.

Editors of the play get quite heated about whether this passage properly belongs in the 'real' text of the play. More intriguing is the sudden opening out on to contemporary history. The boy actors were threatening the established popularity of companies, including Shakespeare's own at the Globe, as the boys performed to smaller and more wealthy audiences in indoor theatres. Hamlet relates this turn in theatrical fashion to Claudius's manipulation of popular opinion, as if both royal succession and theatrical history are merely part of larger struggles over legitimacy. As Hamlet says, there's 'something in this more than natural' (2.2). He may well say that; Shakespeare is (as Empson might have said) getting Hamlet to tell Shakespeare's own Globe audience that he doesn't know either what's going on with these new boy-actor companies elsewhere in London but, whatever it is, he expects it can be used to 'read' the textual problem of Claudius's popularity. I've already used the phrase culture wars, wars notionally over culture that are actually about political power.

Ecology, eloquence, guilt, complicity

I'll return to some broader points about criticism, culture and politics in the last stages of this first chapter. But I'll turn now to an under-appreciated modernist contemporary of Eliot (who admittedly championed him later). This is David Jones and he was also a gifted painter. His First World War novel *In Parenthesis* – prose-poem may be a better word – was published in 1937 and (like Kenneth Burke whom we met in the Introduction), it shows clear and prophetic 'green' awareness of the dangers of progress. His Preface seems to me a particularly moving example of criticism at its simplest and most powerful, as he looks back at his own text and reflects on what he was trying to do, what he didn't really intend to do, and what he now, as a modernist devotee of form in language, assesses critically. As an enforced participant in history, in the trenches, he knows in retrospect what history has now revealed to him about the past and the new modernity.

> This writing has to do with some things I saw, felt, and was part of ... I have only tried to make a shape in words, using as data the complex of sights, sounds, fears, hopes, apprehensions, smells, things exterior and interior, the landscape and paraphernalia of that singular time and of those particular men. I have attempted to appreciate some things, which, at the time of suffering, the flesh was too weak to appraise. There are passages which I would exclude, as not having the form I desire – but they seem necessary to the understanding of the whole ... I did not intend this as a 'War Book' – it happens to be concerned with war. I should prefer it to be about a good kind of peace – but as Mandeville says 'Of Paradys ne can I not speken properly I was not there; it is fer beyond and that for thinketh me. And also I was not worthi.' ... We feel a rubicon has been passed between striking with a hand weapon as men used to do and loosing poison from the sky as we do ourselves ... That our culture has accelerated every line of advance into the territory of physical science is well appreciated – but not so well understood are the unforeseen, subsidiary effects of this achievement. We stroke cats, pluck flowers, tie ribands ... make some kind of love, write poems, paint pictures, are generally at one with that

> creaturely world inherited from our remote beginning. Our perception of many things is heightened and clarified. Yet must we … respond to increasingly exacting mechanical devices, some fascinating and compelling, others sinister in the extreme; all requiring a new and strange direction of the mind, a new sensitivity certainly, but at a considerable cost … For the old authors there appears to have been no such dilemma – for them the embrace of battle seemed one with the embrace of lovers. For us it is different.
>
> (Jones 1963: ix–xv)

I think this connects very well with two critics I want to share with you now. First is the contemporary eco-critic Jonathan Bate thinking about iconic romantic poetry and its environmental lessons for today. What he says has additional poignancy after reading David Jones on the 'unforeseen' effects of advances in science – which he realized presciently were 'at a considerable cost'. And then I'll turn to the great modern poet-critic Geoffrey Hill (more on him and his critical relations with Eliot in Chapter 8) as he too reflects on romantic poetry and its difficult complicity with guilt. (Romanticism is the subject of Chapters 4 and 5 of this book.)

Bate's 2000 book *The Song of the Earth* starts by setting out the need to dream the 'dream of deep ecology' (the impossible wish for a clean-slate return to nature) in the work of the imagination as found pre-eminently in romantic poetry. This is because 'the business of literature is to work upon consciousness' (Bate 2000: 23).

> Central to the dilemma of environmentalism is the fact that the act of identifying the presumption of human apartness from nature as the problem is itself a symptom of that very apartness. The identification is the product of an instrumental way of thinking and of using language. It may therefore be that a necessary step in overcoming the apartness is to think and use language in a different way. Let us begin by supposing that we cannot do without thought-experiments and language-experiments which imagine a return to nature, a reintegration of the human and the Other. The dream of deep ecology will never be realized upon the earth, but our survival as a species may be dependent on our capacity to dream it in the work of our imagination.
>
> (37–38)

Bate adds this on Keats's 'To Autumn'. What Bate says here about being at home in the world connects with a very moving critical passage on the end of Milton's *Paradise Lost* by John Hollander that you'll find in Chapter 3.

> In [a] letter, Keats wrote of his ideal of inter-assimilation between men; in the poem he is inter-assimilated with the environment. Indeed, environment is probably the wrong word, because it presupposes an image of man at the centre, surrounded by things; ecosystem is the better word exactly

> because an ecosystem does not have a centre; it is a network of relations ... A romantic poem is a model of a certain kind of being and of dwelling ... The poem is itself an image of ecological wholeness which may grant to the attentive and receptive reader a sense of being-at-home-in-the-world ... ['To Autumn'] ends with an at-homeness-with-all-living-things ... The movement *of* the poem is ... from culture to nature. But the movement *through* the poem, with its intricate syntactical, metrical and aural interlinkings, is not one which divides the culture from the nature.
>
> (107–10)

And here is Geoffrey Hill. The connection here with David Jones is that where Jones lived through and felt a 'rubicon' being crossed between pre-modern and modern warfare, from 'striking with a hand weapon and loosing poison from the sky', Hill sees romantic eloquence as itself harbouring – even being organically dependent on – its own guilt, as suggested by the very worrying scribbled note by Coleridge.

This extract from Hill starts with a routine description of Michelangelo's unfinished statues – 'figures straining to free themselves from the imprisoning marble' – and Hill says that he's always thought the image applies better to 'those arts which are composed of words'.

> The arts which use language are the most impure of arts ... However much a poem is shaped and finished, it remains to some extent within the 'imprisoning marble' of a quotitian [=everyday] shapelessness and imperfection ... [though] I take no cynical view of those rare moments in which the inertia of language, which is also the coercive force of language, seems to have been overcome ... But Romantic art is thoroughly familiar with the reproaches of life. Accusation, self-accusation, are the very life-blood of its most assured rhetoric. As Yeats puts it, in his poem 'The Circus Animals' Desertion': 'Those masterful images, because complete / Grew in pure mind, but out of what began? / ... I must lie down where all the ladders start, / In the foul rag-and-bone shop of the heart'. How is it possible, though, to revoke 'masterful images' in images that are themselves masterful? Can one renounce 'completion' with epithets and rhyme-patters that in themselves retain a certain repleteness? ... I [ask] in the context of that obsessive self-critical Romantic monologue in which eloquence and guilt are intertwined, and for which the appropriate epitaph would be one abrupt entry in Coleridge's 1796 Notebook: 'Poetry – excites us to artificial feelings – makes us callous to real ones'.
>
> (Hill 1984: 2–4)

Hill, like many others (including myself), draws attention to the repetition of 'forlorn' at the end of the penultimate stanza ('in faery lands forlorn') and then immediately at the start of the last stanza of Keats's 'Ode to a Nightingale' ('Forlorn! The very word is like a bell') and he turns to Coleridge again who noted that his concern was not so much with thought itself but what he called 'the mind's self-experience in the act of thinking'. Hill says this about Keats's 'forlorn'.

> The echo is not so much a recollection as a revocation; and what is revoked is an attitude towards art and within art. The menace that is flinched from is certainly mortality ('Where youth grows pale, and spectre-thin, and dies') but it is also the menace of the high claims of poetry itself.
>
> (5)

The 'menace' of the claims of poetry itself and the notion that poetry – art – can paradoxically make us 'callous' to real feelings have profoundly unsettling implications for criticism. You may well have heard that the Marxist theorist Theodore Adorno said that poetry was impossible after Auschwitz. We know that some of those who ran the Nazi death-camps cultivated the arts in their spare time.

I'll end this section by turning from guilt to the related notion of complicity. The important modern critic Will Norman (we'll meet him again in Chapters 8 and 9), in a forthcoming study of complicity in post-1945 American literature, writes about the way intellectuals were caught up in the three major racial conflicts of the period: the Nazi campaign to exterminate Europe's Jews; the process of Third-World decolonization and the Vietnam war; and the anti-racist struggles of the civil rights movement and Black Power. In relation to the anxiety about race, the liberal establishment published a report in 1944 called *An American Dilemma: The Negro Problem and Modern Democracy*, whose author, Gunnar Myrdal, wrote of how many white liberals suppress the facts of racial injustices in the confusion 'which lurks in the basement of man's soul'.

Norman reads the metaphor there, suggesting as it does that racism is little more than an embarrassing dissonance for liberal Americans, as 'an unusually clear articulation of the complicit structure of feeling' that he explores in his powerful and wide-ranging book. Racism is seen as a 'pseudo-Freudian' matter of 'psychology or morality rather than a systemic or structural problem'. Then Norman says this about Myrdal's metaphor in relation to two classic novels of the period.

> The Black man in the basement was a standard trope in literary writing about race in mid-century America ... The basement is where Bigger Thomas does much of his work as a house servant for the Daltons in Richard Wright's *Native Son* (1940), but more memorably it is where he dismembers Mary Dalton's body before stuffing it into the furnace ... Ralph Ellison chose to reclaim the basement from Wright and use it as a framing device for *Invisible Man* (1952), in which it plays a notably ambiguous role. The basement provides his protagonist with a refuge from the conflicts raging in the streets above his head, but is also the symbol of his alienation.
>
> (Norman: unpublished)

Norman adds that both novels draw on Dostoevsky's *Notes from Underground* (1864), then fashionable among the literary elite. Myrdal's choice of metaphor affiliates his sociological study to the literary field as a means for what Norman calls the 'articulation of complicity'. (I'll just add that we'll meet *Native Son* and *Invisible Man*, and the relations between them and beyond, in Chapter 9.)

Literature, history, ideology: Proust, Flaubert, Swift, Beckett

I want to turn to some key critics writing about the novel, two of the greatest of all novels, and the early realist novel, before I return to poetry, and I'll start with Adorno's friend and colleague Walter Benjamin.

Benjamin, the great Jewish Marxist cultural critic and colleague of Adorno, took his own life in September 1940 on the Franco-Spanish border, which had just been sealed, while fleeing from the Nazis. He was notionally on his way to America. He was 48. His precious library and many of his manuscripts were in the Paris apartment which the Gestapo had seized. Bereft of his books and all other literary resources, he didn't feel particularly drawn to America where (according to Hannah Arendt on whom I'm drawing here) he used to say people would have no use for him 'than to cart him up and down the country to exhibit him as the "last European"' (in Benjamin 1973: 18).

This Jewish refugee from the Nazis came to his dreadful end (and, by a stroke of terrible fortune, the day before his suicide – and a few weeks after it – he would have been able to cross to Spain) while another Jewish refugee, also in flight from Nazi Europe and also bereft of his literary resources, had found himself in Istanbul. That was Eric Auerbach, to whom I'll turn shortly. Auerbach wrote wonderfully about Flaubert's incomparable *Madame Bovary*, as we'll see. Perhaps Benjamin's most eloquent critical essay (from 1929) was about Proust, whose *In Search of Lost Time* is the greatest (and longest) of all novels. (I'll just add that I hope you take these hints and read Flaubert and Proust as soon as you can.)

Proust suffered severely from (and died of) asthma: he wrote his great novel propped up in bed. Benjamin said this, in a marvellous evocation of bodily writing. (As it happens, he mentions Michelangelo, as did Geoffrey Hill.)

> This asthma became part of his art – if indeed his art did not create it. Proust's syntax rhythmically and step by step reproduces his fear of suffocating. And his ironic, philosophical, didactic reflections invariably are the deep breath with which he shakes off the weight of memories. On a larger scale, however, the threatening, suffocating crisis was death, which he was constantly aware of, most of all while he was writing … The closeness of the symbiosis between this particular creativity and this particular malady is demonstrated most clearly by the fact that in Proust there never was a breakthrough of that heroic defiance with which other creative people have risen up against their infirmities … As it was, however, this malady was destined to have its place in the great work process assigned to it by a furor devoid of desires or regrets. For the second time there rose a scaffold like

> Michelangelo's on which the artist, his head thrown back, painted the Creation on the ceiling of the Sistine Chapel: the sickbed on which Marcel Proust consecrates the countless pages which he covered with his handwriting, holding them up in the air, to the creation of his microcosm.
> (Benjamin 1973: 216–17)

Edward Said (again a crucial figure in this book) wrote eloquently about the conditions under which Eric Auerbach wrote *Mimesis* (1953): his study of the 'representation of reality in Western Literature' – and it can hardly be imagined that any critic today would dare aspire to such a task.

> No reader of Eric Auerbach's *Mimesis*, one of the most admired and influential books of literary criticism ever written, has failed to be impressed by the circumstances of the book's actual writing. These are referred to almost casually by Auerbach in the last lines of his epilogue ... 'I may also mention that the book was written during the war and at Istanbul, where the libraries are not equipped for European studies ... On the other hand, it is quite possible that the book owes its existence to just this lack of a rich and specialized library if it had been possible for me to acquaint myself with all the work that has been done on so many subjects, I might never have reached the point of writing'.
>
> The drama of this little bit of modesty is considerable, in part because Auerbach's quiet tone conceals much of the pain of his exile. He was a Jewish refugee from Nazi Europe ... In Istanbul [he faced] ... the loss of texts, traditions, continuities that make up the very web of a culture ... [Moreover,] Istanbul does not simply connote a place outside Europe. Istanbul represents ... Islam, the scourge of Christendom ... The Orient and Islam also stood for the ultimate alienation from and opposition to Europe ... To have been an exile in Istanbul at that time of fascism in Europe was a deeply resonating and intense form of exile from Europe.
> (Said 1983: 5–6)

Here's Auerbach on *Madame Bovary* (from a 1937 article that later became part of *Mimesis*). Auerbach quotes from Part 1, Chapter 9, about Emma's mealtimes with Charles in Tostes that 'were unbearable to her' and in which 'all the bitterness of life seemed served up on her plate'. He contrasts this depiction of a bourgeois interior with the 'peaceful idyll' of a painting 'in the Dutch style' and with burlesque scenes in earlier novels 'where husband and wife are squabbling' – and with earlier literary presentations of despair which were 'always despair over a concrete cause'.

> Here, however, nothing special happens, nor has anything special happened just before. It is an arbitrarily selected moment in that regularly recurring hour, in which husband and wife eat together ... [Emma's despair is] shapeless and purely negative ... and only directs itself *against*, namely against one's

> own condition in its entirety, without knowing what to put in its place ... [Flaubert] was certainly the first to represent [such despair] in people of lower ... social class ... Flaubert also tells only rarely of events that move the plot forward. Purely out of images – shaping the nothingness of the indifferent everyday into a weighty circumstance of aversion, of barrenness, of false hopes, crippling disappointments and pitiful anxieties – a grey and randomly chosen human life glides sluggishly towards its end ... *Madame Bovary* is a mosaic of many, very carefully observed, mostly completely insignificant circumstances and events ... What is presented [in the paragraph discussed] is an everyday image, accompanied by Emma's everyday feelings. No observation or analysis of her psychic life is undertaken that would go beyond this presentation. And yet perfect insight into her existence is achieved.
>
> (In Cohen ed. 2005: 427–34)

In 1863, just a few years after *Bovary*, the poet Charles Baudelaire (who reviewed the novel very perceptively) said that modernity in art sought out the ephemeral, the fugitive and the contingent. Flaubert's letters show his relentless and often agonizing search for the phrases and sentences that enact a process (to use his words) of undoing, unscrewing, unwriting. As Naomi Schor says, following Roland Barthes (about whom more below), for Flaubert 'to convey the inarticulate, one must disarticulate' (in Cohen ed. 2005: 511). Jonathan Culler summarizes what Barthes says about the task of literature in modernity. Flaubert (and Baudelaire) are at the start of this historical process.

> It is not, as is often thought, 'to express the inexpressible' ... but 'to unexpress the expressible' ... to problematise the meanings our cultural codes otherwise confer, and thus to unwrite the world as it is written by prior discursive practices.
>
> (Culler 2002: 129)

Nothing happens in that paragraph of Flaubert's. And, as the saying goes, 'nothing happens, twice' across the two acts of Beckett's *Waiting for Godot*. Well, as it happens (if I can put it like that), in a book written in a startlingly different critical mode, only nine years after Auerbach's *Mimesis*, Flaubert was the first of the three great novelists (with the 18th century satirist Jonathan Swift as an eerie antecedent) who with James Joyce and Samuel Beckett made up the subject matter of Hugh Kenner's *The Stoic Comedians* (1962). This is perhaps the most stylish and funniest short critical book of its generation. He starts from the notion that three hundred years after the Gutenberg Revolution, writing, which used to be the 'graph of speech', now implies a 'wholly typographic culture'.

> We have grown accustomed at last not only to silent reading, but to reading matter that itself implies nothing but silence. We are skilled in a

> wholly typographic culture, and this is perhaps the distinguishing skill of twentieth-century man ... [After Gutenberg and the Enlightenment] printers stunned spelling into conformity, lexicographers language, and encyclopaedists opinion, so that Posterity could enjoy the convenience of forming its words, its sentiments or its notions out of interchangeable parts. And there came into being likewise a class of man whose business it was to set ideas, or sentences or letters, into one likely order or another, to the end that the printing presses might be kept busy and Posterity enlightened ... [Swift's] Lemuel Gulliver [in *Gulliver's Travels* Book 3] reported helpfully on how the craft was managed in Lagado with a machine which shook the entire vocabulary into chance arrangements; and wherever thirty-six scrutineers 'found three or four words together that might make part of a sentence, they dictated to the four remaining boys who were scribes'.
>
> (Kenner 1962: xv–xvi)

Kenner traces the ensuing development of the novel, with its twin requirements to meet 'verisimilitude' and 'plausibility', the latter to 'satisfy criteria of reason, since it is the reader's belief that his own actions are reasonable, and he will employ his book-reading time on nothing less' (xvii). This connects well with what Lennard Davis says about what novel readers want, or have been conditioned to want, from 'characters' and the ideological reasons underpinning that desire: I'll be sharing Davis's important critical ideas with you very soon.

Kenner crucially adds about the novel that 'the form so circumscribed has this peculiarity, that it tempts subverters', an early example being Jane Austen, and the subversion reaching a crisis-point with Flaubert whose *Madame Bovary*, which gave the middle-classes the scientific rationale that 'they had always clamoured for', disturbed them so much that they ordered the book to be 'placed on trial as a massive affront to morals and religion' (xvii). I'll add that, unsurprisingly, what really riled the trial prosecutors was Flaubert's mild, as if clinical, observation that Emma found in adultery all the banality of marriage.

Kenner's point there about the early novel tempting subverters gives me the chance to add that modern critics have been concerned to revise Ian Watt's 1957 standard and overly linear account of the rise of the novel (a narrative reflecting the rise of economic individualism in early capitalism and starting with Daniel Defoe, which we met in the Introduction). Michael McKeon, for instance, argues, like Kenner but more elaborately, for a more dialectical model – Kenner would say subversive – in which it is typical that Defoe's earnest and placid *Robinson Crusoe* is gleefully undermined just a handful of years later by the satiric attacks on early novelistic methods in *Gulliver's Travels* (which Watt fails to mention). And Nancy Armstrong points out, in her compelling book *Desire and Domestic Fiction* (1987), also met in the introduction and to which I'll return in Chapter 6, that Watt ignores the vital work of a woman novelist like Aphra Behn (see the end of Chapter 3) whose focus, very much the opposite of Defoe, is on love and desire.

Kenner's point is that the novelist as comedian writes not from some sense of confident power that other critics suggest but from unease and inadequacy.

> The writer's work is to write. He writes, however, under some disadvantage, for others are so much more fluent than he ... [But] he can, thanks to his detachment from the heat of creation, at least set periods and commas exactly right, depart from sound grammar only knowingly, and be at pains to verify the quantities of useful information for which we look to fiction ('Constipation is a sign of health in pomeranians', Beckett informs us, he who is so chary of risking information) ... We have been working our way for centuries through a world fragmented into typographical elements, and lo, the Comedian has gone before us.
>
> (xviii)

Before we turn to Lennard Davis, I'll just add a crucial extract on Swift whom Kenner rightly places at the start of his tradition of subversive novelistic comedians. Claude Rawson wrote the best and strongest recent book on Swift and he provides a very different angle on Swift's historical relevance, one that takes us back to Benjamin, Auerbach and their personal experiences of Nazism.

Rawson's *God, Gulliver, and Genocide* (2000) says this.

> Swift's works are a meeting-house for some of the most troubling moral nightmares of European intellectual history in the last five hundred years: war, imperial conquest, the impulse to exterminate. His major satires, especially *Gulliver's Travels* and *A Modest Proposal*, contain remarkable configurations, not always attractive to a modern sensibility, of later fantasies and anxieties about these subjects ... and those figures who have sometimes simultaneously combined the roles of alien and home-grown pariah, particularly the Irish and the Jews ... The Yahoos in *Gulliver's Travels* ... are Swift's version of what we have sometimes chosen to call the 'other', whom we distinguish from ourselves and whose all too probable kinship with ourselves has always disturbed our consciousness, as well as our conscience ... *Gulliver's Travels* [anatomizes] many representative myths of the savage-civilised encounter ... [especially] the death-dealing talk of xenophobic threats and the murderous genocidal realities which reach their ultimate monstrosity in the Nazi camps ... If the Yahoos represent a deprived humanity, how are we to interpret the Houyhnhnms' serious debate as to whether 'they should be exterminated from the face of the earth', especially when we recall that God expressed the same intention in the same language before unleashing the Deluge? or the fact that the Nazis used the same language, from Luther's Bible, about the Jews? ... That the Nazis also used the language of Genesis, or that Swift prefigured in fantasy, and in disconcerting detail, much of what the Nazis actually did, is a fact to be confronted.
>
> (Rawson 2000: 1–15)

After what Rawson says there, we can understand the desire, as we read Swift, to flinch and to resist. Resisting novels more generally is the subject (and the title) of a little-known and important 1987 book by Lennard J. Davis on ideology and the need to resist.

'Ideology' is a word I'm using a lot. What I mean by this often controversial word (and here I'm following the French Marxist Louis Althusser) is a set of ideas that make up our imaginary (but seriously believed) relations to the real conditions of our lives. Ideology, and its component ideas, of course vary over time and between people, but one core aspect of the idea is that ideological beliefs underpin the way we think about aspects of our world as just the way things are. Roland Barthes called this 'mythology' and showed that myths look like and are meant to look like 'nature' (the unchangeable 'way things are') when they are actually due not to nature but to history – which can be changed. Criticism should therefore be about working to expose 'nature' as 'history'. Do read Barthes's wonderful *Mythologies* (1957) which analyses everyday cultural 'myths' like wrestling and soap-powder ads. Exposing nature as history may not be easy, because ideology itself keeps us from enquiring into the conditions of our lives. Ideology comes into our lives as friendly and reassuring presences, like the education system, the media and the church. Althusser called these and other institutions the 'ideological state apparatus' (to distinguish them from the state's 'repressive' apparatus like the police or the army).

What's this got to do with critically thinking about characters in books? Davis makes the point that, once characters in fiction are written down, they are (in effect) not so much like real people as dead people. Crucially he distinguishes between character (the ideological constructs of fiction) and personality (you and me).

> As we spend time with real people we get to know more about them and, even if still a mystery finally, they grow more understandable. With a fictional character, time may give us insights into formal elements of the narrative, but we do not really come to understand the main character any better after the initial two or three readings … To be married to Elizabeth Bennett in the world of reader-character relations would amount to being trapped in a Dantesque circle of hell in which only the same information could be presented over and over … Personality is what living beings have. Our personalities may not be coherent; they may not be readily understood [even] by us; they may be misinterpreted or not even accessible to others; but they are what we refer to when we refer to ourselves. 'Character' on the other hand is what people in novels have. They are characters with characteristics. The biggest ideological presupposition that novel readers are encouraged to make is to think that characters in novels have personalities. That distinction, or in my view misconception, is the essence of novel reading … [Moreover,] the coherence of character can be a kind of substitute for the formlessness and irrational nature of modern consciousness and culture … The feeling that we get when we are watching a complex character is largely an illusion created by

> the opposite – the relatively small number of traits that make up a character … In the 19th century, the novel was seen as important for the furthering of civilization and culture [and] the ideological role of character was certainly part of the civilising or, if you will, the socially indoctrinating aspect of the novel … Ideologically speaking, then, character gives readers faith that personality is, first, understandable and, second, capable of rational change.
>
> (Davis 1987: 110–119)

A related point about ideology and the rise of the realist novel itself was recently made by Ryan Ruby in an account of the new 'internet novel'. He identifies one problem for this new genre as the 'formal mirroring problem' – how can the narrative perspective of the realist novel respond to the perspectives of online media? Ruby says this about the early realist novel and its need to make its voice 'natural' (apparently free from ideology).

> The realist novel is itself an attempted solution to a 'formal mirroring problem', namely, how to translate the medium of oral storytelling, which requires the simultaneous co-presence of storyteller and audience, to written storytelling, in which the author is separated both physically and temporally from the reader. Up through the eighteenth century, authors were anxious enough about whether readers would accept this translation that they often found it necessary to account for the existence of their texts before settling down to tell their stories. The frame narrative, the found manuscript, and most famously the epistolary novel are nothing more than a series of narrative bootstrapping carried out for an audience that had yet to be trained to find the realist novel's autonomous narrative 'voice' plausible. Another device, borrowed from the theatre – a genre that, like oral storytelling, requires the physical co-presence of actor and audience – was direct address, such as Fielding, for example employs in *Tom Jones*.
>
> (Ruby 2021: online)

Antony Easthope – to move from the realist novel to the most prestigious form of poetry – made related points about ideology and the rise of the iambic pentameter.

You might have heard it said that the iambic pentameter is 'natural' to English speech. As easily the most dominant metrical pattern in English verse, from Shakespeare to the Victorian period, you might well think that must be true. But the dominance of the pentameter, its place as the default pattern for all high-art poetry before modernism, is the work of ideology and a kind of cultural displacement.

Pentameter came into English poetry (after it first emerged in Chaucer's Middle English only to disappear with the huge changes in the language as 'Middle' became 'Modern' English) in the early 16th century, imported from Italy.

Like so many other examples in our culture of what Barthes, as we've just said, called the workings of myth, which aims to pass off as 'natural' what is actually a matter of history, with the effect that the so-called natural seems always to have been eternally 'just there', pentameter (a five-stress line in a fixed pattern of ten syllables) replaced and pushed into the margins the much older four-stress line (in which the four stresses are fixed but the number of syllables can vary). The older four-stress line comes from the Anglo-Saxon period and, when pentameter (and other 'accentual-syllabic' patterns) replaced the older ('accentual') verse, the latter became relegated to less prestigious, culturally 'lower' and less 'properly' poetic forms of verse like children's nursery rhymes, marching songs, football chants and so on. If you glance at *Macbeth* you'll see the point clearly. Everyone speaks pentameter – apart from the marginalized witches who speak accentual four-foot lines (and the Porter who speaks in prose).

Easthope's 1983 book *Poetry as Discourse*, which attracted some flak from traditional critics, shows how the opposition between pentameter and the old accentual verse, with the former displacing the latter as 'art', is nothing to do with the English language 'naturally' falling into pentameters. The metrical context is the crucial deciding factor in 'placing' words into the expected pattern, words which in themselves have no 'natural' metrical identity but only a random one. Following Raymond Chapman, Easthope takes these words from daily speech (admittedly ten syllables, to prove the point simply), 'the stated price is subject to review', and inserts them into two 'opposite' metrical contexts. First, he puts them as a replacement for the last line in Milton's poem 'Lycidas' and then into a nursery rhyme. (It might help with the latter if you clap your hands with the four stresses.) Easthope says this.

> [The] sentence from daily speech ... can turn into pentameter when inserted into that metrical context:
>
> At last he rose and twitched his mantle blew:
> The stated price is subject to review.
>
> But the same utterance ... will also function perfectly as a four-stress line in accentual metre.
>
> Little maid, pretty maid, whither goest thou?
> Down in the meadow to milk my cow.
> Shall I go with thee? No, not you,
> The stated price is subject to review.
>
> (Easthope 1983: 59)

Easthope notes that Beckett's *Waiting for Godot* has a speech (prose, of course) that slips rather grandly into disguised pentameter, including a variation on what Easthope calls the 'most famous line of pentameter in English', to parody the 'humanist rhetoric' behind the domineering establishment of pentameter itself: 'Let us not waste our time in idle discourse ... / Those cries for help still ringing in our ears ... / What are we doing here, *that* is the question' (Act 2).

And even a high-modernist poem like Eliot's 'Prufrock' (see Chapter 8), which purports to be in the free verse that Eliot's mentor Pound said was necessary to 'break' the authority of the pentameter, turns out to be in (very) loose pentameter.

Easthope adds some further thoughts about pentameter and its role in ideology in relation to the older accentual pattern. Because pentameter in practice demands, unlike accentual verse, a counterpoint between the abstract pattern and the actual 'performance' of subtle, slight and dramatically 'characterising' variations from the rule (try saying Hamlet's 'to be or not to be' line to hear the slight variations which 'perform' his thought), it encourages the illusion of a 'free' subjectivity.

> Through counterpoint the abstract pattern of the metre is ... backgrounded ... The work of metric *production* – and so of the poem as constructed artifice – is suppressed in favour of a notion of the poem as spontaneously generated *product* ... Counterpoint requires that a complex abstract pattern be performed as though it were extemporary. The pattern learned by effort is presented as though it were unstudied.
>
> (67)

The political implications of this were realized as early as 1910 when the metrical historian George Saintsbury claimed that, in the counterpoint of pentameter, 'the claims of Order and Liberty are jointly met as in no other metrical form' (quoted in Easthope: 67), and then again by Robert Graves and Laura Riding in 1925.

> Metre considered as a set pattern approved by convention will stand for the claims of society as at present organized: the variations on metre will stand for the claims of the individual.
>
> (Quoted in Easthope: 68)

Easthope puts it like this.

> Counterpoint ... corresponds to the ideological opposition between the 'social' and the 'individual', an opposition which envisages society as a 'necessity' against and within which the individual finds his or her 'freedom'.
>
> (68)

The 'free' subjectivity suggested in the counterpointing of pentameter is free in the sense of apparently free from ideology and history: its 'voice' is lifted into what Easthope calls a 'kind of transcendence'. This is what Yeats wanted when rejecting Pound's free verse: he needed the metres of pentameter (and others in the accentual-syllabic tradition) to ensure that the personal is 'packed in ice or salt' and thereby raised towards 'impersonal meditation' (quoted in Easthope: 71–72). In contrast to this privileging of the apparently autonomous individual in the smooth poise of the 'voice', accentual verse calls for the performance, typically in groups, of emphatically stressed accents.

> [The] performance [is] typically recited or chanted, often in association with rhythmic gestures, clapping, dancing. In chanting, rhythmic repetitions take complete priority over natural intonation, subsuming it, and this is the metrical space for a collective voice … Instead of the collective voice of accentual metre, pentameter gives space to the [ideologically constructed] 'natural' intonation and so to a single voice in the closure of its own coherence.
>
> (73–74)

Meaning and its subversions, desire and power: Woolf and the *Alice* books

Let's move from the potential subversiveness of the collective voice in the accentual verse of childhood chant to a truly subversive writer of childhood literature who was more than happy for children to make, collectively or otherwise, whatever meanings they wanted from his work. I mean, of course, Lewis Carroll's *Alice* books. Juliet Dusinberre in her excellent and ground-breaking 1999 book *From Alice to the Lighthouse* writes particularly well about the subversiveness of Carroll's entire writing strategy, not only its language, and its refusal to signal towards traditional notions of depth, and she connects this with the modernism of Virginia Woolf. (We'll met Woolf in Chapter 8.) Here's Dusinberre.

> When [Woolf] asserted, to an audience of schoolchildren, that the reader must be the author's writer and accomplice, she proposed a new contract which had been pioneered in … [Carroll's] *Alice*. In this new relationship the child was not a tool fashioned to relieve adult guilt and cultural weariness, but an independent resistant being. … The absence of a deliberately pointed moral, and of linear direction in narrative, the abdication of the author as preacher, and the use of words as play, all of which were pioneered in children's books in the latter half of the nineteenth century, feed into the work of Virginia Woolf and her generation of writers … In *To The Lighthouse* Virginia Woolf offers the reader no definite standpoint from which to interpret the fictional world and to partake in the author's control of it … What is communicated is not the understanding which emerges from the author's interpretation of her own text, but the reeling dizziness of trying to understand, in which reader and writer are equally caught up … The voice of the author, if it can be heard at all, is never the voice of Providence, as it is for … George Eliot. Both Woolf and Joyce rebelled against the privileged discourse through which the author commands his own creatures. But that form of insurrection by the author on behalf of the reader had begun much earlier in the children's book.
>
> (Dusinberre 1999: xxi, 41)

Dusinberre refers to Humpty Dumpty's claim that words mean whatever he wants them to and to Carroll's claim that he was happy for readers to decide what (if anything) his books meant. As Dusinberre suggests, Roland Barthes's famous 1968 essay 'The Death of the Author' is the direct descendant of Carroll's proto-modernist ideas. This is the Barthes, already mentioned above, who is, for me and for many others, the most exhilarating of all modern theorists. He said this.

> Literature (it would be better from now to say *writing*), by refusing to assign a 'secret', an ultimate meaning, to the text (and to the world as text), liberates what may be called an anti-theological activity, an activity that is truly revolutionary since to refuse to fix meaning is, in the end, to refuse God and his hypostases – reason, science, law.
>
> (Barthes 1977: 147)

The challenging modern theorist Gilles Deleuze also wrote on the *Alice* books and makes similar points. For him the subversive refusal to mean is because of surfaces that scandalously deny the usual notion of depth. (He draws on the fact that Carroll had a stammer.)

> A strange evolution takes place throughout all of Alice's adventures. One can sum it up as the conquest or discovery of surfaces. At the beginning of *Wonderland*, the search for the secret of things and events goes on in the depths of the earth … [But] the sinking and burrowing movements give way to lateral, sliding movements … Here lies the secret of the stammerer – it no longer consists in sinking into the depths, but in sliding along in such a way that depth is reduced to nothing but the reverse side of the surface … There are no adventures of Alice; there is but *one* adventure: her rising to the surface … and her discovery that everything happens at the borderline … This is even more true of … *Looking Glass*. Events, in their radical difference from things, are … at the surface: a mirror that reflects them, a chess-board that 'flattens' them. By running along the surface, along the edge, one passes to the other side; from bodies to incorporeal events … This discovery that the strangest things are on the surface … would be unimportant if it did not carry with it an entire organisation of language: Carrollian language.
>
> (In Harari ed. 1980: 280–81)

The later work of Roland Barthes went further in exploring the notion that any single text's refusal to mean in the old stable sense was due to its difference (a key word in modern theory) from itself. Barbara Johnson in her excellent 1980 book *The Critical Difference* (more in Chapter 7) shows how Barthes's *S/Z* (originally 1970) placed particular emphasis on this idea of the text's difference from itself. This is how Johnson puts it.

> A text's difference is not its uniqueness, its special identity. It is the text's way of differing from itself ... It is not a difference between ... but a difference within. Far from constituting the text's unique identity, it is that which subverts the very idea of identity, infinitely deferring the possibility of adding up the sum of the text's parts or meanings and reaching a totalised, integrated whole.
>
> (Johnson 1980: 4)

Johnson uses the example of Rousseau's early romantic *Confessions*. He claims that he is 'unlike anyone I have ever met ... I am like no one in the whole world', but this later shifts to a very different conception of his self: 'there are times when I am so unlike myself that I might be taken for someone else' (quoted in Johnson: 4). Deconstructive criticism, as championed by Johnson (after Jacques Derrida and others), is accordingly based on the 'teasing out of warring forces of signification within the text' – a text as exemplified by that internal contradiction in Rousseau – in order to destabilize the 'claim to ... domination of one mode of signifying over another' (4–5).

We saw above that Virginia Woolf wanted the reader to be the author's 'writer and accomplice'. Her own critical writings were founded on a sense that literature is (in Carol Atherton's words, following Gertrude Stein) 'a history of you' rather than 'a history of it', thus signalling a return of authority to the individual reader as opposed to 'the structures and methods of academia' (Atherton 2005: 106). Woolf foreshadows what Barthes also said in *S/Z* was necessary for criticism: for the text to be what he called 'writerly' in order to 'make the reader no longer a consumer, but a producer of the text'. The opposite is what Barthes called the 'readerly' text, one that 'can be read, but not written' by the reader. Barthes called 'readerly' texts 'classic' (we might call them 'classic-realist' – see Chapter 6), those that position the reader as a passive consumer, and the 'writerly' text would be modernist or, like the *Alice* books, proto-modernist, those that demand a more active and interrogative reader. Here's Johnson.

> The readerly is constrained by considerations of representation: it is irreversible, 'natural', decidable, continuous, totalizable, and unified into a coherent whole ... The writerly is infinitely plural and open to the free play of ... difference, unconstrained by representative considerations, and transgressive of any desire for decidable, unified, totalized meaning.
>
> (Johnson 1980: 5–6)

I want to move now to another key French critical theorist whose ideas, like those of Barthes (and Foucault), have had the effect of radically destabilizing some conventional and 'common sense' ideas and have had a major impact on modern literary criticism. For Barthes, as we've seen, these are ideas around the free play of meaning, the text's difference from itself and the vital role of 'writerly' criticism. For Foucault, the key terms for critical enquiry are around the intimate relations between knowledge, discourse and power (and his influence can be most clearly seen in the work of Nancy Armstrong, whom we'll meet again later).

I turn now to the third of these theorists, René Girard, author of the landmark study *Desire, Deceit and the Novel* (originally 1961), which we'll see later in this book influenced important critics such as Eve Sedgwick. This study pioneered the notion that desire is imitative and triangulated, that we desire someone else's desire and identify with that other person's desire before desiring ourselves. This approach to desire is grounded in anthropological studies (of women as commodities exchanged between men) and has ideas in common (as Girard himself said) with Denis de Rougemont's wonderful *Love in the Western World* (originally 1939), which crucially emphasized that desire above all seeks out obstacles. (This connects with what we'll see Slavoj Žižek say about love when we look at Shakespeare's Sonnets in Chapter 2.) Girard contributed a lively analysis of *A Midsummer Night's Dream* to a very influential collection called *Textual Strategies* (1980). What he says about desire and triangulation here is vivid and serves to illustrate far more than a single Shakespeare play.

> The only constant element in the configuration is the convergence of more than one desire on a single object, as if perpetual rivalries were more important to the ... characters than their changing pretexts ... Even though obsessed with the flesh, desire is divorced from it; it is not instinctive and spontaneous; it never seems to know directly and immediately where its object lies; in order to locate that object, it cannot rely on such things as the pleasure of the ... senses ... Desire must therefore trust in another ... desire on which it patterns itself. As a consequence, desire ... perpetually runs to desire just as money runs to money in the capitalist system ... The most crucial point [is] the necessarily jealous and conflictual nature of mimetic convergence on a single object ... Each [lover] is an obstacle to the other in a game of imitation and rivalry that is their mode of alienation, and this alienation finally verges on trance-like possession ... There is a passion which is primarily the copy of a model, a passion that is destructive not only because of its sterile rivalries but because it dissolves reality ... The model may be present in the flesh ... and it may also rise from the pages of a book, come out of the frame of a picture, turn into the worship of a phantom, verbal or iconic.
>
> (In Harari ed. 1980: 190–93)

Among Michel Foucault's most influential books, and certainly his most accessible, was the first volume of his *The History of Sexuality* and, while Girard displaced desire from its unitary and unexamined place in Western culture and relocated it in networks of imitation and illusion, Foucault argued that power operated through discourse and its strategic mechanisms to produce sexuality itself.

Power for Foucault operates not to repress sex (the fallacy of the 'repressive hypothesis' in Victorian society) but the opposite – to produce, construct and regulate sex through discourse (a key word for Foucault), the discursive production of sexuality and of sexual subjects. For Foucault discourse, and discursive formations, refers to all the ways by which language in society operates to constitute knowledge and forms of subjectivity, and to exert mechanisms of power and control, both through domination and resistance. For Foucault, power is not a unified state apparatus but 'the multiplicity of power relations' in any particular area.

> Power is everywhere: not because it embraces everything, but because it comes from everywhere ... Power is not an institution, not a structure, nor a possession. It is the name we give to a complex strategic situation in a particular society.
>
> (Foucault 1978: 93)

Far from being silent about sex, the Victorian age, with its rage to classify, saw, in Foucault's words, the 'dispersion of devices invented for speaking about it, for having it be spoken about, for inducing it to speak of itself ... a whole network of varying, specific, and coercive transpositions into discourse ... a regulated and polymorphous incitement to discourse' (34). Instead of repressing different sexualities, they were isolated and incorporated in power mechanisms through the discourses of (for instance) medicine, the law and education. These mechanisms were the means of producing sexuality itself. Foucault put it like this.

> Sexuality is the name that may be given to a set of interlocking historical mechanisms ... a great surface network on which the stimulation of bodies, the intensification of pleasures, the incitement to discourse, the formation of sciences, the strengthening of controls and resistances are linked together in accordance with a few great strategies of knowledge and power.
>
> (105–06)

Four particularly strategic locations or unities centred on sex with their own 'specific mechanisms of knowledge and power' (103) were identified by Foucault as four ideologically necessary bodies or figures, saturated with anxiety and subjected to the need for control and surveillance: the hysterical or nervous woman (and thus inadequately moral mother); the self-pleasuring boy; the couple dependent on birth-control policies; and the 'perverse' adult, pathologized as the 'other' to the 'normal', 'healthy' man.

I'll add that a follower of Foucault, the historian David Halperin, quotes a gruesomely comic list from ancient Athens (that will remind you of Borges's encyclopaedia entry that Foucault was so taken with) and it certainly puts the Victorian classifying anxieties and rage to discourse about sex into perspective. The list is of things men do without any notion of mutuality.

> Namely, speaking, singing, dancing, fist-fighting, competing, hanging oneself, dying, being crucified, diving, finding a treasure, having sex,

vomiting, moving one's bowels, sleeping, laughing, crying, talking to the gods, and the like.

(In Richter ed. 2007: 1727)

'Culture is ordinary', politics and education: the exemplary Milton

It's time to move to the last phase of this first chapter and I want to move to some broader issues of culture and the more immediate impact on culture of politics. I start with a simple narrative of what happened around the word 'culture' between the 1950s and today.

In the 1950s, the great radical critic Raymond Williams insisted that culture was ordinary. In the 2010s the leaders of what came to be called the alt-right (now dominating mainstream populist-conservative thinking in many countries) insisted that culture is upstream from politics. Being upstream from politics, the implied task for culture is to enact what Walter Benjamin warned was the fascist agenda: to aestheticize politics. (Benjamin's counter-demand was to politicize aesthetics.)

Williams was concerned (from the left) to answer conservative critics like T.S. Eliot and F.R. Leavis for whom an implicitly elitist notion of culture was one that needed a kind of secular priesthood for protection and continuity in the threat of what they saw as the commercialism and vulgarity of 'mass-culture'. Those waging today's culture wars see the weaponization of culture as the principal means to advance the politics of populist division and fear. Narratives are produced and amplified in whatever media are available to demonize perceived enemies such as those easily labelled as 'others', especially immigrants.

From Williams, wanting to open out culture to the desires and hopes of everyone (culture from below), to today's empowered populist politicians deploying culture to achieve what they really want (power without accountability, decisions taken with impunity), is the story of the last sixty years. It's a culture war that it's easy to conclude that has been lost.

How might criticism respond? One response is to share with you what Edward Said argued about traditional literature and criticism. In it, the 'process of representation … reinforces the known at the expense of the knowable' and seeks 'to obliterate the traces of other relationships within literary structures' – ones that may be 'based principally on acquisition and appropriation. This is the great lesson of Raymond Williams's *The Country and the City*.' In his reading of 17th century country-house poems 'Williams teaches us to … remember that for every poem or novel in the canon there is a social fact being requisitioned for the page, a human life engaged, a class suppressed or elevated' (Said 1983: 22–23).

This famous passage from Williams has often been quoted (including in my last book). Williams's tone is suddenly charged with passion and anger when he urges us to respond with our fully sentient selves when we visit the grand country-houses of England and turn from them, as he says we should, to look at the small and isolated working farms and cottages in the area.

> But stand at any point and look at that land ... Think it through as labour and see how long and systematic the exploitation and seizure must have been ... to produce that degree of disparity, that barbarous disproportion of scale ... What these 'great' houses do is ... a visible stamping of power, of displayed wealth and command ... And will you then think of community? You will see modern community ... in the surviving exploiters and in their modern relations – the corporation country-house, the industrial seat, the ruling-class school.
>
> (Williams 1973: 132–33)

This connects directly with the 'heritage industry' and with debates around the curriculum in the UK. The 1980s National Curriculum placed what critics saw as a mythologized English identity at the heart of the history curriculum. Let me share with you Robert Hewison in 1987 (who pointed out that rather than manufacturing goods, the country was producing heritage) and Patrick Wright in 1985 (who wrote about the morbidity of heritage culture) – and then we'll look at Paul Gilroy on what he called postcolonial melancholia.

Patrick Wright said this about our preserving of country-houses as a means of collapsing current conflicts into an eternal and authentic Englishness.

> History [becomes] purged of political tensions; it becomes a unifying spectacle, the settling of all disputes. Like the guided tour as it proceeds from site to sanctified site, the national past occurs in a dimension of its own – a dimension in which we appear to remember only in order to forget.
>
> (Wright 1985: 69–70)

And Robert Hewison saw the heritage industry as a neurotic response to Britain being 'gripped by the perception that it is in decline'.

> The heritage industry is an attempt to dispel this climate of decline by exploiting the economic potential of our culture, and it finds a ready market because the perception of decline includes all sorts of insecurities and doubts ... Looking at a Laura Ashley catalogue ... we imagine ourselves living in a museum.
>
> (Hewison 1987: 9–10)

The enormous popularity of TV series like *Downton Abbey* is, of course, one clear manifestation of this cultural phenomenon, to mystify, glamourize and retreat to a conflict-free vision of the past that Williams saw in the country-house poetry of the 17th century.

Paul Gilroy's landmark 2005 *Postcolonial Melancholia* built on the findings of Freud and other psychoanalysts, especially those working on the German refusal to accept collective responsibility for Nazism, and argued (as they did) that the same applied for the evasion of collective responsibility in ex-colonial powers like Britain. This is felt as a 'loss of fantasy of omnipotence' and manifested in what Wright called remembering 'in order to forget' as well as a neurotic obsession not only with heritage but also with what we've already noted as today's 'culture wars' and the manipulation of antagonism towards 'others' (Gilroy 2005: 208–09).

In particular, Gilroy shows how the Second World War becomes a crucial cultural resource to be read as our finest hour before the impact of multiculturalism, the moment frozen in nostalgic misremembering as Britain's social body somehow untainted by race. (See also Dworkin 2009.)

The modern sociologist William Davies put it like this (in an article for *the Guardian* in late June 2021, as I finished writing this book).

> Freud made a distinction between 'mourning', in which a person suffers some loss or injury which they slowly and painfully move on from, and 'melancholia', in which they turn in on themselves in a hateful search for what's been lost, refusing to accept that it is gone. In [2005], cultural theorist Paul Gilroy adopted the same language to diagnose Britain's 'postcolonial melacholia', suggesting that the unrelenting culture and flag-waving and Churchill-worship signified an unhappy, angry quest for something that had been mislaid. Our new era of enforced union jacks … has proved Gilroy more right than he could possibly have feared. Boris Johnson didn't invent this melancholic culture, but he has encouraged and exploited it ruthlessly. It is there in the jingoistic headlines of tabloids, just as it is there in … confected 'culture war' issues … [and] the insistence that the future cannot – *must* not – be better than the past … [This is] the self-punishing aspect of melancholia that Freud identified.
>
> (Davies 2021: online)

The Harvard professor of history Timothy Snyder refers to sado-populism, which you might like to explore further.

Literary criticism may seem an almost irrelevant pursuit in the cultural landscape just outlined. But another look at what Eliot and Leavis found so worrying, and Williams found so empowering, may help us – may help you – to retain faith in critical thinking and critical reading as morally as well as culturally necessary. Chris Baldick said this about Leavis.

> What was new and threatening in the post-First World War world was precisely that the 'mass' was beginning actively to challenge the status of the minority, creating an oppositional language subversive of cultural authority.
>
> (Baldick 1987: 163)

The threat was to the guardians of 'high' minority culture. It's startling, even now, to recall how Leavis defined that minority. In what one critic has called the 'amazing' language of 'literary-critical eugenics' (Lane 2006: 199), Leavis speaks of these privileged few as the 'consciousness of the race', guardians of the standards 'upon which fine living depends', those entrusted to uphold the nation's 'health' and 'strength' and who guard against its 'decline'. A poet worth reading and studying is, for Leavis, 'more alive than other people … more himself than the ordinary man can be', but bound to be read properly by only a few because the 'ordinary cultivated reader is ceasing to be able to read poetry'.

The three poets chosen by Leavis, in his 1932 *New Bearings in English Poetry*, to carry the flame were Hopkins, Eliot and Ezra Pound. Richard Lane notes that Leavis's terms of praise for such poets derive partly from Pound himself, who said that the function of literature 'in the aggregate of humans … has to do with maintaining the very cleanliness of the tools, the health of the very matter of thought itself' (in Lane: 199–200). Eugenics is a strong word. But Pound and Eliot were very sympathetic to currents of political thought that invite such a word in this context. Frank Kermode put it in a very understated way in his excellent 1967 *The Sense of an Ending*.

> The radical thinking of the early modernists about the arts implied, in other spheres, opinions of a sort not normally associated with the word radical … It appears, in fact, that modernist radicalism in art … involves the creation of fictions which may be dangerous in the dispositions they breed towards the world.
>
> (Kermode 1967: 110–11)

In 1948 Leavis chose an equally, indeed even more controversially, restrictive list of novelists for *The Great Tradition* which centred on George Eliot, James and Conrad. Of all the responses I've seen to Leavis's notion that those three – with Jane Austen and D.H. Lawrence – were necessary (with Pound and Eliot's poetry) to combat the decline of the West, Terry Eagleton's has the advantage of being the funniest, though perhaps the humour is more desperate than anything else.

> It was doubtless comforting to feel that by reading Henry James one belonged to the moral vanguard of civilization itself; but what of all those people who did not read Henry James, who had never even heard of James, and would no doubt go to their graves complacently ignorant that he had been and gone? … Many of these people seemed morally serious and sensitive enough: they showed no particular tendency to go around murdering, looting and plundering, and even if they did it seemed implausible to attribute this to the fact that they had not read Henry James.
>
> (Eagleton 1983: 34–35)

Not that long before Leavis's polemical restrictions of the canon to those poets whom he called the 'consciousness of the race', the Newbolt Report of 1919 wrote of the post-war political urgency for education to use the 'confort' and 'mirthe' of literature to promote social cohesion. Terence Hawkes quotes from the Report. You'll see that what we called at the start of this chapter liberal-humanist or essentialist criticism lies behind the thinking here.

> Literature seems to be classified by a large number of thinking working men [sic] with … [the] unintelligible and futile trivialities of 'middle-class culture' … We regard the prevalence of such opinions as a serious matter, not merely because it means the alienation of an important section of the population [sic] from the 'confort' and 'mirthe' of literature, but chiefly because it points to a morbid condition of the body politic which if not taken in hand may be followed by lamentable consequences … For if literature be, as we believe, an embodiment of the best thoughts of the best minds, the most direct … communication of experience by man to men [sic] … then the nation of which a considerable proportion rejects this means of grace … must assuredly be heading for disaster.
>
> (In Hawkes 1986: 113)

Hawkes notes that one member of the Newbolt committee was more blunt. 'Deny to working class children any common share in the immaterial and presently they will grow into the men who demand with menaces a communism of the material' (in Hawkes: 113). In Chapter 6 we'll see Thomas Carlyle's warning, in similar though more socially liberal language, about the danger to Victorian England if the Chartists' demands weren't met.

It's words like 'grace' in the Newbolt Report that mark out the evangelizing and patrician tone and attitude, the top-down response of Eliot and Leavis. So it may be timely to share with you a contemporary critic (and educator) who describes clearly and movingly what is at stake in reading and thinking about literature, in sharp contrast to those like Eliot and Leavis for whom the 'properly' literary-critical was only fit for the selected few. This is Richard Rylance.

> The style of intensely dialectical, often unresolved exploration that characterises the intellectual achievement of major literary texts is a style of thinking appropriate to our times and the human situation in which … values are mainly provisional and consensual. I believe that the mode of knowledge with which we engage when we discuss literature – open, discursive, provisional, revisable, intersubjective – is emblematic of the ways values should operate in a society such as our own. I also believe in the value of clear, successful communication and … that it is a political and ethical imperative to spread this as widely as possible.
>
> (Rylance 2007: online)

Elaine Showalter put it like this. The teaching of literature is a 'humane, humanistic, value-laden art' (Showalter 2003: 136). As I write this, the news is of a rapid decline in those studying literature at 16 plus, and therefore at university, in the UK. This is due to the slow but very marked impact of an instrumentalist attitude towards education (long fostered by conservative government), despite the findings of reports like one that showed how children who read the Harry Potter books were more inclined to sympathy and kindness towards those judged different, than those who didn't read them.

John Milton (more on this greatest of poets in Chapter 3), in his pamphlet *On Education* (1644), put the teaching of poetry at the centre of a properly humanist education, arguing that it may be less 'subtle and fine' than rhetoric (traditionally with grammar at the cornerstone of the curriculum) but that it is 'more simple, sensuous and passionate'. Culture is ordinary and registered on and through the body. It is also expanding.

At the beginning of his landmark first book, *Culture and Society* (1958), Williams put it clearly. 'We live in an expanding culture, yet we spend much of our energy regretting the fact, rather than seeking to understand its nature and conditions' (Williams 1963: 12). And in a 1963 Postscript to the book' Williams turned to Milton and his later pamphlet *The Ready and Easy Way* (1660) in which he argued again for a republican commonwealth, just when the restoration of the monarchy was imminent. Milton stresses the crucial role in such a commonwealth of education for the diffusion of culture as well as the 'heat of government'.

> They should have ... schools and academies at their own choice, wherein their children may be bred up in their own sight to all learning and noble education; not in grammar only but in all liberal arts ... This would soon spread much more knowledge and civility ... by communicating the natural heat of government and culture... [which] would soon make the whole nation more ... ingenious at home [and] more honourable abroad. To this a Free Commonwealth will easily assent ... for of all governments a Commonwealth aims most to make the people flourishing, virtuous, noble and high-spirited.

In a marvellous image, Milton adds that monarchy aims instead to 'fleece' ordinary people for the 'supply of regal prodigality' and to keep people 'softest, basest ... servilest, easiest to be kept under ... in mind also sheepishest' (in Williams 1963: 326). That takes me to Robert Lowell's landmark poem 'For the Union Dead' (1964), which ends with the appalled perception of society run by a 'savage servility', sliding by 'on grease'.

Edward Said (drawing on Williams) wrote powerfully about oppositional criticism and its importance as (in Rylance's words) 'a political and ethical imperative'. Said's final words here are strikingly similar: criticism's support for the advancement of alternatives is a 'fundamental human and intellectual obligation'. The positions outlined here by Rylance, Williams and Said should perhaps be our critical touchstones.

> Were I to use one word consistently along with *criticism* ... it would be *oppositional* ... If [criticism] is to be in the world and self-aware simultaneously, then its identity is its difference from other cultural activities and from systems of thought or of method: in its suspicion of totalising concepts, in its discontent with reified objects, in its impatience with ... orthodox habits of mind ... 'Ironic' is not a bad word to use along with 'oppositional' ...

> Criticism must think of itself as life-enhancing and constitutionally opposed to every form of tyranny, domination, and abuse; its social goals are noncoercive knowledge produced in the interests of human freedom. If we agree with Raymond Williams, 'that however dominant a social system may be, the very meaning of its domination involves a limitation or selection of the activities it covers, so that by definition it cannot exhaust all social experience, which therefore always potentially contains space for alternative acts and alternative intentions which are not yet articulated as a social institution or even project' [Williams 1979: 252], then criticism belongs in that potential space inside civil society, acting on behalf of those alternative acts and alternative intentions whose advancement is a fundamental human and intellectual obligation.
>
> (Said 1983: 29–30)

Works cited

Carol Atherton, *Defining Literary Criticism* (Palgrave: 2005)
Eric Auerbach, *Mimesis* trs. Willard Trask (Princeton U.P.: 2003)
Chris Baldick, *The Social Mission of English Criticism* (Oxford U.P.: 1987)
Francis Barker, *The Tremulous Private Body* (Methuen: 1984)
Roland Barthes, *Mythologies* trs. Annette Lavers (Paladin: 1972)
Roland Barthes, *Image, Music, Text* trs. Stephen Heath (Fontana: 1977)
Jonathan Bate, *The Song of the Earth* (Harvard U.P.: 2000)
Walter Benjamin, *Illuminations* ed. Hannah Arendt, trs. Harry Zohn (Fontana: 1973)
Margaret Cohen ed., *Flaubert: Madame Bovary* (Norton: 2005)
Jonathan Culler, *Roland Barthes* (Oxford U.P.: 2002)
William Davies, 'Punishing the young serves Johnson's politics of nostalgia', *Guardian* 22 June 2021.
Lennard J. Davis, *Resisting Novels* (Methuen: 1987)
Denis de Rougemont, *Love in the Western World* trs. Montgomery Belgion (Princeton U.P.: 1983)
Juliet Dusinberre, *From Alice to The Lighthouse* (Macmillan: 1999)
Dennis Dworkin, 'Paul Gilroy and the cultural politics of decline', *Rethinking History* Vol. 13, Issue 4: 2009.
Terry Eagleton, *Literary Theory* (Blackwell: 1983)
Anthony Easthope, *Poetry as Discourse* (Methuen: 1983)
William Empson, *Essays on Shakespeare* (Cambridge U.P.: 1986)
Michel Foucault, *The History of Sexuality* Vol. 1 trs. Robert Hurley (Random House: 1978)
Paul Gilroy, *Postcolonial Melancholia* (Columbia U.P.: 2005)
René Girard, *Desire, Deceit and the Novel* trs. Yvonne Freccero (Johns Hopkins U.P.: 1976)
Josue V. Harari ed., *Textual Strategies* (Methuen: 1980)
Terence Hawkes, *That Shakespeherean Rag* (Methuen: 1986)
Robert Hewison, *The Heritage Industry* (Methuen: 1987)
Geoffrey Hill, *The Lords of Limit* (Oxford U.P.: 1984)
Peter Humm *et al.* edd., *Popular Fictions* (Methuen: 1986)
Barbara Johnson, *The Critical Difference* (Johns Hopkins U.P.: 1980)

David Jones, *In Parenthesis* (Faber: 1963)
Hugh Kenner, *The Stoic Comedians* (California U.P.: 1962)
Frank Kermode, *The Sense of an Ending* (Oxford U.P.: 1967)
Frank Kermode ed., *T.S. Eliot: Selected Prose* (Faber: 1975)
Richard J. Lane, *Fifty Key Literary Theorists* (Routledge: 2006)
Kathi Maio, 'Disney's Dolls', *New Internationalist* 5 December 1998.
Claude Rawson, *God, Gulliver, and Genocide* (Oxford U.P.: 2000)
David Richter ed., *The Critical Tradition* (Bedford/St. Martin's: 2007)
Ryan Ruby, 'Reading the Room', *New Left Review: Sidecar* 22 February 2021.
Richard Rylance, 'But … Why Study English?' *English Subject Centre* 2007.
Edward Said, *The World, The Text, and The Critic* (Harvard U.P.: 1983)
Eve Sedgwick, *Between Men* (Columbia U.P.: 1985)
Elaine Showalter, *Teaching Literature* (Blackwell: 2003)
Raymond Williams, *Culture and Society* (Penguin: 1963)
Raymond Williams, *The Country and the City* (Chatto and Windus: 1973)
Raymond Williams, *Politics and Letters* (New Left Books: 1979)
Patrick Wright, *On Living in an Old Country* (Verso: 1985)

2 Shakespeare

with Sean McEvoy

Henry IV Part 1, Hamlet, Othello, King Lear, Macbeth, Twelfth Night, the Sonnets

You will have noticed that Shakespeare is alone in this book in having a chapter devoted solely to himself, and you may be wondering why. There are many reasons why his work has become central to the subject of English literature, with an influence that extends over all those writers who have followed. The origins of English literary criticism can be seen to lie in 18th century writers on Shakespeare like Maurice Morgann and Samuel Johnson (both of whom we'll meet below), and there is a huge body of Shakespeare criticism that has set the agenda for work on other writers. But though he was recognized in his time as a major playwright and poet, at his death in 1616 it would no doubt have astonished his contemporaries to see the dominant position in English literature and national (and, as we'll see shortly, American) culture that he was to reach. In England he is the only author that school students must study by law, and there is a large, state-funded theatre company dedicated to the performance of his plays (the Royal Shakespeare Company). In America he is studied in over 90 per cent of schools. The intention, explicit in the case of the British school curriculum, is that the study of a such an essentially English writer will help foster a sense of national unity in an increasingly diverse and multicultural country.

Whether the same can be said in the case of America is the subject of a quite remarkable book by James Shapiro, *Shakespeare in a Divided America*, published in 2020. This seems a good place to start our thinking about the place of an iconic cultural figure like Shakespeare in the broadest critical contexts.

Shapiro presents a series of chapters focused on highly charged moments in American history in which Shakespeare and productions of his plays were (as Fintan O'Toole put it in his review for the *Irish Times*, on 7 March 2020) a 'catalyst for conflict and a weapon in the culture wars'. Shapiro admits that Trump's 2016 election was his own catalyst to write about Shakespeare in a divided America, just when another distinguished Shakespearean, Stephen Greenblatt, was openly comparing Trump to a Shakespearian tyrant. And in the summer after Trump's 2016 inauguration there was a momentous production of *Julius Caesar* in Central Park, New York, for which Shapiro was an advisor, and in which the

DOI: 10.4324/9781003127567-3

director Oscar Eustis was specifically aiming for a cathartic experience for the very many people who were then feeling a kind of political vertigo. Shapiro's book begins and ends with this production in which a very evidently Trump-like Caesar is assassinated, to the ensuing fury of the right-wing media.

Other chapters deal with extraordinary events like the bloody riot of 1849 outside a production of *Macbeth* in New York's Astor Place theatre against which a huge crowd had mobilized in (O'Toole's words) 'populist rage against the establishment … If this were now, the rioters would surely be wearing MAGA hats'. (For more on this riot, see McEvoy 2016.) A dozen or so years earlier the former president John Quincy Adams had argued (in two articles of 1835) that the message of *Othello* was that to intermingle black and white blood is a 'gross outrage upon the law of Nature; and that, in such violations, Nature will vindicate her laws'. For Adams, any terror or pity felt as we watch Othello killing Desdemona will 'subside immediately into the sentiment that she has her deserts'. And Shapiro illuminatingly shows how the 1998 film *Shakespeare in Love* was, in the process of its production, purged of its more subversive and potentially homoerotic features. (The producer was Harvey Weinstein.)

Here's Shapiro, from his Introduction, on Shakespeare's central place in the American educational and cultural systems.

> At first glance it seems almost perverse that Americans would choose to make essential to their classrooms and theatres a writer whose works enact some of their darkest nightmares or most lurid fantasies: a black man marrying then killing a white woman; a Jew threatening to cut a pound of a Christian's flesh; the brutal assassination of a ruler deemed tyrannical; the taming of a wife who defies male authority … As I write these words in November 2018, a news report describes how parents of students at [a high school in] North Carolina were shocked to discover that a performance of the satirical 1987 adaptation *The Complete Works of William Shakespeare (Abridged)* at the school included 'suicide, alcohol consumption and bad language'. What they seem to have found even more objectionable was a same-sex kiss.
>
> (Shapiro 2020: 2)

The parents (after gathering in a prayer circle) organized a petition to ban any such promotion of homosexuality or suicide in their school district, in what Shapiro calls an 'example of how Shakespeare speaks to the fears that divide us as a nation'.

> His writing continues to function as a canary in a coal mine, alerting us to, among other things, the toxic prejudices poisoning our cultural climate.
>
> (2)

In terms of Britain and its projection of itself as the undivided imperial nation, the idea that Shakespeare was archetypically English in what he wrote and how he wrote it made him a powerful cultural icon, almost a national totem during Britain's rise to global dominance in the late 18th and 19th centuries. By 1840 Thomas Carlyle could declare Shakespeare to be 'the grandest thing we have yet done', pointedly adding that he was worth more to England than the 'Indian Empire' and that he could imagine him 'radiant aloft over all the Nations of Englishmen [i.e. English-speaking nations], a thousand years hence' (in Foulkes 2002: 6–7).

Carlyle's point about Shakespeare being worth more than the Indian Empire is pointed (in retrospect) by what postcolonial readings of Shakespeare, especially *The Tempest*, have shown about the role of the plays in the British Empire. They were performed in India as part of the colonial project, to justify imperialism to its subjects and to convey the ideological argument for the superiority of Western values.

There is no doubt that Shakespeare as a national, imperial icon was crucial to his central place as English developed as a subject at the end of the 19th and beginning of the 20th centuries. Indeed, by the 1980s there would be a backlash against this dominance for exactly those associations, so that the plays would be seen, according to David Margolies, as deliberately employed to 'represent a class position that accords with an elitist notion of culture and a ruling-class view of the world' (in Holderness ed. 1988: 45).

But that can't explain the continuing presence of Shakespeare as a world dramatist at a time when British international prestige and influence has never been weaker. This is not because the plays are 'universal' in the sense often claimed, that there is some insight into 'human nature' in them that makes them apply to all peoples in all places. In large parts of the world, after all, he is unread and unperformed. The historical legacy which Shakespeare brings with him is certainly important to his prominence in literary studies. But there are other factors, too. Shakespeare was one of the most acute and insightful writers at the dawn of the modern period, a time when the ways of ordering our world with all its hierarchies had not yet become fixed and the world need not have taken the direction it took. As Hugh Grady puts it, 'precisely because these plays estrange what four centuries of history have made us perceive as normal and natural, they take on a significance now that they never could have had for those audiences' (Grady 1996: 24–25). For Kiernan Ryan, there is in fact a kind of historical universality in the plays.

> [They embody a] commitment to the cause of humanity as a whole … [a] *capacity for communication*, for creating and addressing a community of minds united in a common cause … [Shakespeare's drama] is shaped and phrased in such a way as to activate our awareness of the potential we share with the protagonists, and with all human beings then and now, to live more fulfilling lives than those we find ourselves compelled to live by the place and time we happen to inhabit.
>
> (Ryan 2015: 13–14, 26)

For Ewan Fernie, 'Shakespeare means freedom. That is why the plays matter, and not just aesthetically but also in terms of the impact they have had and can continue to have on personal and political life in the world' (Fernie 2017: 1).

What Fernie and Ryan say about freedom and community is well said and important, but we might also remember that community in Shakespeare's plays can be built on what Shapiro calls 'its principle of exclusion'. This, as he points out, certainly applies to awkward figures like Shylock and Malvolio who, in effect, have to be excluded and ejected in order to ensure the 'charmed circle' of the endings of *The Merchant of Venice* and *Twelfth Night* (in which, as we'll see, the same is true of Antonio). As nations as well as individuals, 'we define ourselves against those whom we reject, keep out, or lock up' (Shapiro 2020: 3).

Let's now move to some, highly selective, ways of thinking about Shakespeare and his plays in general before we look at six particular plays (and this chapter will end with his Sonnets). One starting point might be a quality in his plays that for a long time was rather unfashionable to talk about in critical circles: his richly credible characters, their verisimilitude. This was most memorably written about as early as 1777, in a book ostensibly about Falstaff, by a civil servant called Maurice Morgann. And it's an extraordinary and extensive footnote he suddenly adds when writing about Shakespeare's 'dramatic characters'. Here's the heart of it. Morgann notes that, for theatre audiences, we necessarily see the characters 'only in part' but as 'capable of being unfolded and understood in the whole; every part being in fact relative, and inferring all the rest'.

> Very frequently, when no particular point presses, he boldly makes a character act and speak from those parts of the composition, which are *inferred* only, and not distinctly shown. This produces a wonderful effect [of] a felt propriety and truth from causes unseen … It may be fit to consider [Shakespeare's characters] rather as historic than dramatic beings; and, when occasion requires, to account for their conduct from the *whole* of character, from general principles, from latent motives, and from policies not avowed.
>
> (In Smith ed. 1946: 172)

One random example follows: when the absurd Andrew Aguecheek, in *Twelfth Night*, after Toby Belch casually mentions how much he's adored by Maria, suddenly says 'I was adored, once, too' (2.3), the ground seems to open out beneath him as the audience is suddenly (and momentarily) made to supply what is only inferred or unseen, a presumably wish-fulfilling back-story.

The apparent solidity of Shakespeare's characters, 'whole' and 'original' compared to what Morgann calls 'mere imitation' in other writers, is approached in another way by Janet Adelman at the start of her great 1992 book *Suffocating Mothers*, a searching exploration of masculinity and the maternal body in Shakespeare, when she looks at what she calls the 'extraordinary moment' in the early history play *Henry VI Part 3* when the man who will become Richard III speaks of his plans to compensate for his deformity (and, therefore, lack of fulfilling love) by plotting for the throne.

> We hear – I think for the first time in Shakespeare – the voice of a fully developed subjectivity, the characteristically Shakespearean illusion that a stage person has interior being, including motives that he himself does not fully understand … The explanation Richard gives himself turns on his construction of a psychic myth of origins … What he speaks about is the origin of his aggression in the problematic maternal body.
>
> (Adelman 1992: 1–2)

We'll see more from Adelman later in her excellent reading of Gertrude in *Hamlet.*

Rosalie Colie, in the last pages of her important book *Shakespeare's Living Art* (to which we'll also return later in relation to the Sonnets), comes at the illusion of interiority in Shakespeare by looking at its unusual absence in the bitter satire-comedy *Troilus and Cressida*, which, systematically, operates an emptying out of the usual plenitudes and richnesses of Shakespeare's craft, not least in its anti-characterization, its cruel belittlement of Homer's archetypes that provided his source material. Colie contrasts this play with what is more usually characteristic.

> Words can annihilate as well as create: characteristically, we have watched how Shakespeare recreates language by enriching its outworn ground, by replanting it with newer, finer referents. Here, he shows us how words detached from their received referents can unmake … can show us [characters] conniving at that dismantling, trading their enriched inherited identities for counters in a game without rules, impoverishing themselves and their tradition … Such an exercise in 'undoing' allows us to see … Shakespeare's customary habits of 'doing', of examining and enriching traditions. His renewing and reanimating of literary forms by realigning them with a more imaginatively conceived mimetic reality becomes even more remarkable when we realize, by studying the emptying-out of *Troilus and Cressida*, how fully he understood … how precarious the relation is between morality and literary technique.
>
> (Colie 1974: 349–51)

What both Morgann and Colie say about Shakespeare's craft, in relation to modes of reality and the forms of its representation, can be usefully situated when we think about the broader shifts in cultural and socio-political practices and ways of organizing and perceiving the world and the staged world in Shakespeare's life-time. One simple example (to which we'll return below) is to note that the world of *Hamlet* dramatizes a shift from, and an implicit conflict between, two world-views corresponding to Hamlet's two fathers: the feudal world of old Hamlet (ritual, ceremony, inherited forms of community, duty and blood-ties) and the early-capitalist world of Claudius, Hamlet's other 'father' (geo-political manoeuvring, the surveillance-state, the alienated and isolated individual). C.L. Barber in 1959 writes very well about a version of this shift, the 'moment when educated men were modifying a ceremonial conception of human life to create a historical conception'.

> The ceremonial view, which assumed that names and meanings are fixed and final, expressed experience as pageant and ritual – pageant where the right names could march in proper order, or ritual where names could be changed in the right, the proper way. The historical view expresses life as drama. People in drama are not identical with their names, for they gain and lose their names, their status and meaning – and not by settled ritual: the gaining and losing of names, of meaning, is beyond the control of any set ritual sequence. Shakespeare's … pageants are regularly interrupted, the rituals are aborted or perverted; or if they succeed, they succeed against odds or in an unexpected fashion. The people in the plays try to organise their loves by pageant and ritual, but the plays are dramatic precisely because the effort fails.
>
> (Barber 1959: 220–21)

A few years after Barber wrote that in his study of the comedies, Northrop Frye wrote this (originally in 1966) about the tragedies, or rather about the experience of tragedy.

> If there is anything more than absurdity and anguish in the death of Lear or Othello, it comes, not from anything additional that we can see in or know about the situation, but from what we have participated in with them up to that moment. When Macbeth sees life as a meaningless idiot's tale, we can see that such a vision of absurdity is right for Macbeth at that point, and is therefore true for him. But it is not the whole truth, even for him, because he is capable of articulating it, nor for us, because we have shared with him, however reluctantly, an experience too broad and varied to be identified with its inevitable end, however desired an end. Tragedy finds its ultimate meaning neither in heroic death nor in ironic survival, nor in any doctrine deducible from either, but in its own re-enactment as experience … At the end of a comedy a new society is created or restored and the characters go off to a new life out of our reach … At the end of a tragedy … there is a far greater sense of mystery, because (paradoxically) it is not what the characters have learned from their tragic experience, but what we have learned from participating in it, that directly confronts us.
>
> (Frye 1967: 117–19)

We'll turn now to six plays (and the Sonnets) and to what critics have said about them from the 18th century to today.

However profoundly Shakespeare explores human psychology and relationships, his theatre was inevitably intertwined with political power and its expression in his time. Not only was the publication and performance of his plays subject to licensing by a state censor (the Master of the Revels) but actors themselves were required by law to be in the service of a nobleman – or even of the monarchy or members of the royal family. The company to which Shakespeare belonged became the King's Men on James I's accession in 1603.

How the monarchy operated was very much the focus of the history plays he wrote in the final years of the sixteenth century. In these plays the idea that monarchs had become themselves primarily performers, as Machiavelli said they must, is subtly and provocatively made part of the theatrical event.

In ***King Henry IV** Part 1* Prince Hal tells the audience that he is spending his time with Falstaff and his crew only to create a startling impression of his virtue at his chosen moment of moral reformation, when he will appear 'like bright metal on a sullen ground' (1.2). In these plays the legitimacy of monarchy has become dependent not upon blood but upon the convincing performance of the role, once power has been seized. Jean Howard explains how Richard II (who was deposed by Hal's father Henry IV in the play's prequel) had 'probably the best blood claim to the throne in any of the Shakespearean history plays'. But that doomed monarch only produced 'gorgeous but ineffective rhetoric' and 'histrionic poses', serving only to 'reveal the emptiness of legitimate titles severed from pragmatic skills necessary to invest them with meaning' (Howard 1994: 141). Hal's father also thinks a king must keep himself apart from his people so that, 'being seldom seen', he might 'like a comet' be best 'wondered at' (3.2). Hal knows different.

In the (very Elizabethan-seeming) tavern in *Henry IV* Part 1, Hal and Falstaff both play the king to entertain the regulars in a piece of improvised comic theatre (2.4). Howard says this.

> The most astonishing thing about their play-acting sequence is that it makes kingship so self-consciously into a role to be performed. The conventions of the stage provide languages for rendering that role … Their playlets, moreover, are performed before the admiring and critical eyes of other tavern-goers, suggesting that there are informed consumers of theatrical art ready to judge the performance of any would-be king. Even Mistress Quickly, not the most sophisticated of critics, praises Falstaff for how he 'holds his countenance' and says his performance is 'as like one of these harlotry players as ever I see'. This is an urban culture accustomed to consuming theatrical fare, and is accustomed to seeing any social role, even that of the king, turned into the matter for any harlotry player to imitate.
>
> (Howard 1994: 142–43)

There is a way to perform kingship effectively, and the theatre both demonstrated this and was integral to the model of how kingship functioned in the world – and to an audience that appreciated it. Stephen Greenblatt (in his celebrated essay 'Invisible bullets') goes further in suggesting that the play shows how the performer-monarch, needing an audience to impress and justify his power, makes his audience of subjects complicit in the whole performance.

> Prodded by constant reminders of a gap between real and ideal, facts and values, the spectators are induced to make up the difference, to invest in the illusion of magnificence, to be dazzled by their own imaginary

> identification with the conqueror. The ideal king must be in large part the invention of the audience, a product of a will to conquer which is revealed to be identical to a need to submit.
>
> (In Dollimore and Sinfield edd. 1985: 43)

Greenblatt shows that Hal's playing of multiple roles in the play underpins the subversive notion that the monarch is not divinely ordained, but a human like the rest of us – a reading already contained in the notion of kingship that we buy into in the theatre.

> Hal's characteristic activity is playing or, more precisely, theatrical improvisation – his parts include his father, Hotspur, Hotspur's wife, a thief in Buckram, himself as prodigal and himself as penitent – and he fully understands his own behaviour through most of the play as a role that he is performing ... [So] subversion is the condition of power ... [and] theatricality ... is not set over against power but is one of power's essential modes.
>
> (33, 45)

As for Falstaff, Hal's alternative father figure, David Scott Kastan argues that his particular subversiveness, rather than just legitimized by royal power, is more potentially politicized.

> [His] role-playing may have appeared less productive of power than a challenge to it, and the comic plot may seem indeed to give compelling voice to what aristocratic history would repress ... [His mimicry] exposes the narrow self-interests of those in power and those who seek it. His improvisatory clowning challenges the illusionistic representation of history, directly engaging the spectators in the yard, even as history insists on their respectful distance ... Falstaff's exuberance refuses to be dominated by any authority, resisting incorporation into or containment within the stabilizing hierarchies of the body politic or indeed the well-made play.
>
> (Kastan 2002: 38–39)

Falstaff's extensive role-playing includes playing dead on the battlefield at Shrewsbury to save his life (5.4). Jean Howard adds about this that, since the King himself has other warriors in the battle dressed as himself, when Falstaff 'feigns death in order to avoid having to engage in battle and then pretends to have killed the already dead Hotspur ... he indirectly implicates Henry IV in similar crimes' (Howard 1994: 145). This serves to destabilize yet further the legitimacy of kingship and is yet another example of the self-awareness in the history plays of the theatricality of politics and the politics of theatricality.

Hamlet is very famously concerned with, even obsessed with, theatricality and the performative, but it's also the case that it lends itself to the notion that there has been some kind of rupture within history – time being now 'out of joint' (1.5) – into which Hamlet finds himself thrust. Paul Cantor, for instance, sees Hamlet's potential role as a would-be hero undermined by the world and time he is obliged to inhabit. His attempts to dress up his father in classical terms, as Hyperion, Jove, Mars or Mercury, his mother as a potential Niobe, or himself in his vision of the classical avenger Pyrrhus through the Player King's speech, are futile in this new haunted world. The only time Hamlet acts with heroic decisiveness, when he kills Polonius, 'he literally does not know what he is doing' (Cantor 2004: 48).

> [Heroism] has become deeply problematical where … he is haunted by visions of a world beyond … Heroic action begins to lose some of its lustre when viewed from the perspective of eternity … [And he dies in] a game that is not really a game, a battle that is not really a battle, fighting against his opponent who is not his true opponent, in a cause that is not his true cause.
>
> (24, 43, 49)

This connects with what we saw in the introduction to this chapter about Hamlet and his impossible place between two worlds and two fathers. Denmark itself is on a fault line between the 'Homeric' classical heroism of Hamlet's dead father, who took on opponents in single combat, and the modern Machiavellian world of Claudius. This conflict is complicated further by the principles of Christian piety and passivity which run contrary to both. Hamlet is very much the man of his time.

> [He is] a quintessential tragic figure of the Renaissance [where] … the inner contradictions of the era come to consciousness in his alert and capacious mind … Trying to combine disparate ethics, he exposes the profound tensions between those ethics, ending up in a tragic situation in which his own principles make contradictory demands upon him and hence paralyse him … His intellect is constantly leading him to deny meaning to the very acts he feels impelled to perform … In the process [of destroying Claudius] he ends up destroying much that is good in Denmark as well, including himself.
>
> (49–55)

Ultimately, he refuses to shape the course of action anymore. And it's a kind of world-weary suicide that comes to him of its own accord, like the Gravedigger's water (5.1).

Michael Neill locates the tragic time-rupture even more precisely in England's cultural history, in the post-Reformation world where the dead were now beyond the help and the prayers of the living. In Protestant England the church's teaching required people to abandon their centuries-old belief in Purgatory. Revenge tragedies like *Hamlet* were implicated in the new relationship with the dead that was required; the avenger is like the new Protestants.

> [They wrestle to] redeem the dead from the shame of being forgotten, even as they struggle to lay those perturbed spirits to rest and thereby free themselves from the insistent presence of the past.
>
> (Neill 1997: 246)

Again, there is a difficulty in meaningfully connecting the past to the present. Neill shows that, in *Hamlet*, this anxiety is strong, and it emerges in the play's unfinished stories (such as Barnardo's in 1.1, or the play *The Murder of Gonzago* which of course ends abruptly in 3.2) and also in the 'insultingly stunted or indecorous' (246) funeral rites such as those for Polonius (4.5) and Ophelia (5.1). The demands of the ghost also place an intolerable burden on the present.

> [Hamlet's] tormenting paradox [is that the] dream of remembering the violated past and destroying its tainted order is fulfilled at the cost of repeating the violation and spreading the taint.
>
> (251)

Hamlet's attempt to rejoin the past and present is endlessly deferred, as 'every avenger becomes his antagonist's double' (260).

The ghost, whilst demanding attention to history, pours its own poison into Hamlet's ear and usurps him, requiring him to forget all other events and to become a kind of ghost himself, haunting and marginalized. The commitment to put past and present together again in an act of restorative justice leads only to the oblivion of death, for 'nothing short of death will satisfy the ghost, but it also arouses a curiosity nothing short of death will answer' (256). Even Hamlet's own play-memorials become hopelessly equivocal: Priam in the Player King's speech (2.2) is both Old Hamlet and Claudius; Gonzago's poisoner (3.2) is both Claudius as murderer and Hamlet as avenger. Acutely aware that he is living in a fractured time, until he resigns into an anti-climactic quiescence Hamlet cannot put his story together so that it makes clear sense.

We'll look, finally on *Hamlet*, at another way of thinking about this complicatedly troubling play.

In her very close and compelling reading of Gertrude in *Hamlet*, one that perhaps more than any other faces directly the problem of the character's unknowable opacity in relation to her motives and possible complicity in the murder, Janet Adelman says this about what she calls 'the first mother to reappear' in the plays since the mother so symptomatically blamed as origin of deformity in the passage that we looked at from *Henry VI Part 3* at the start of this chapter.

> The first mother to reappear in Shakespeare's plays is adulterous, I think, because maternal origin is in itself felt as equivalent to adulterating betrayal of the male, both father and son; *Hamlet* initiates the period of Shakespeare's greatest tragedies because it in effect rewrites the story of Cain and Abel as the story of Adam and Eve, relocating masculine identity in the

> presence of the adulterating female ... Less powerful as an independent character than as the site for fantasies larger than she is, she is pre-eminently mother as other, the intimate unknown figure around whom these fantasies swirl ... Her body is the garden in which her husband dies, her sexuality the poisonous weeds that kill him, and poison the world – and the self – for her son ... Here, as in Shakespeare's later plays, the loss of the father turns out in fact to mean the psychic domination of the mother: in the end, it is the spectre of his mother, not his uncle-father, who paralyses his will.
>
> (Adelman 1992: 30)

Let's turn to ***Othello*** (which we noted at the outset of this chapter much exercised the mind of John Quincy Adams) and say first that of all Shakespeare's protagonists Othello has been often seen by critics as, even more than Hamlet, caught in an irreconcilable conflict between different historical forces. As a black Moorish general, a convert from Islam to Christianity in the service of Venice who marries the daughter of a Venetian senator, he becomes, as Karen Newman sees it, 'a monster in the Renaissance sense of the word ... both hero and outsider' (Newman 2009: 57, 53): a startling hybrid, half-one thing, half-another.

In his wooing of Desdemona, he charms her through tales of his African origins and exotic adventures (1.3) at the same time as he 'submits and embraces the dominant values of Venetian culture' (49). Her falling in love with him will conveniently align female sexuality with monstrosity within a society dominated by 'the white male hegemony that rules Venice, a world of prejudice, ambition, jealousy and denial of difference'. Desdemona expresses the doubleness of Othello in Venetian eyes when she says that 'I saw Othello's visage in his mind' (1.3), but 'far from washing the Moor white, as the line seems to imply, [it] emphatically affirms Othello's link with Africa and its legendary monstrous creatures' (52), rendering her monstrous, too.

> As the object of Desdemona's illegitimate passion, Othello both figures monstrosity *and* at the same time represents the white male norms the play encodes through Iago, Roderigo, Brabantio. Not surprisingly, Othello reveals at last a complicitous self-loathing.
>
> (52)

Newman sees Iago as both a 'cultural hyperbole', the essence of 'cultural norms' (50) but also embodying the anxieties that dominate the city: masculine individualism, amoral competitiveness in the pursuit of wealth and sex. The play works to expose starkly the fault lines that run through this society, where the warrior hero's fate is sealed by a woman's handkerchief.

> Othello's tragic action revolves not around a heroic act or even object ... but around a feminine toy. Instead of relegating *Othello* to the critical category of 'domestic tragedy', always implicitly or explicitly pejorative

> because of its focus on women, jealousy and a [love] triangle, we can reveal *Othello* from another perspective, also admittedly historically bound, that seeks to displace conventional interpretations by exposing the extraordinary fascination with and fear of racial and sexual difference that characterizes Elizabethan and Jacobean culture ... [But at the same time] by making the black Othello a hero, and by making Desdemona's love for Othello, and her transgression of her society's norms for women in choosing him, sympathetic, Shakespeare's play stands in a contestatory relation to the hegemonic ideologies of race and gender in early modern England.
>
> (57–58)

Kiernan Ryan also sees the play as a challenge to dominant patriarchal ideas. Ryan quotes Emilia's 'trenchant, impassioned' speech to Desdemona (4.3) where she talks of 'the injustice built into marriage' (Ryan 2002: 87), embodied in the male double standard and in the husband's claim to possession of his wife, enforced by violence if necessary. Many critics look no further than the idea that the tragedy springs from the fact that Othello's jealousy is groundless, as if 'the killing of Desdemona would have been justified if Othello had been right and his wife *had* been cuckolding her husband with Cassio' (88). But Emilia's speech works otherwise.

> This startling passage invites us to recognise that the true sexual tragedy springs from Othello's thraldom to the male version of marital jealousy and the male presumption of dominion and possession from which such jealousy is the outcome. Emilia's argument leaves us no room to doubt that sexual deceit and vengeful jealousy, whether justified or not, are the predictable results of organized inequality and oppression, and that they cannot be understood, never mind judged, as transgressions solely attributable to the individual in question ... Its egalitarian female perspective defines the play as a specific masculinist tragedy: a tragedy produced not only by Iago's prejudiced hatred of the Moor, but by Othello's adherence to the prevailing sexual ideology.
>
> (88)

As he commits suicide at the end of play, Othello identifies himself with an enemy of the state, a Turk he once slew in Aleppo (5.2). Ryan says this.

> What we have here is nothing else than a compressed definition of the whole tragedy ... Othello portrays himself both as a servant and instrument of the Venetian state and as the Turk, the 'circumcised dog' whom Venice feels threatened by and whom it despises. He correctly perceives himself to have been both the alien victim of Venetian society and the active, though unwilling, accomplice of its destruction of him ... [in a] socially scripted production, in which Othello now sees himself to have been fatally miscast.
>
> (88–89)

But he does see that miscasting, ultimately. The conflict is within himself, and in a particular kind of tragic recognition he perceives this. Looking back, he can distance himself from it, as he points to 'that's he that was Othello; here I am' (5.2).

> By insisting on the distinction between the self disclosed by the catastrophe and the fatal part he has had to play as the noble Moor and jealous husband 'Othello', Shakespeare drives home the revelation that destinies such as this are neither natural nor inevitable, but the resistible result of a world that can be changed.
>
> (89)

A world that can be changed. What Shakespeare's next and greatest tragedy ***King Lear*** confronts is the irresistible force of what is, certainly in contrast to *Othello*'s naturalistic domesticity, an ironically driven mythic structure (modernist and anti-naturalistic) that Lear unwittingly releases at the start of the play and that ends, with appallingly cruel logic, in the most painfully shocking death in Western literature. Dr Johnson, until faced with editing the play, simply couldn't read it. He famously endorsed Nahum Tate's rewriting of the play, especially its ending, that replaced the original on the London stage from the late 17th to the early 19th century. Johnson said this about Tate.

> In the present case the public has decided. Cordelia, from the time of Tate, has always retired with victory and felicity. And, if my sensations could add anything to the general suffrage, I might relate I was many years ago so shocked by Cordelia's death that I know not whether I ever endured to read again the last scenes of the play till I undertook to [read] them as an editor.
>
> (In Cruttwell ed. 1968: 296–97)

Northrop Frye, in his 1966 lectures on Shakespeare's tragedies, also confronts the end of *King Lear*, refusing the consolations of redemptive readings (like the influential late Victorian A.C. Bradley's). His use of the word 'absurd' at the end of this extract connects inevitably with the famous and influential readings of the tragedies by Jan Kott, whose work appeared at almost exactly the same time.

> *King Lear* has been called a purgatorial tragedy, and if that means a structure even remotely like Dante's *Purgatorio*, we should expect to see, as we see in Dante, existence being taken over and shaped by a moral force. Our understanding of the tragedy, then, would have that qualified response in it that is inseparable from a moral or conceptual outlook. It is true that Lear has suffered terribly, but he has thereby gained, etc. Suffering is inevitable in the nature of things, yet, etc. But, of course, Lear is not saying anything like this at the end of the play: what he is saying is that Cordelia is gone, and will never, never come back to him. Perhaps he thinks that she is coming back to life again, and dies of an unbearable joy. But we do not see this: all

> we see is an old man dying of an unbearable pain. The hideous wrench of agony which the death of Cordelia gives to the play is too much a part of the play even to be explained as inexplicable. And whatever else may be true, the vision of absurd anguish in which the play ends certainly is true.
>
> (Frye 1967: 135)

Jan Kott's chapter is called '*King Lear*, or Endgame' and throughout it evokes the early plays of Samuel Beckett (the most famous of which we will meet later in this book). Kott's reading is closely associated with what was perhaps the greatest of all 20th century productions of the play, directed by Peter Brook and starring Paul Scofield in 1962 (which in turn led to an enormously influential film of 1971). Here is Kott, on the play's most astonishing scene, 4.6, and its 'comedy of the grotesque' (the phrase is from the landmark *Lear* chapter in G. Wilson Knight's 1930s book *The Wheel of Fire*, which Kott acknowledges).

> After his eyes have been gouged out, Gloucester wants to throw himself over the cliffs of Dover into the sea. He is led by his own son, who feigns madness … He lifts his feet high pretending to walk uphill. Gloucester, too, lifts his feet, as if expecting the ground to rise, but underneath his foot there is only air. This entire scene is written for a very definite type of theatre, namely pantomime … This is a scene in which a madman leads a blind man and talks him into believing in a non-existing cliff. In another moment a landscape will be sketched in … No other Shakespearian landscape is so exact, precise and clear as this one. It is like a Brueghel painting; thick with people, objects and events … [But] the landscape is now just a score for the pantomime … a landscape which is only a blind man's illusion … The scene of the suicidal leap is also a mime … Gloucester knelt down on an empty stage, fell over and got up … The non-existent cliff is not meant just to deceive the blind man. For a short while we, too, believed in this landscape and in the mime … The Shakespearian precipice at Dover exists and does not exist … For once, in *King Lear*, Shakespeare shows the paradox of pure theatre.
>
> (Kott 1967: 111–15)

One detail about the 1962 Brook/Scofield production, which many of those who saw it found 'revelatory', and Scofield's austere reading of the role 'devastating', connects with Kott's emphasis on the meta-theatrical. Stanley Wells was there and says this.

> No one present at the first night will forget the sight of the cruelly blinded Gloucester groping his way toward the wings as the house lights slowly rose to signal the interval.
>
> (Wells ed. 2000: 75–76)

But perhaps the most systematically argued modern reading of *Lear*, again as it happens from 1966, was offered in a ninety-page essay, not by a literary critic but by a professor of philosophy, Stanley Cavell, in his 'The Avoidance of Love'. This account breaks with a number of critical orthodoxies and really needs to be read in full. His most striking reading is of the play's opening scene in which, Cavell says, Lear is motivated, as throughout the play, by the attempt to avoid 'the shame of exposure, the threat of self-revelation' (286). Denying that Lear at the start is acting out of blind, puerile or senile belief in what Goneril and Regan say or that the whole process is 'incomprehensible conduct', Cavell calls it, 'in fact, quite ordinary'.

> A parent is bribing love out of his children; two of them accept the bribe, and despise him for it; the third shrinks from the attempt, as though from violation. Only this is a king, this bribe is the last he will be able to offer; everything in his life, and the life of his state, depends upon its success. We need not assume that he does not know his two older daughters, and that they are giving him false coin in return for his real bribes, though perhaps like most parents he is willing not to notice it. But more than this: there is reason to assume that the open possibility – or the open fact – that they are *not* offering true love is exactly what he wants ... Lear knows it is a bribe he offers, and, part of him anyway, wants exactly what a bribe can buy: (1) false love; and (2) a public expression of love. That is: he wants something he does not have to return *in kind* ... and he wants to *look* like a loved man ... He is perfectly happy with his little plan, until Cordelia speaks ... Cordelia is alarming precisely because he *knows* she is offering the real thing ... putting a claim upon him he cannot face. She threatens to expose ... the necessity for [his] plan: his terror of being loved, of needing love.
>
> (Cavell 1969: 288–90)

Tracing the emotional logistics of Cordelia's behaviour (and her asides) in response, Cavell goes on to argue for the wider philosophical ramifications of the avoidance of love, and more generally shame, to the play's wider concerns and its plot, particularly the more problematic aspects of plot (like why Edgar fails to reveal himself to his father till the moment of the father's death). Particularly moving is Cavell's reading (again against the critical tradition) of the opening of the play's last scene (5.2) in which 'again Lear abdicates, and again Cordelia loves and is silent'. Lear refuses to see the older daughters and chooses the fantasy of a life with Cordelia in prison (where they'll 'sing, and tell old tales, and laugh'), which Cavell says is 'not the correction but the repetition of his strategy in the first scene'.

> He cannot finally face the thing he has done; and this means what it always does, that he cannot bear being seen ... he has found at the end a way to have what he has always wanted from the beginning. His tone is not: we will love *even though* we are in prison; but: because we are hidden

> together we can love. He has come to accept his love, not by making room in the world for it, but by denying its relevance to the world.
> (296–97)

The next 'great' tragedy is ***Macbeth*** and the critical consensus is that, in terms of the density of its language, it's the most intensely concentrated of the plays, the only other contender, *Anthony and Cleopatra*, being concentrated in a more discursive and relaxed way. This has something to do with the fact that the play centres, uniquely among the tragedies, on the claustrophobic analysis of a relationship – between Macbeth and Lady Macbeth – which is of such an intimacy, and where earlier roles and power positions between them are so seamlessly reversed, that it can exclude what would be commonplace in normal dialogue. Nicholas Brooke puts it like this.

> In Act 1 they did not hear each other's soliloquies, but always knew each other's thoughts. It is some while before Duncan's murder is made explicit between them, but they know at once that it is in each other's mind ... It is their relationship which is the focus of real interest in the play. It changes radically in 3.2, and they are never intimate again; simultaneously their roles are reversed, and he now displays the determination on blood which was once hers alone, but which she can no longer sustain.
> (Brooke ed. 1990: 19)

Also excluded in this play, again to an unusual degree and as Brooke argues further, are issues such as sexuality, politics, and larger social concerns: as Brooke says 'there is no sign of the populace, or of any concern for people at large ... It is the Porter alone who, in his brief scene, reminds the audience of the world that the play elsewhere so completely excludes' (20).

The Porter, or rather the knocking at the gate which summons the Porter, elicited what might be the most eloquent moment in romantic criticism of the plays, Thomas de Quincey's 1823 essay. He starts by recalling how, as a boy, he 'always felt a great perplexity' about the knocking at the gate after the murder of Duncan. He shows how, leading up to and for the murder itself, 'another world has stepped in', and the normal world 'must for a time disappear'.

> The murderers, and the murder, must be insulated – cut off by an immeasurable gulf from the ordinary tide and succession of human affairs – locked up and sequestered in some deep recess ... ordinary life is suddenly arrested – laid asleep – tranced – racked into a dread armistice; time must be annihilated; relation to things without abolished; and all must pass self-withdrawn into a deep [suspension] of earthly passion. Hence it is, that when the deed is done, when the work of darkness is perfect, then the world of darkness passes away like a pageantry in the clouds: the knocking at the gate is heard; and it makes known audibly that the reaction has commenced; the human has made its reflux upon the fiendish; the pulses

> of life are beginning to beat again; and the re-establishment of the goings-on of the world in which we live, first makes us profoundly sensible of the awful parenthesis that had suspended them.
>
> (In Smith ed. 1946: 335–36)

Macbeth's soliloquies are where the density of poetic language is at its most knotted, complex and hypnotic. William Empson, subtlest and most dazzling of all close readers, in his first book *Seven Types of Ambiguity* (1930, largely written in his undergraduate years), wrote about the speech, which has these famous opening lines (from 1.7).

> If it were done when 'tis done, then 'twere well
> It were done quickly: if the assassination
> Could trammel up the consequence, and catch
> With his surcease success …

Empson's detailed and agile analysis of the speech swoops suddenly on the word 'catch'.

> And *catch*, the single little flat word among these monsters, names an action; it is a mark of human inadequacy to deal with these matters of statecraft, a child snatching at the moon as she rides thunderclouds. The meanings cannot all be remembered at once, however often you read them; it remains the incantation of a murderer, dishevelled and fumbling among the powers of darkness.
>
> (Empson 1949: 50)

About this moment in Empson, Michael Wood, himself now in turn among the subtlest of today's critics, says this.

> It is an act of alert critical reading to spot the action word among the proliferating concepts; and generous to suggest that Macbeth … can still represent a more ordinary human disarray among matters that are too large, too consequential for us … But then to call the other words 'monsters', to identify the small verb as a 'child', and to introduce the moon and the thunderclouds, is to create a whole separate piece of verbal theatre, and to create something scarcely recognisable as criticism. And when at the end of the passage Empson widens his frame, returns to Macbeth's full anxious meditation … he sees our failure to grasp all the meanings as an achieved Shakespearian effect [and] finds a figure of speech for the character and the situation. The word becomes a whole passage, the child becomes a fumbling and dishevelled magician, and the moon and thunderclouds become the powers of darkness … [Empson's] metaphors bring the life of these words incredibly close to us. The child

> snatches and Macbeth fumbles; but the child herself is a verb; and Macbeth is a man using words to keep his mind away from a deed.
>
> (Wood 2016: online)

We go now to ***Twelfth Night***, widely regarded as the most beautiful and moving of the comedies (it is also the last, contemporary with *Hamlet*). But one measure of the precariousness of its beauty, especially when we watch the coming together of the couples at the end, is its dependence on what James Shapiro (at the start of this chapter) calls the 'principle of exclusion' (Shapiro 2020: 3). This is most telling, and also most troubling, in the cases of Antonio (who loves and is now losing Sebastian) and Malvolio (who is duped into believing himself loved by Olivia). We'll look at these two separately. Emma Smith says this about Antonio.

> Antonio is a character not really needed by the plot … Except, that is, thematically. Antonio's desire for Sebastian resonates with Orsino's for Cesario and with Olivia's for Viola, which is to say that however hard we might want to try, it is hard fully to straighten out this play and reconcile it to the conventional drive towards heterosexual marriage.
>
> (Smith 2019: 184)

Some critics and directors have tried to resist the play's homoerotic current by suggesting that Orsino finds Cesario's apparent femininity alluring, but this doesn't alter the case with Antonio. His love for Sebastian has an obstinacy of self-abasement (very much in line with Shakespeare in his Sonnets) which is as blazingly clear (in 2.1) when he says to Sebastian: 'If you will not murder me for my love, let me be thy servant' as it is when he then tells the audience directly that he 'adore[s]' (2.1) the younger man, a word that Shakespeare only uses to mean 'religious devotion or idealized romantic love' (183).

> Even if we are convinced, or prefer to believe, that Orsino falls for a woman underneath convincing male disguise, that can't help us with Olivia, who also does. Or rather, it moves the frisson of same-sex desire across, mobilizing the relationship between the two women – or even the two male actors playing women – as further instance of homoerotic attraction … Sexual transgression, then, is part of *Twelfth Night*'s queer comedy, and Antonio's role enables us to see more clearly, making it harder to dismiss or de-authenticate the play's other expressions of same-sex desire.
>
> (186)

When there are three couples set up to be married in the final minutes of the play Antonio remains apart, haunting them with the perspective he has brought to the expression of sexual desire in the play.

> [His] presence at the end of the play gives a different, oblique perspective on its resolution, and his irreconcilability into the married world of the finale complicates *Twelfth Night*'s movement from queer to straight, from homoeroticism to heterosexuality. His is the desire that cannot be contained in the marital conclusions typical of romantic comedy … The play's conclusion calls time – almost – on the erotic alternatives with which it keeps flirting. But, as Antonio witnesses, it is a bittersweet conclusion, shot through with losses as well as gains.
>
> (191–92)

An intriguing critical approach to the play is to connect the gender transvestism, as in Viola dressing and playing the role of the boy Cesario, with the class 'transvestism' of Malvolio falling for the trick of believing that Olivia wants to see him in yellow stockings and cross-gartered. This is clothing that, in Dympna Callaghan's words, 'might be suitable if worn by a young gentleman suitor to Olivia but is incongruous and ridiculous' in an older servant, though a privileged one, and, in terms of Elizabethan homilies, 'a violation of both decorum and decree' (Callaghan 1999: 33).

To connect these versions of transvestism in *Twelfth Night* is to recognize that Malvolio's transgression is the more troubling and threatening to the play's romantic comedy. The only record we have of a Renaissance performance, John Manningham's diary, places the Malvolio plot at the centre, and a performance of the play in 1623 calls it *Malvolio*. Callaghan says this about the last scene (5.1).

> Malvolio does not merely upstage the comedy of the main plot: he notoriously disrupts the festive spirit of *Twelfth Night*. The unrecuperable 'I'll be revenged on the whole pack of you' troubles all the charm and delight [of] the play. It is also possible that Malvolio's desire for revenge is directed … at Olivia quite specifically for her 'Alas, poor fool, how they have baffled thee!'. It would seem, then, that class transvestism is more threatening than that of gender, which can be resolved rather more readily … because it is Malvolio who menaces the romantic coupling with which the play concludes.
>
> (34)

To look more closely at that ending is to query if the gender issues, or anything else, can be 'resolved' quite so 'readily'. Callaghan quotes Stephen Orgel, from his celebrated article of 1989 ('Nobody's Perfect').

> Viola announces in the final moments … that she cannot become a woman and the wife of Orsino until her woman's clothes have been recovered … and that this will require the release of the sea captain who alone can find them, which in turn will necessitate the mollification of the enraged Malvolio, who has had the sea captain incarcerated: this all

> materializes out of nowhere in the last three minutes of the play. And Malvolio ... offers no assistance but runs from the stage shouting [revenge]. For Viola to become a woman requires, in short, a new play with Malvolio at its centre.
>
> (Orgel 1989: 27)

The difficult energies and currents ruffling the surface of this 'golden' comedy are found in their most raw and intense form in the extraordinary book of poems that was issued in 1609 called ***Shakespeare's Sonnets***. We'll end this chapter with the Sonnets and a sampling of the mountain of critical comments that they have attracted, some of it (especially in the 19th and early 20th centuries, in relation to the homoeroticism we've just been thinking about in *Twelfth Night*) decidedly unfriendly.

In Sonnet 76 Shakespeare might have been referring to Donne's lyric poems, poems more obviously fashionable than his own, sequences of sonnets themselves being rather unfashionable when Shakespeare wrote or at least published his. (Here I assume that he shaped the book and authorized the publication of the 1609 volume, unlike Donne whose love poems circulated only in manuscript before his death.) And we'll see in Chapter 3 that Donne may have been referring to Shakespeare's Sonnets in one of his poems.

> Why is my verse so barren of new pride?
> So far from variation or quick change?
> Why, with the time, do I not glance aside
> To new-found methods and to compounds strange?

But, as even these lines suggest, one clear difference between the love poetry of Shakespeare and of Donne is that Shakespeare's is – even more so than the rich tradition on which he draws – about poetry itself as much as it is about love. This was put very well by Rosalie Colie in her great book *Shakespeare's Living Art* (1974).

> By the *Sonnets* we are ... invited to become critics, urged to experience something about the writing of poetry, the making of fictions, and the meanings of poetry to a poet ... [They] dramatize literary criticism ... [and] animate, among other significant and characteristic conventions of the genre, the self-referential, self-critical tendency in sonneteering itself.
>
> (Colie 1974: 51)

This self-referential tradition Colie traces to, among others, Dante and his wonderful *Vita Nuova* where a prose commentary is threaded among the love poems, commenting on and analysing them. (Do please read this lovely short book.) Colie says this about what she identifies as the dramatic nature of the Sonnets, to which I'll just add that it's the larger dramatic structures within the whole sequence that make these poems, as a whole, quite different from the miniaturized dramas within some of Donne's poems. For Colie, what makes the sequence so remarkably different from others – though on reflection one might think that we shouldn't be surprised by it – is its 'loose but nonetheless involved and involving "plot"'. (The looseness, for me, is part of the surprise and the point: this magician of dramatic plots has both supplied and dis-articulated a 'plot' across 154 poems. The plot is both 'there' and on the edge of our critical vision.)

> The arrangement of the characters into two triangles – poet-friend-mistress; poet-friend-rival poet – is, so far as I know, unparalleled in Renaissance sonneteering … This triangulation of personalities … turns tradition upside down and inside out to examine the 'real' implications of conventional utterance and, in some cases, to force these implications to new limits in the situation, poetical as well as psychological … Merely in the development of his psychological story, Shakespeare has managed to make important statements about the relation of a literary love-code to specific experiences of loving … Shakespeare manages to treat the human relationships postulated in his sonnets so problematically, to make such 'real' problems of them, that a standard self-analytic pose has been considerably enriched and deepened … One cannot help noting how deviant [and] how peculiarly personal the poems are, within a genre in which conventions of self-expression, self-analysis, and self-reference are extremely highly developed.
>
> (51–53)

In her following chapter Colie also notes how (painfully) open to the world is the action of the 'plot', as opposed to the assumption of closed privacy (which the reader is allowed to share vicariously) in more conventional sequences. She says we sense that the poet is never really alone with either of his lovers; and with the triangulation 'their experiences interlock, and each is too knowing not to know that each one knows too much about the others' (133). The self-analyses in the poems are played out against worldly attitudes and feelings of social guilt. I'd add that if Donne is always self-dramatizing in his love poems, Shakespeare characteristically accuses himself of being led away from attention to his love by, precisely, his social role in the dramatics of his job, as in Sonnet 110. 'Alas 'tis true, I have gone here and there, / And made myself a motley to the view … / Most true it is that I have looked on truth / Askance and strangely …'.

The 'plot' is famously complicated by the sexual entanglement of the loved boy of Sonnets 1–126 (the 'friend' and almost certainly aristocratic patron) with the mistress of Sonnets 127–152, at the expense of Shakespeare. The betrayal of the poet by both the lovers gains plausibility by being mirrored or at least echoed in the many betrayals, or denials, that drive the most painful moments of plot in the plays, of which Sebastian's apparent betrayal of his older lover Antonio in *Twelfth Night* and the new King Henry's denial and rejection of Falstaff in *Henry IV Part 2* are perhaps the most pertinent.

At the level of psychodrama, these two larger groups of sonnets reverse or undermine the usual and expected polarities of gender and erotic drive, with the mistress (dark-haired rather than the fashionable blonde) evoking sexual disgust (Sonnet 135 calls her 'will' – her vagina – 'large and spacious'), or at least an amused resignation about their lying to each other, as much as the usual courtly worship, which is instead focused on the boy and, in turn, complicated by ironic manipulations of the Petrarchan conventions. This is most acutely realized in the great Sonnet 57 ('Being your slave ...') which, in a dizzying spiral of ironic 'turns', says three things simultaneously. 'I'm happy to be your slave in the devotedly powerless tradition. / How dare you treat me as a slave, with such thoughtless cruelty and negligence? / There may at least be some comfort in being allowed to love you at all, despite the humiliations that come with such love.'

About the homoerotic content of Sonnets 1–126 the critical arguments have often clustered around the notorious (that is, brilliant) Sonnet 20, which, obligingly, says (on the surface) both that the poet is not interested in the boy's sexual body and (more mutedly and through a series of puns that work like an extended wink at the more knowing readers) that he is very much interested in just that. I'll just add that when Jessica in *The Merchant of Venice* leaves her Jewish home to elope with the Christian Lorenzo – and, in the process, stealing her father Shylock's wealth to give to him – she is commended by Lorenzo for disguising herself in 'the lovely garnish of a boy' (2.6). Calling the boy 'the master-mistress of my passion' and claiming that his 'one thing' (his penis) is 'nothing' to the poet's purpose (but 'nothing', as Ophelia for one would have known, could mean the vagina), the poem ends (with modernized spelling) like this. 'But since she [nature] pricked thee out for women's pleasure, / Mine by thy love and thy love's use their treasure'. Stephen Orgel outlines the alternative, subversive reading (restoring the old spelling which has no apostrophes).

> In this reading 'But' signals a reversal of the argument, and means 'on the other hand': the 'womens pleasure' the friend is 'pricked out for [= selected for] is not the pleasure he gives women but his ability to take pleasure as women do; 'loves' in the last line is then not a possessive but a plural, and 'use' is a verb – the line without its modern apostrophe need not be a renunciation at all [meaning instead]: 'let my love be yours, and let your loves make use of their treasure'.
>
> (Orgel 1996: 57)

Colin Burrow, in his very well-balanced and scholarly edition, says this.

> The form of sexuality presented in the Sonnets feeds off all the various ways of writing about love between men in this period, and delights in their incompatibility. It consequently upsets several dominant paradigms. One widespread model of same-sex affection in the period is of a social superior and older man who supports a younger social inferior, whom he

> might adopt as his favourite, whose career he might advance, and to whom he might give a place in his bed ... The Sonnets begin with an experimental reversal of this form of relationship ... and the socially inferior poet's authority over the 'lovely boy' grows as the sequence moves forward.
>
> (Burrow 2002: 128)

But what Burrow also insists on, reading the sub-sequence of Sonnets 104–126, which were the latest of all the sonnets to be written (the poems to the mistress 127–154 were the earliest, perhaps as much as ten years earlier), is the increasing instability of any authority the poet might feel let alone exercise over this young man, even (as the most complex of these poems suggest) when the poet exacts some kind of paying-back for the boy's earlier unkindness. This, as Burrow says, is very different from the figure of the 'lowly poet' suggested in the first 17 sonnets who sounds 'like a schoolmaster paid by a noble family to advise their son to marry' (137), which, I'll just add, is exactly what I think did happen (but we won't get into the biographical fog).

> In this later body of work the things which the poet wishes to say in praise of his addressee and what he recognises to be true about him are entangled to the point of anguished inseparability ... They try to praise while gesturing towards circumstances which make praise untrue ... Knowledge is blurred and diffracted by self-persuasion that things might be otherwise than they appear, and by the actual opacity of the friend's emotion. The friend is never a narcissistic mirror of the poet's desire ... [but] a love-object whose conduct and nature and sensibility are unknowable.
>
> (135–37)

That opacity, the boy's refusal to participate in mutuality and mirrored recognition, is addressed directly, in a kind of awed wonder, at the start of Sonnet 53. 'What is your substance, whereof are you made, / That millions of strange shadows on you tend?' Love (as post-Freudian theorists like Jacques Lacan and after him Slavoj Žižek have shown) is like that: the beloved is a figment or displacement of impenetrable part-objects and unreachable illusions, always slipping away. Žižek has a very striking insight that he develops from Freud and Lacan and that also resonates with what we saw in Chapter 1 with Denis de Rougement and his notion that love needs obstacles to thrive. Žižek says this.

> [It's] not simply that we set up ... hindrances in order to heighten the value of the [loved] object: external hindrances that thwart our access to the object are there precisely to create the illusion that without them, the object would be directly accessible. What such hindrances thereby conceal is the inherent impossibility of obtaining the object ... The [object] functions as a kind of 'black hole' around which the subject's desire is structured.
>
> (In Richter ed. 2007: 1186)

C.L. Barber, in his classic 1960 essay, says this about the opening of Sonnet 53.

> It is clear that the strange shadows come not from the friend, but from the poet … Sonnet 61 recognises this fact in answering another arresting question: 'Is it thy will thy image should keep open / My heavy eyelids to the weary night?' The conclusion is a troubled recognition that it is the poet's will, not the friend's: 'For thee watch I, whilst thou dost wake elsewhere, / From me far off, with others all too near'.
>
> (Intro. Barber 1960: 23–24)

This leads me to Stephen Orgel, again, and to his own Introduction to another edition. Like Rosalie Colie, with whom we started, he identifies the 'single overriding subject' of the Sonnets as the writing and making of meanings, 'the imagination's attempt to re-form the realities of human relationships'. What Orgel says here is (to end on a personal note) as good and as sad as anything I've read on these poems, after living with them (and their critics) for fifty years.

> Though it is a commonplace to praise the overwhelming force of Shakespeare's imagination, the theme as expressed in the Sonnets is of relentless failure; the poems, over and over, are about self-deception and betrayal, and about the inadequacy of the mind, or the imagination, or of poetry, to have any effect, even on the poet's own feelings. Where poetry for Donne … could serve as a celebration of [his] erotic conquests, Shakespeare's volume of love poems stands as a monument to frustration and loss, anatomising the inadequacies and the radical loneliness of the self, and the ultimate elusiveness of the Other.
>
> (Intro. Orgel 2006: 20)

Works cited

Janet Adelman, *Suffocating Mothers* (Routledge: 1992)
C.L. Barber, *Shakespeare's Festive Comedy* (Princeton U.P.: 1959)
C.L. Barber intro., *Shakespeare: The Sonnets* (Dell: 1960)
Nicholas Brooke ed., *Shakespeare: Macbeth* (Oxford U.P.: 1990)
Colin Burrow ed., *Shakespeare: The Complete Sonnets and Poems* (Oxford U.P.: 2002)
Dympna Callaghan, *Shakespeare Without Women* (Routledge: 1999)
Paul A. Cantor *Shakespeare: 'Hamlet'* (Cambridge U.P.: 2004)
Stanley Cavell, *Must We mean What We Say?* (Cambridge U.P.: 1969)
Rosalie Colie, *Shakespeare's Living Art* (Princeton U.P.: 1974)
Patrick Cruttwell ed., *Samuel Johnson: Selected Writings* (Penguin: 1968)
Jonathan Dollimore and Alan Sinfield edd., *Political Shakespeare: New Essays in Cultural Materialism* (Manchester U.P.: 1985)
William Empson, *Seven Types of Ambiguity* (Chatto and Windus: 1949)
Ewan Fernie, *Shakespeare and Freedom: Why the Plays Matter* (Cambridge U.P.: 2017)

Richard Foulkes, *Performing Shakespeare in the Age of Empire* (Cambridge U.P.: 2002)
Northrop Frye, *Fools of Time* (Toronto U.P.: 1967)
Hugh Grady, *Shakespeare's Universal Wolf: Studies in Early Modern Reification* (Oxford U.P.: 1996)
Graham Holderness ed., *The Shakespeare Myth* (Manchester U.P.: 1988)
Jean E. Howard, *The Stage and Social Struggle in Early Modern England* (Routledge: 1994)
David Scott Kastan, 'Introduction', in Shakespeare *King Henry IV Part One* (Thomson: 2002)
Jan Kott, *Shakespeare Our Contemporary* (Methuen: 1967)
Sean McEvoy, *Theatrical Unrest: Ten Riots in the History of the Stage, 1601–2004* (Routledge: 2016)
Michael Neill, *Issues of Death: Mortality and Identity in English Renaissance Tragedy* (Oxford U.P.: 1997)
Karen Newman, *Essaying Shakespeare* (Minneapolis U.P.: 2009)
Stephen Orgel, 'Nobody's perfect, or why did the English stage take boys for women?', *South Atlantic Quarterly* Vol. 88: 1989
Stephen Orgel, *Impersonations: The Performance of Gender in Shakespeare's England* (Cambridge U.P.: 1996)
Stephen Orgel intro., *Shakespeare: The Sonnets* (Cambridge U.P.: 2006)
David Richter ed., *The Critical Tradition* (Bedford/St. Martin's: 2007)
Kiernan Ryan, *Shakespeare* (Palgrave: 2002)
Kiernan Ryan, *Shakespeare's Universality: Here's Fine Revolution* (Bloomsbury: 2015)
James Shapiro, *Shakespeare in a Divided America* (Faber: 2020)
D. Nichol Smith ed., *Shakespeare Criticism 1623–1840* (Oxford U.P.: 1946)
Emma Smith, *This Is Shakespeare* (Penguin: 2019)
Stanley Wells ed., *Shakespeare: King Lear* (Oxford U.P.: 2000)
Michael Wood, 'We do it all the time: Empson's intentions', *London Review of Books* Vol. 38, Issue 4: February 2016

3 Early modern literature 1590–1690

with Sean McEvoy

John Donne, Andrew Marvell, John Milton, Christopher Marlowe, Ben Jonson, John Webster, Aphra Behn

The previous chapter mentioned **John Donne**'s love lyrics (the elegies and 'songs and sonnets') in relation to Shakespeare's Sonnets and so it might be helpful to start this chapter with a thought about the differences between these two more or less contemporary sets of poems. (Dates of composition in both cases are not clear but, in both cases, probably ranged from about 1595 to about 1605.) The clearest difference is in the evoked personal voice. In Donne it is unashamedly vivid in its immediacy of presence and apparent transparency. In the famous lines that open 'The Good Morrow', the very sexy jokes ('did', 'sucked', 'country') leap off the page, but what is even more alive is the voice that knows – in a kind of magnificent confidence – that it can get away with such shock tactics, even in the face of what was, when he was writing these early poems, hostility from the church authorities towards erotic texts that were deemed dangerous enough to ban (this affected Marlowe); thus, presumably, Donne's decision not to publish them.

> I wonder, by my troth, what thou and I
> Did, till we loved? Were we not weaned till then?
> But sucked on country pleasures, childishly?

At the other extreme of the emotional range his greatest poem, 'The Nocturnal', is no less shamelessly centred on Donne's ego in full flight or voice.

> But I am by her death (which word wrongs her),
> Of the first nothing, the Elixir grown [...]
> But I am none; nor will my Sun renew [...]

Donne knew exactly who the readers of his manuscript-poems were, a series of coterie readerships as identified by Arthur Marotti, 'a series of social relationships spread over a number of years'. Some of Shakespeare's early sonnets may well have circulated among his friends but Marotti is arguing that Donne's

DOI: 10.4324/9781003127567-4

target readers were much more specifically and strategically targeted and that such coterie relationships led to what he calls the 'metacommunicative (or meta-poetic) level of discourse' in Donne's verse.

> Any time he suggested by direct or indirect means that he knew that his reader knew or that he knew that his reader knew that he knew something, he emphasised the metacommunicative aspect of his verse.
>
> (Marotti 2008: 20–21)

Philip Martin, in his 1972 book on Shakespeare's Sonnets, refers to Donne's poetic self as 'self-dramatizing, aggressive even when most disheartened', while Shakespeare's is 'self-effacing'. Martin says this about the typical role of the image in the Sonnets, which connects with a subtle point made by C.L. Barber about how Shakespeare's love is in effect 'left behind' or 'fulfilled in what it is compared to', when absorbed into the image (intro. Barber 1960: 12). Martin quotes the opening of Sonnet 73 where the poet compares his age to trees – with 'yellow leaves, or none, or few' – shaking 'against the cold'.

> It is surprising how quickly the 'I' ceases to be the centre of attention, for the speaker as well as for us: the poet dissolves into the images of his state ... If, as many readers think, the Sonnets are among the most *mature* love poems in the language, it is largely because of [their] willingness to feel one's way through a situation rather than impose oneself masterfully upon it. The address, the posture, are the antithesis to Donne's.
>
> (Martin 1972: 139–43)

We could simply say that Donne's love lyrics are very conscious of their own status as performances. These are poems staged with their interlocutors not just addressed – usually women ordered about and cajoled – but positioned as part of the drama, as when the woman in 'The Flea' squashes the creature between two of the verses or (silently) argues with him, again between verses, in the 'Valediction: Forbidding Mourning'. (He moves from 'Our two souls, therefore, which are one ...' to 'If they be two ...', implying her silenced interjection 'They're not one! They're two!')

It's regularly charged that the libertine poetry of the later 1590s, especially Donne's, reinforce what Martin, just quoted, described as a masterful imposition and David Norbrook calls the 'acquisitive, domineering male ego', one which (famously in 'To his Mistress Going to Bed' – more on which below) reflects the 'new scientific mentality with its mastering gaze, its passion for mapping the world in order to gain power over it' (intro. Norbrook 1993: 43). But Norbrook qualifies what Martin called the typical aggressiveness of Donne's attitude and what Norbrook himself describes as a poetry 'designed to shock ... sensibilities'. One point is that some of the later love lyrics from the first years of the new century appear to reflect a more serious commitment to a mutuality that has (perhaps a little romantically) been connected with Donne's marriage.

> If [Donne's attitude] often seems aggressive, reducing the woman's body to a terrain to be colonised, his cartographical conceits can also indicate the delicacy and vulnerability of a mutual relationship, the mapped globe quivering with the surface tension of a tear [in 'A Valediction of Weeping'] … What Donne's verse does suggest is that the dialogue between assertive masculine libertinism and a more mutual idea of love … was taking place within individuals [in his milieu].
>
> (46)

Norbrook gives the example of 'Love's Growth' where Donne insists on the material nature of his love, 'mixed of all stuffs, paining soul or sense'.

> Donne deploys the language of the humanist exaltation of the active life: 'Love sometimes would contemplate, sometimes do'. In a bawdy pun, 'doing' or making love becomes an exemplum of the active life in the world … What is at issue [is] the revelation of ever-new facets of the original relationship, and these are now figured by the stars around the sun, the budding blossoms, and the ever-increasing circles spreading from the loved one.
>
> (57–58)

The woman's body is at the centre, even in another bawdy pun on 'concentric' (the spreading circles are 'concentric unto thee'), as she and it are at the end of the 'Valediction, Forbidding Mourning' where the poet, anticipating his return to their physical love, says it 'makes me end, where I begun'.

These are poems, in that and many other ways, that are very conscious of their modishness, with their differences from earlier or more conventionalized love lyrics insisted upon, as when Donne says, in that same poem 'Love's Growth', that 'Love's not so pure, and abstract, as they use / To say, which have no mistress but their muse'. That's aimed at conventional Elizabethan sonneteers, perhaps even at Shakespeare's earliest sonnets, which Donne may have seen in circulation. This is a poetry that more than anything needs to sound contemporary, to attain to a context-free plenitude of presence. It's almost as if Donne was waiting for T.S. Eliot to champion him as exemplary of the undissociated consciousness, for whom a thought was a feeling. Eliot indeed enlisted Donne as his prime example of a poetics that he championed in his campaign that, as we'll see, was concerned to dislodge Milton from his pre-eminence.

It's a corrective to read Thomas Docherty, in *John Donne, Undone*, who is concerned to question what he characterizes as 'the modernist construction of Donne' as the poet of essential individualism. Dochery reads the poems as 'modes of therapy' in the face of the specific cultural problems of Donne's time, including the challenges made by science to secular history, readings that propose an advance on 'much of what passes for contemporary criticism of Donne', which he summarizes as the repeating of old ('New Critical') formulas such as 'the dramatic voice', 'witty invention', 'originality', 'masculine persuasive force' and 'strong lines'. Docherty says that the Donne that we conventionally read is a post-Eliot Donne. The therapy that Docherty sees as necessary for Donne becomes re-inscribed, in the post-Eliot modernist tradition, as therapy for modern readers.

> What Eliot seems to have admired in Donne is a materiality of thought, a poetry which passes itself off as *pure* medium … of the experience of poetry itself … This poetry is validated in the course of English literature as a means of countering the effects of the English Revolution, that intellectualising 'dissociation of sensibility' which has, according to Eliot, marred the poetic consciousness of everyone since Milton … The poetry of Donne thus becomes a means of *therapy* for the modernist poet or reader, suffering from our split consciousnesses and in need of restitution, wholeness and pure individuality … There are, then, fairly clear ideological reasons for such an understanding of Donne, as poet of the individualist voice, an inviolable voice announcing, among other things, the values of English Literature in a strident, clear and 'fascinating' medium or voice.
>
> (Docherty 1986: 1–5)

Michael Schoenfeldt writes about the importance of body–soul relations in Donne, which we saw also emphasized by David Norbrook. Schoenfeldt refers to this typical moment in William Empson.

> To revere the dichotomy between matter and spirit leads to hopeless confusion when reading Donne, because though he too is badgered by it, he keeps playing tricks with it, feeling that it ought to be transcended. What is more, though I presume he knew they were tricks, he did not think of them as such completely wild tricks as the hardening of our intellectual outlook makes us do now.
>
> (Empson 1993: 99–100)

Schoenfeldt puts it like this, trying – after Empson – to 'soften our outlook a bit' (in Raynaud ed. 2002: 32).

> Throughout his career, Donne was fascinated and troubled by the relationship between bodies and souls. As Robert Ellrodt argues, 'the soul or the spirit, the body or the flesh, are indeed the two poles of Donne's speculation: his mind, alert and tense, moves along an axis which at once opposes and unites them' (Ellrodt 1999: 188) … One of the signature genres and gestures of Donne's poetry, the Valediction, takes on such profound meaning for him because of his deep investment in the embodied nature of the self … The speaker of 'A Valediction: Forbidding Mourning', [if] he were indeed certain that they were not such terrestrial lovers, could have ended the poem at line 20, with the confident declaration that their refined if ineffable love is so 'inter-assured of the mind' that they 'care less, eyes, lips, and hands to miss'. But … this

> blazon of body parts that he pretends not to miss betrays in its [slowed rhythm] the emotional weight these body parts … truly hold for the speaker, [who] knows, with the seductive speaker of 'The Ecstasy', that 'pure lovers' souls' must 'descend / To affections, and to faculties, / Which sense may reach and apprehend, / Else a great prince in prison lies'.
>
> (28)

For me, the most striking and eloquent critical contribution to this idea of the body–mind dynamic in Donne is a fine essay by the novelist A.S. Byatt called 'Feeling thought: Donne and the embodied mind'. She starts by recalling her puzzlement as a student over Eliot's dissociation of sensibility argument with his insistence that, compared to Donne, Tennyson didn't feel his thought. Byatt knew that Tennyson was, largely because of Eliot, despised but seemed to her to feel his thoughts very immediately, whatever 'feeling your thought' might mean. She revises Eliot's notion by saying that what Donne feels, and makes his readers feel, is 'the peculiar excitement and pleasure of mental activity itself'.

> The pleasure Donne offers our bodies is the pleasure of extreme activity of the brain. He is characteristically concerned with the schemas we have constructed to map our mental activities – geometry, complex grammatical constructions, physiology, definitions. He is thinking about thinking.
>
> (In Guiborry ed. 2006: 248)

Byatt says that as a schoolgirl Donne excited her 'because he was a pattern-maker – with light and language' and she connects Donne in this respect with Wallace Stevens (whom we'll meet at the end of Chapter 8).

> I think both Donne and Stevens describe not images, but image-making, not sensations but the process of sensing, not concepts but the idea of the relations of concepts.
>
> (249)

Describing her excitement in reading Elaine Scarry's *Dreaming by the Book*, Byatt looks at Donne's 'Air and Angels' in the light of what Scarry calls 'radiant ignition'. Byatt says that we see neither angel nor woman in the poem but 'mental flashings' as when Donne refers to 'things / Extreme, and scattering bright'.

> There is a kind of *intellectual-bodily* imagination of the embodied soul. Donne's soul 'takes limbs of flesh, and else could nothing do'. At the end of the poem we imagine the embodiment of the angel which takes 'face, and wings / Of air, not pure as it, yet pure' … It is a poem haunted by the brightness of the unseen, the embodying of the bodiless.
>
> (251–52)

Byatt refers to the famous image of the compasses in the 'Valediction: forbidding mourning', which appears after what she rightly calls 'one of the most beautiful images of radiant ignition' when Donne describes the lovers' souls as really one soul enduring not a beach but 'an expansion, / Like gold to aery thinness beat'.

> We see and don't see the beaten gold – which is impossible as a solid because its thinness, like the shapeless flame of 'Air and Angels', is *aery*. As in that poem Donne follows the arresting brightness with the geometry of the stiff twin compasses.
>
> (252)

Byatt ends by looking at the intensely erotic elegy 'To His Mistress Going to Bed' and its famous request to the woman to 'license my roving hands and let them go, / Before, behind, between, above, below' and she quotes this marvellous passage from Elaine Scarry's book about the arrival of pictures in the imaginer's mind. (A footnote is here incorporated.)

> Half in the imperative and half in the voice of petition John Donne addresses his mistress for permission to let him move his hands across her undressed body … but it is also the imaginer who is being solicited to make the picture of Donne's hand move across the picture of the woman's body, a sense of movement achieved by a sequence of five stills, five locations on the woman's body … [Donne] immediately follows the five stills with a line of awed exclamation … 'O my America, my new found land'. It is as though he had said to the reader, Please do this, and a moment later, Thank you for doing that, and in the momentum of being thanked we had the impression of the pictures having been successfully made.
>
> (Scarry 1999: 106, 271)

Byatt closes with these words about 'before, behind, between, above, below', a 'flow of movement … parts of speech evoking a sensuous graph'.

> [These are] locations on the body of both writer and reader, the more powerful because the more purely *brief* firings in the mind of a deep habit imagining motion in the body, and linking these images to other emotions to form concepts and map them with grammar.
>
> (In Guiborry ed. 2006: 257)

We'll turn now to the lyrics of **Andrew Marvell**, which appear startlingly different from those of Donne – and, even more so, of course, from the poetry of John Milton to which we'll turn after we look at Marvell. In the cases of Donne and Milton we are confronted by a vividness of poetic presence and voice (Milton painfully voicing his blind isolation in *Paradise Lost*), an obtruding personality, or at least – in the case of Donne – the dramatic presentation of such a personality, a performative sensibility, sensibility as performance. In sharp contrast, and as Rosalie Colie says in her excellent 1970 book on Marvell, *My Ecchoing Song*, Marvell's vision is 'thoroughly mediated; his was no sensibility laid bare to perception'; what he wrote was always carefully 'processed', a poetry 'nervous, cerebral, yet spirited'. Compared to both Donne and Milton, Marvell is a 'poet-without-persona' or 'poet-with-too-many-personas', always aware of the 'lapse' between language or languages and human needs and desires (Colie 1970: 4–5). I'd add that in this sense Marvell is proto-modernist. Here is Colie.

> Experienced readers, even experienced Marvellians, often find themselves curiously denied thorough satisfaction in the poet's verses, precisely because of an elusiveness and mysteriousness at variance with the apparent precision of the poet's language. Setting and occasion are left unexplained: what are the Bermudians up to? On what errand do the wanton troopers ride? Sometimes a poem ends abruptly where a reader hopes for more, and might legitimately have expected more; sometimes there are disjunctions in a poem which would seem beyond bearing, except that the words are so beautifully said … He is … a poet of highly polished surfaces. Surfaces: yet no critic has felt him a superficial poet; even to those readers unconcerned with his Platonism, his Puritanism, his republicanism, and so forth, his poetry gives the impression, or the illusion, of great depth – a smooth inviting pool beneath the surface of which are caverns measureless to man.
>
> (3)

What are the Bermudians up to? The poem 'Bermudas' is one of Marvell's most beautiful but there is, about the song the pilgrims are singing in their boat, a characteristic 'elusiveness and mysteriousness'. Barbara Everett says this.

> The boat moves, it is unclear where, and the song rises, it is unclear from whom or to whom – indeed it seems unclear to the singers themselves, whoever they are.
>
> (Quoted in Goldberg 1986: 163)

And, even more tellingly, Christopher Ricks, in his book on Milton's grand style, says this about 'Bermudas', nothing that the Bermudas were traditionally thought of as Paradise and the poem encodes 'a brilliantly unobtrusive insight into labour before the Fall' (Ricks 1967: 143). The poem ends like this.

> Thus sung they, in the English boat,
> An holy and a cheerful note,
> And all the way, to guide their chime,
> With falling oars they kept the time.

Ricks says this.

> The point is made so unobtrusively that some readers never seem to notice it at all; without any nudge, Marvell tells us that they *rowed* in order to keep time in their song – not, as we would expect in this fallen world, that they sang in order to keep time in their rowing.
>
> (Ricks 1967: 143)

In 1946 Christopher Hill wrote about what Colie called the 'lapse' between desire and the real, and for Hill it helps us see how important is Marvell's humour (or that of his personas). His version of the Fall, for instance, is a stylish joke. This is from his great 'The Garden'.

> The nectarine, and curious peach,
> Into my hands themselves do reach;
> Stumbling on melons, as I pass,
> Ensnared with flowers, I fall on grass.

And in his wonderful long poem 'Upon Appleton House' Marvell's disillusioned vision of the fallen world is almost jaunty.

> Tis not, what it once was, the world,
> But a rude heap together hurled,
> All negligently overthrown,
> Gulfs, deserts, precipices, stone.

Hill is concerned to read Marvell in his difficult context and so he sees 'The Definition of Love' as a Civil War poem with its awareness that 'Fate does iron wedges drive / And always crowds itself betwixt'.

> [It] shows his attempt to come to terms with and to control the contradictions between his desires and the world he has to live in, his ideals and the brutal realities of the Civil War … the conflict between Love and Fate, desire and possibility. Fate 'defines' Love in both senses of the word – it both limits it and expresses its full significance … Fate is symbolised by the products of one of the industries that were transforming rural Britain, by the conventional symbol for warlike arms; and it 'crowds itself betwixt' with irresistible force: here Fate is thought of as a … multitude of human individuals, as well as abstract military and industrial processes.
>
> (Hill in Carey ed. 1969: 77–79)

There is a grim humour in the poem's claim that the speaker's love is the result of a coupling of parents called Despair and Impossibility but it's a poem that still unsettles with its insight into the elemental loneliness of human longing, that lovers in even parallel unity 'can never meet'.

If the soul–body relation was a dynamic and volatile process for Donne (as we saw), for Marvell, in another of his great lyrics 'A Dialogue Between the Soul and Body', the antithesis, says Hill, is 'not just between soul and body, for the soul may betray the body as well as the body the soul; it is a complex, four-handed conflict' with 'opposite concepts jostling in Marvell's mind' (81). Thus the extraordinary, but also extraordinarily casual, paradoxes and the sense, as we read the dialogue, that this is not so much a dialogue as a Beckett-like blind signalling across huge distances between body and soul, each imprisoned in isolation. If Donne, as we saw, sensed in 'The Ecstasy' that souls need to descend and work in bodies 'Else a great prince in prison lies', for Marvell the two entities are both imprisoned and both the other's jailer: to coin a phrase, definitely dissociated. The Soul, for instance, says this.

> O who shall, from this dungeon, raise
> A soul enslaved so many ways?
> With bolts of bones, that fettered stands
> In feet; and manacled in hands.

A poem in which soul and body not only speak separately but show no awareness of being in the dialogue of their poem is both richly comic and a nightmare. The speaker-protagonists of Marvell's lyrics (quite unlike Donne's vivid presences) are, as Colie says, a series of personas, more or less abstracted and ironically conventionalized, like his Mower (who, in a wonderful comic touch of self-in-turning, cuts himself down with his own scythe). In a useful footnote Hill says of Marvell's Mower (and his gardens) that, as with such symbols, any significance varies.

> The Mower is now the power of Love, now the scythe of Death or Fate; now the armies of the Civil War; at other times he stands for a pre-commercial simplicity which acquires an elemental force in contrast to the sophistication of the garden. So too the garden itself stands for different things in different poems.
>
> (86)

The exceptions to these variously symbolized personas are the nymph 'Complaining for the Death of Her Fawn' (a quite wonderful poem) and the speaker of Marvell's best known but perhaps least characteristic poem 'To His Coy Mistress' who speaks, and indeed argues, like Donne. But Marvell argues only up to a point like Donne. (The biographical record suggests he preferred drinking wine alone at home to womanizing. And his great poem 'The Garden' has a joke about how the garden of Eden would have been 'two paradises in one' if Adam – or anyone – could 'live in Paradise alone'.)

The logical argument itself, though strenuous, is on examination illogically fallacious and I think intentionally and comically so. This is very true of Donne as well. Frank Kermode said in 1971 that Donne's signature argumentation relies heavily on 'dialectical sleight-of-hand' and 'syllogistic misdirections' so that in a poem like 'The Flea' he is 'wooing by false syllogisms' (Kermode 1971: 121–22). In effect the argument in the 'Coy Mistress' says this: *if* we had all the time in the world then you needn't go to bed with me; *but* we haven't got all the time in the world; *therefore* you must go to bed with me. But, unlike in Donne where the woman is at least arguably (in both senses) present, in Marvell there is a void where there should be at least the spectral presence of the woman. A void and her body parts. Francis Barker, in his brilliant book *The Tremulous Private Body* (which we met in Chapter 1), puts it like this. (We saw above the woman's implied responses in the pauses of the 'Valediction'.)

> She does not speak, not even with an implied speech suggested by momentary pauses for response, or other hesitations, in the inexorable male voice which utters the poem. In a place which the poem addresses and labels 'Mistress', 'Lady' – woman – there is silence … The male voice can be understood as crying vaingloriously and even somewhat pathetically into a silence it doesn't notice.
>
> (Barker 1984: 91–93)

In that sense this rather un-Marvell-like poem could be read as subverting and exposing the muted aggressions in Donne's lyrics of seduction and conquest that it apparently imitates. If we read the 'Coy Mistress' like this, and in the way that Barker does, we are a very long way from Eliot who saw the poem as the best example of Marvell's polished and gentlemanly wit, which he called tough and reasonable (reasonable: that worms will 'try' the dead woman's virginity?) beneath the graceful surface.

'The Nymph Complaining' is at once the most fully realized and persuasively ventriloquized realization of a 'character' in Marvell – a teenage girl who has lost both her unfaithful lover and now as well the substitute lover (and substitute child), the fawn that he gave her (it was casually shot dead by 'wanton troopers', Civil War soldiers on what the word 'wanton' suggests was a riot of raping) – and an astonishing dramatization of what many of the Marvell lyrics suggest, that desire gets nowhere. This is the sharpest distinction from Donne, where desire has implicit or explicit success built in. Marvell is the poet of loss (and thus, much the more modern poet) and, in the 'Nymph' poem as in others, his lyrics read like a series of displaced responses, as Hill suggests, to their political-historical moment, and voiced as strangely charged sorrows and isolations.

Annabel Patterson lists some of the interpretations of the 'Nymph Complaining' that for her are merely partial.

> A full-fledged religious allegory; a study in female naivety … hence the childishness of some of her sentences and the bathos of some of her lines; a feminist treatise about seduction, even rape and illegitimate birth; an exercise in Derridean deconstruction. This poem has made readers … so

> uncomfortable that they have moved to resolve their discomfort by exclusion and systematization.
>
> (Patterson 1994: 64)

The follower of Derrida mentioned there is Jonathan Goldberg whose 1986 essay (drawing on the Narcissus-Echo narrative) very reasonably sees the fawn as an emblem of desire's illusionary goals, a substitute in a chain of merely repeating substitutes, an 'it'. Remarkably, Goldberg counts 26 references to the fawn as an 'it' in 38 lines (lines 55–92). This 'it' is an impossibility, a dream-object. Goldberg notices the lines about the fawn playing a version of hide and seek with the nymph ('twould stay, and run again, and stay') and he connects this with Freud's classic account of the child's *Fort! Da!* game designed to normalize the mother's absence and return (and eventual final absence). Goldberg says this.

> Playing with the object it becomes the object with which it plays. To preserve itself, voice objectifies itself in its identification with the object of play. The game is one of substitution, making a replacement object serve when the real object is gone – and becoming that object, having *it* as one's own.
>
> (Goldberg 1986: 26)

Patterson quotes Rosalie Colie on this extraordinary poem: 'Something is exhausted in this poem; but I am not quite sure what it is' (Colie 1970: 61). And she adds this.

> Marvell … saw that religion, sex and politics are names for the different (and sometimes crossing) paths of desire towards its unknown object … When the nymph concludes her lament by imagining herself turned to a miraculous marble statue ('For … I shall weep though I be stone'), and the fawn cut out of a different and more precious material ('purest alabaster'), we … [can] see it as an almost pure expression of desire in its essence in which the difference between the nymph's naivety and Marvell's sophistication has been erased.
>
> (Patterson 1994: 64)

To turn from the poetry of Marvell to his friend and contemporary **John Milton** (as an MP, Marvell might have helped save Milton from those seeking his life at the Restoration) can be a shock. If Marvell's poetry reflects displaced responses to the Civil War, with *Paradise Lost* the critics have historically engaged in a more recent civil war, a version of the war in Heaven which is where the poem chronologically starts (as told in Book 6). This is because, more than any other great text, the poem is itself divided or conflicted between its ostensible surface narrative and purpose (to justify God's ways to man) and Milton's pro-revolutionary and republican impulses, as in the very public role he played in the English Revolution, in his vigorous and vigilant defence of liberty and in his passionate belief that we are all born free.

Famously, Blake (and Shelley) saw that Milton's sympathies were with Satan (who knows, after all, that he is doomed to fail) rather than God. Satan and Milton share many characteristics as well as their opposition to arbitrary and oppressive power. Blake said that 'without contraries is no progression' and Milton said that trial purifies us through 'what is contrary', with truth dynamically flowing in 'perpetual progression'. In David Loewenstein's words, progress for Milton is 'by challenging and disrupting tyrannical custom, mindless conformity and old orthodoxies' (Loewenstein 2004: 13–14).

Radical critics who follow Blake and Shelley, most notably Christopher Hill, and those influenced by Hill, like David Norbrook, counter the older view, that the poem reflects Milton's post-revolutionary despair and retreat after the Restoration into the kind of orthodoxy that C.S. Lewis influentially argued for in his 1942 study. They insist instead on the subversive and contrary energies within the text, those that even question the nature of the Fall itself, energies, and critiques that 'institutional Christianity represses' (126). Hill and those who follow him reach a kind of novelistic climax in Philip Pullman's *His Dark Materials* which, like Milton, rewrites the Fall – against, as it happens, C.S. Lewis's Narnia books.

Here's Christopher Hill, from his great *The World Turned Upside Down*, written a few years before his more extended study *Milton and the English Revolution* (1977). Hill looks at Milton's prose pamphlets in connection to the revolutionary radicals like Gerrard Winstanley and then turns to *Paradise Lost*.

> It is not only in his prose pamphlets that we can see affinities between Milton and the radicals. It is the poetry that is truly subversive … He treats hell … in the same mythological way as Winstanley, as a means of depicting inner psychological conflicts … Classical and Biblical myths are mingled in a way which shows that neither is to be taken literally. Hell is internal. Heaven is an allegory for the earth. When at the crisis … Adam realises that Eve is lost because she has eaten the apple he cries out [to himself]: 'How can I live without thee, how forgo / Thy sweet converse and love so dearly joined / To live again in these wild woods forlorn …' Adam's fall was due not to pride or intellectual curiosity, as it well might have been if Milton had followed Genesis and the commentators. It was due to love, love for woman; and to a preference for society rather than a lonely rectitude in individual isolation. … And the conclusion of *Paradise Lost* – 'a Paradise within thee, happier far' – [is] an elaboration of the radicals' view that man can attain to a pre-lapsarian state here on earth.
>
> (Hill 1975: 397–98)

I'll be writing about Eve very soon but will just say here how astonishing, and marvellous, it is that Eve expresses the heart of Milton's political ideas most simply when, in Book 9, wondering whether to hide from Adam her newly awakened power after eating the apple, she considers that it might make her 'more equal' to him: 'for inferior who is free?'

Adam's choosing love of Eve over obedience to God reflects the unashamed (literally) emphasis in the poem on Adam and Eve's pre-fallen and mutually fulfilled and fulfilling love-making, a clear breaking from the biblical and post-biblical notion that sex came in at the Fall (and is shameful because of it). David Loewenstein says this on Adam and Eve and human sexuality, noting the way the poem is nonetheless conflicted in terms of what I'd call their sexualized mutuality and socialized hierarchy.

> The challenge Milton faces as a fallen poet is how to write about such intimate lovemaking and mutuality in Eden … [He] dissociates the poet's erotic subject and writing from its more tainted Renaissance and Cavalier manifestations, where love and revelling are often associated with 'court amours' … or 'wanton masque' … and 'the starved lover … quitted with disdain' by his 'proud' mistress. Significantly, Satan later begins his temptation of Eve with the lavish rhetoric of Petrarchan love poetry … In offering a rich exploration of human sexuality and passion, *Paradise Lost* is too complex to conform to a consistent or unified model of sexual relations … Indeed, the more carefully we read *Paradise Lost* the more we notice the poet's conflicting impulses.
>
> (Loewenstein 2004: 84–85)

Loewenstein gives the example of Eve's wonderful love song to Adam in Book 4 which is prefaced by her addressing Adam with what Loewenstein calls 'a series of Pauline clichés, appealing to masculine authority by calling [Adam] "author and disposer"' (St Paul insisted on the man being the head of the woman). But her love poem that follows undermines those platitudes. Here it is.

> With thee conversing I forget all time;
> All seasons, and their change, all please alike.
> Sweet is the breath of morn, her rising sweet,
> With charm of earliest birds: pleasant the sun,
> When first on this delightful land he spreads
> His orient beams, on herb, tree, fruit, and flower,
> Glistering with dew; fragrant the fertile earth
> After soft showers; and sweet the coming on
> Of grateful evening mild; then silent night
> With this her solemn bird, and this fair moon,
> And these the gems of Heaven, her starry train:
> But neither breath of morn, when she ascends
> With charm of earliest birds; nor rising sun
> On this delightful land; nor herb, fruit, flower,
> Glistering with dew; nor fragrance after showers;
> Nor grateful evening mild; nor silent night,
> With this her solemn bird, nor walk by moon,
> Or glittering star-light, without thee is sweet.

Loewenstein says this.

> Her sensuous, lyrical voice is underscored [as] … only with Adam are all these delightful, natural moments 'sweet', the word which begins and ends her sixteen-line love-song … Here is one place, then, where we can see her own rich poetry undermining the Pauline model of masculine authority. Her sensuous, passionate poetry, moreover, aligns her creative powers with the poetics of Milton himself, who believed that poetry should be 'simple, sensuous and passionate' [In Milton's *Of Education*].
>
> (85–86)

Diane Mccolley, in a fine essay on Milton and the sexes, summarizes the long critical debate over how Milton reads and presents Eve (is he upholding or undermining the traditional patriarchal stereotype of Eve, and woman, as vain, weak and liable to fall – or is it an unstable mix of the traditional and the more sceptical?), noting the depressingly dismissive comment in the widely used *Riverside Milton* edition (edited by Flannagan in 1998) that 'skips over three decades of reassessment by stating that "There is no evidence in *Paradise Lost* that Eve's proper role according to Milton is anything other than meek submission"' (in Danielson ed. 1999: 177). Mccolley's judgement is generously balanced.

> Those who love Milton's poems find that his high regard for the quality of human beings of both sexes offers more towards mutual respect than the problem of equality can undo … He incorporates in Adam and Eve the fusion of nature and spirit – not allegorically divided between them, but processive in each and reciprocated in their marriage – that for him defines human (and all) life … Although his hope of spiritual rebirth for the body politic was disappointed, he never abandoned his hope for the rebirth of the specific men and women who would read his poem … [He] provided prose arguments and poetic experience designed to expand the disciplined liberties of a regenerate people.
>
> (177)

Mccolley's conclusion is that 'the woman question' in Milton will never be finally decided and nor should it be. But she insists that Milton was radical in making Eve as she is in the poem, among many other things the 'leader in peace-making' after the Fall. (She also has the poem's last spoken words, breaking with tradition.) Milton, in her reading, is at once more serious and more hopeful about 'relations between the sexes' than any poet of his or perhaps any other time.

> His loving portrait of Eve … raises her immeasurably above other Eves of art and story, opening new possibilities of dialogue for [readers] at every

> turn. To the small degree that Adam and Eve are 'higher' or 'lower' they are two strings tuned to different pitches, to make harmony.
>
> (189)

Another kind of war has been fought over *Paradise Lost* and Milton, one that is not so much due to the poem's internal self-divide and conflicted energies between surface orthodoxy and more deeply located radical questioning, but a war waged by those critics, especially T.S. Eliot and F.R. Leavis, who would rather the poem didn't exist at all, particularly in the English tradition as played out in school curricula. Rather than attack the poem and the poet for what these critics really disliked – its politics – they chose to attack it for its style. Margarita Stocker has set this out clearly.

> There has been, in our [20th] century, no comparable attack of such force, by critics of such considerable influence, upon any other 'classic' writer. When he launched what became known as the Milton Controversy in 1936, Eliot's influence as a poet-critic was at its apogee. He derogated Milton's style, the pernicious influence of which upon English poetry must now be recognised: no modern could or should learn from Milton. Equally, Milton's religious ideas were repugnant. To second Eliot, came a critic whose ideas and practice were to affect the study of English for decades, and whose influence is only now beginning to recede. F.R. Leavis described Milton's verse as suffering from the tyranny of sound over sense, as essentially un-English, unintelligent, and musically monotonous. He confidently pronounced Milton's reputation dead, and the burial effected with 'remarkably little fuss'. He was remarkably wrong.
>
> (Stocker 1988: 13)

The attempt to demote Milton was part of the strategy to promote Donne and the so-called metaphysical poets in his place. Raymond Williams spoke in an interview very sharply about this happening in Cambridge in his day.

> I said to people here in Cambridge: in the thirties you were passing severely limiting judgements on Milton and … favourable judgements on the metaphysical poets, which in effect redrew the map of 17th-century literature in England. Now you were, of course, making literary judgements … but you were also asking about ways of living through a political and cultural crisis of national dimensions. On the one side, you have a man who totally committed himself to a particular side and cause … On the other, you have a kind of writing … that is a way of holding divergent attitudes … in the mind at the same time … I said that when you were making your judgements about these poets, you were not only arguing about their literary practice, you were arguing about your own at that time.
>
> (Williams 1979: 335)

In 1966 John Holloway in a lecture (later revised for his 1977 book *The Proud Knowledge*) tactfully remarked that 'to some extent, we have cozened ourselves into thinking that Milton lacks any close grasp of fact' and that 'when we reject this, our evidence also shows how distinctively Milton used his grasp of fact', though very differently from Shakespeare (Holloway 1977: 43). This is tactful as it clearly has Eliot and Leavis's charge-sheet in view in suggesting that their attacks have made readers cozen themselves. A tactful response to Eliot and Leavis also plays out quietly in the pages of vigorous close reading in Christopher Ricks's *Milton's Grand Style* mentioned above (and in my view, Ricks's best book), as when he says mildly of Leavis's charge that, when Milton chose the style of the poem, he in effect renounced the English language, 'does not seem true' (Ricks 1967: 117).

And on the specific accusation that Milton's so-called grand style was un-English (Leavis), and as if written in a dead language (Eliot), Holloway (again without engaging directly with either critic) makes the simple point that the poem, at multiple moments of especially intense emotion, is written in a style that is the exact opposite of 'Latinate copiousness and melodious amplitude' (Holloway 1977: 39), the style that Eliot condemned as unduly dictated by the auditory imagination rather than actual speech or thought. And about this latter charge of Eliot's, Ricks, again gently but a little less so, says 'the more one looks closely at Milton's word-order, the less truth there seems to be' (Ricks 1967: 102). Holloway gives a dozen or so examples of this charged and simple language. Here are three, first Satan in Book 4 and then Eve in Books 9 and 12.

> [Adam and Eve] enjoy their fill
> Of bliss on bliss, while I to Hell am thrust …
> Yet let me not forget what I have gained
> From their own mouths …
>
> Adam shall share with me in bliss or woe:
> So dear I love him, that with him all deaths
> I could endure, without him live no life.
>
> … but now lead on;
> In me is no delay; with thee to go
> Is to stay here …

Holloway says this.

> The terse, close-packed style, blunt and clipped, running line after line in almost uninterrupted monosyllables, can be seen only as a deliberate extension of the vernacular. It is a *calculated* plainness, a calculated commonness, that goes beyond what those things are in themselves … Such bluntness and terseness is itself part also of the epic tradition. Nor, in

> Milton, does it come alone: it comes as part of the variegated spectrum of style over which his poem continually plays.
>
> (Holloway 1977: 40)

On broader issues about the poem, and distinguishing Milton here from predecessors like Shakespeare, Holloway, arguing for Milton's essential modernity, writes very well about what he calls 'a great fact about Milton's place in the development not only of our literature but also of our culture ... More and more ... one comes to sense the poem as a *striving to know*'.

> What [Milton] rehearses, over and over again, is the *activity of enquiry itself*, the quest for insight ... [Since] Shakespeare, the European consciousness has undergone a profound modification. Before this modification took place, men believed that the great decisive truths about themselves and their place in the cosmos were known ... already established and known once for all ... We now believe that the major truths ... have only just been discovered; or indeed, are about to be discovered; or most of all, perhaps, that every man must undertake his own personal voyage of discovery and re-discovery. Milton stands at the opening of the new era. He belonged to the older world, the world of Shakespeare, in that his ultimate convictions were the traditional ones. But he did not accept them as mere traditions ... He approached them in the new spirit: he fearlessly lent them a new meaning, whenever he thought it right; he found them out once again, as if they were new; and he filled them with an individually realised cogency and life. He was, in a word, the first of our great Moderns.
>
> (51–53)

The most important recent book on literature and politics in the revolutionary years is David Norbrook's 2000 *Writing the English Republic*. He writes eloquently about the moment in Book 4 when Satan first sees Adam and Eve, 'one of the poem's key points of sublimity', and relates it to European republicanism. Norbrook refers in passing (and without quoting it) to Eliot's remark (or sneer) that he could only derive pleasure from those lines by a 'deliberate effort' not to visualize Adam and Eve at all. This elicited a sharp reply from Fredric Jameson.

> It is no secret, if still mildly paradoxical and unaccountable in a Puritan writer, that Milton is the great poet of sex in the English language. We may today reread with a certain pity, if not contempt, T.S. Eliot's once influential remarks about [his effort not to visualise the naked Adam and Eve], an effort, one would have thought, a good deal more puritanical than anything in Milton himself.
>
> (In Barker ed. 1981: 330)

Norbrook says this about Satan's first sight of Adam and Eve – in effect of ourselves.

> We can encompass the experience of looking at humanity from the outside, as a species just created, and sharing the wonder. The tableau of Adam and Eve can be seen as a republican icon. The narrator lays great emphasis on their nudity – so much so that Eliot found this spectacle more shocking than Milton's Hell … a reminder of how deliberatively provocative Milton was being in glorifying his characters' sexuality. He would have known how Michelangelo's David had embodied the spirit of the young Florentine republic; in their different way the newly-created Adam and Eve speak for a republican delight in returning to the beginning, in stripping away false customs.
>
> (Norbrook 2000: 481)

And Norbrook returns to that passage in his very moving account of the end of *Paradise Lost.*

> The image of God that shone so brightly in our first view of the couple has been dimmed; but in mourning its loss so powerfully, the poem also raises the possibility of its recovery, albeit in a different form of 'restoration' … It is Eve who is given the last word spoken in the poem. Her 'restore' refers us back to the 'greater Man' of the poem's opening who will 'Restore us'. By the time the poem was published, the word could be taken as a direct, polemical contrast with Charles's Restoration. In the context of the poem's origin, however, it would have retained a more radical, republican meaning, one that looked back to a pristine liberty and revived a longing for its return.
>
> (490)

This connects tellingly with what John Hollander writes about the end of the poem. This wonderful critical summary is, I feel, the appropriate and best last word on Milton for the moment.

> We are all the children of Adam and Eve, who were at home everywhere there was for them; it was only by losing this privileged human place forever that they entered a world in which they would have to internalise, and go on successfully internalising, the place of being-at-home … It is only after the fall from perfection into nature that 'being-at-home' could ever be localised in something like a house. What [has been called] 'Adam's house in Paradise' applies to the visions and desires of fallen, natural human consciousness … From the Edenic standpoint, Adam and Eve had no house because they were so purely at home … For Milton, the essence of the original, paradigmatic condition of being-and-feeling-at-home consisted in the unfallen matrimonial domicile, that the relationship between two persons generated a space and an enclosure that superseded literal emplacement. They leave their lost Paradise bearing the invisible germ of at-homeness that will flower when they have by hard labour wrenched, urged, twisted a place of dwelling out of the earth.
>
> (Hollander 1998: 69–70)

While poetry possessed a narrow, elite readership in Elizabethan and Jacobean England, the theatre brought literary writing to a mass audience. The big public outdoor London theatres such as the Globe or the Rose may each have accommodated as many as three thousand spectators for an afternoon performance. How that public theatre depicted, reflected and commented on politics and society has been a particular focus of criticism in the last forty years.

The first of London's commercial theatres opened in 1574 and **Christopher Marlowe** was its first star writer. A controversial figure in his own day, he may have been a government spy and was certainly accused of atheism and homosexuality before his sudden violent death in 1593 at the age of 29. His *Doctor Faustus* was one of the most enduring plays of the entire period, still in performance when the Civil War closed the theatres in 1642, and, it was reported, capable of making its audiences anxious that real devils might be summoned up by its dynamic stagecraft.

Jonathan Dollimore pointed out that up until 1984, when he published *Radical Tragedy*, literary critics had very often either seen the play as essentially a Christian morality tale or a depiction of a more or less heroic Renaissance aspiration to strive for human knowledge and dominion against the constraints of medieval superstition and religious dogma (despite how Faustus actually spends his time). In the words of Harry Levin's 1961 study, *Christopher Marlowe: the Overreacher*, Marlowe's hero was like his creator.

> Living in a day when controls were external and ubiquitous and high-handed, he boldly asserted the values of freedom … Subsequently … Faustianism has become the veritable ideology of liberal man, the principal myth of western civilization.
>
> (Levin 1961: 188)

Dollimore argued that this critical dichotomy was a false one. The play is full of contradictions and cannot be so simplistically reduced. In fact, it is 'not an affirmation of Divine Law, or conversely of Renaissance Man, but an exploration of subversion through transgression' (Dollimore 1984: 109). In transgressing against divine law and rebelling against God himself, Faustus subverts the very idea of an all-powerful, just creator and ruler of the universe. The play's hero is seen to be trapped in a cosmic battle between God and Lucifer for his soul.

> Not only heaven and hell but God and Lucifer, the Good Angel and the Bad Angel, are polar opposites whose axes pass through and constitute human consciousness … From Faustus' point of view … God and Lucifer seem equally responsible in his final destruction, two supreme agents of power deeply antagonistic to each other yet temporarily co-operating in his demise. Faustus is indeed their subject, the site of their power struggle. For his part God is possessed of tyrannical power … [while] Lucifer, Beelzebub and Mephistophilis enter syndicate-like 'To view the subjects of

> our monarchy' (Sc. xix) ... [Faustus] is located on the axes of contradictions which cripple and finally destroy him.
>
> (111–12)

The subversive consequence of this is to reveal that it is not divine justice that underwrites God's power, but the other way round. In Marlowe's London, Protestant Christianity was dominated by the teachings of Jean Calvin according to whom God had decided even before the human race was created which few individuals would be saved, and there was nothing any individual person could do about it. But even without such a notion of divine tyranny, Faustus's rebellion discloses a human moral sense which is permanently independent from God, for, as the Greek philosopher Plato had seen, if God approves justice because it is just, then it is not of his creation; but if what is justice is only what God decrees, then justice is merely his will enforced by his power.

> The final chorus of the play tells us that Dr Faustus involved himself with 'unlawful things' and thereby practised 'more than heavenly power permits' (Epilogue). It is transgression which has revealed the limiting structure of Faustus' universe for what it is, namely, 'heavenly *power*'. Faustus has to be destroyed since in a very real sense the credibility of that heavenly power depends upon it. And yet the punitive intervention that validates divine power also compromises it: far from justice, law and authority being what legitimates power, it appears, by the end of the play, to be the other way round: power establishes the limits of those things.
>
> (118)

Dollimore places what the play proposes in the context of the contemporary resistance to political tyranny which would result in the Civil War of the 1640s.

> As an embodiment of naked power alone, God could so easily be collapsed into those tyrants who, we are repeatedly told by writers in this period, exploited Him as ideological mystification of their own power ... Not surprisingly, the concept of 'heavenly power' interrogated in Dr Faustus was soon to lose contemporary credibility, and it did so in part precisely because of such interrogation.
>
> (119)

By 'ideological mystification' Dollimore means that tyrants explained their right to rule by appealing to their God-given right to do so, as part of the natural order of the Christian universe. In Marlowe's play *The Jew of Malta* (1589), that order is challenged by a Machiavellian Jew, Barabas. But the Christian rulers nakedly use their Christianity to justify what they do to him as a Jew, such as take away half of his wealth. In fact Barabas is lucky they let him, or any Jew, have any money at all, only allowed by the Governor 'through suffrance of your hateful lives, / Who stand accursed in the sight of heaven' (1.2).

The Christian rulers of Malta regard Barabas as a despised member of the people who crucified Jesus, to be excluded from their community and rightfully exploited. But they themselves (like their Turkish enemies) are entirely motivated by 'the wind that bloweth all the world besides: / Desire of gold' (3.5), and whose rule is based on slavery, exploitation and expropriation of others' property. Stephen Greenblatt notably argued that Barabas is in fact a creation of that society and an embodiment of the capitalist values it does not consciously recognize in itself.

> The true emblem of the society of the play is the slave market, where 'Every one's price is written on his back' (2.3) … At this level of society, the religious and political barriers fall away: the Jew buys a Turk at the Christian slave market … It is important to grasp the extent to which Barabas expresses in extreme, unmediated form the motives that have been partially disguised in the spiritual humbug of Christianity, indeed the extent to which Barabas is *brought into being* by the Christian society around him. His actions are always *responses* to the initiatives of others: not only is the plot of the whole play set in motion by the Governor's expropriation of his wealth, but each of Barabas's particular plots is a reaction to what he perceives as a provocation or a threat.
>
> (Greenblatt 1980: 205–06)

Furthermore, Barabas's language itself betrays how he is constructed as the image of all the rapacious, exploitative qualities of Christian Malta, even to the point where his character loses its individual identity the more the play progresses.

> For not only are Barabas's actions called forth by Christian actions, but his identity itself is to a great extent the product of Christian conceptions of a Jew's identity … His sense of himself, his characteristic response to the world, his self-presentation are very largely constructed out of the materials of the dominant, Christian culture. This is nowhere more evident than in his speech, which is virtually composed of hard little aphorisms, cynical adages, worldly maxims – all the neatly packaged nastiness of his society.
>
> (207)

But Greenblatt sees any genuine rebellion against the dominant ways of thinking and behaviour as impossible: even what is seen as the enemy of society is a construction of 'the immense power of the social system in which such systems play their part … In this effacement of Barabas's identity, Marlowe reflects not only upon his culture's bad faith, but also upon the tragic limitations of rebellion against this culture' (209).

These two influential leaders, Dollimore and Greenblatt, of what became known as the Cultural Materialist and New Historicist schools of criticism in the 1980s found in Marlowe's work not just the desire to shock of the Bad Boy of Elizabethan theatre, but a way of reading the plays as subversive of the deep structures of belief that kept the rule of the elite in place: the ideologies of their societies. For the New Historicist Greenblatt, however, it was a subversion that those trapped within those ideologies were unable to see any means of escape.

Marlowe's father was a shoemaker. **Ben Jonson**'s step-father was a bricklayer, a trade which the writer himself practised, as well as those of a soldier and actor, before eventually becoming the first Poet Laureate for James I in 1616. In the first two decades of the seventeenth century it was Jonson's comedies that stood out for his contemporaries. *Volpone* (1605–06) is set in Venice, a republic famous for its rational, ordered political constitution but also for its mercantile power (and commercial cunning). Volpone's pleasure in his cunning trick, to pretend to be seriously ill in order to secure rich presents from greedy citizens who wish to be named as his heir, is one that from the beginning of the play he invites the audience to share. These tricks he will pull on them all even get to the point of persuading one would-be legatee – the otherwise paranoidly jealous Corvino – to supply his wife Celia as the 'young woman … lusty and full of juice' who is supposedly required 'to sleep by' Volpone for the sake of his health (2.6).

In the open-air, daylight public theatres (such as the Globe where *Volpone* was first performed) the audience was packed close to the stage. The relationship between performer and audience was something Jonson loved to play with and explore. John Creaser identifies Volpone's 'most marked characteristic' as his 'delight in play'.

> He is constantly playing with words ('these turdy-facy-nasty-paty-lousy-fartical rogues' (2.2)) or enjoying some form of role-play, whether he is encouraging others to perform, or is himself a performer. In his first speech he is a worshipper, in his second a social critic, then a variety of sick old men, a mountebank, a wooer, a *commandadore* [court officer], and finally he unties the knot of the play with the theatrical gesture of 'uncasing' (5.12) himself.
>
> (Creaser 1975: 336)

The process of watching the play is one of being morally compromised, to be drawn into enjoyment of seeing the brilliant Volpone and his servant Mosca cheat, lie and extort from the stupid and greedy.

> Jonson manages to walk a knife-edge between moral condemnation and existential admiration. He does this by setting *Volpone* among characters whose disabilities emphasise the human importance of those qualities – neither moral nor immoral in themselves – which Volpone so brilliantly possesses and which they so signally lack. In the Venice of the play, Volpone is outstanding not for corruption but for intelligence … [The reason] why our delight in Volpone is not neutralised by moral condemnation lies in his outstanding theatrical presence. The actor playing him can hardly fail to establish a unique rapport with the audience.
>
> (344)

Lorna Hutson has placed the moral compromising of the audience that Creaser discusses most sharply in its historical moment. She notes how the 'artistry' of 'the play as a whole imbues its most outrageous moments with an aesthetically satisfying emotional logic'. But this can be seen as underpinned by a new relativism.

> [This is a] newly pragmatic conception of the relation between the human passions and the well-being of the political state ... a doctrine of support for free trade and capitalism, on the grounds that what in an individual was a vice (avarice, social competitiveness), might become, in aggregate, a virtue (national prosperity, civilized manners).
>
> (Hutson in Rowland ed. 1998: xxviii–xxix)

Volpone seduces us to an awareness of the modern delight in the acquisition of goods and wealth which renders boring the moral conditions in which that wealth is produced. This is all achieved through self-conscious, inventive performance: Volpone's 'luxurious inversions of customary roles and routine performances ... make him a proleptically satirical figure for our own equation of free state and free market' (xxix). The play turns upside-down our conventional moral responses in favour of the theatrically satisfying in emotional terms, but foreshadows a world where unlimited individualist economic activity can dissolve both fixed morality and identity, and yet be celebrated. Volpone's final casting off of his last disguise to defeat Mosca's double-cross restores him as the sovereign individualist. John Creaser puts it like this.

> [It] neatly reverses the traditional uncasing of the disguised fox by the powers of 'virtue'; it is another 'device' that is 'rare' and ingenious; it upstages Mosca and makes Volpone once more actor-manager in his own play; and it restores, though in a new form, his sense of power and of splendid isolation.
>
> (Creaser 1975: 351)

Volpone is harshly punished by the Venetian judges, but he turns their punishment into a joke. 'Volpone cannot be forgiven within the play', notes Ann Barton, but 'The Fox, like Face, can rely on the spectators to acquit him of any crime committed against the spirit of comedy, for being predictable, unimaginative or tedious' (Barton 1984: 119).

Face, aka Jeremy the butler, is a protagonist in another of Jonson's plays where the 'spirit of comedy' works energetically to undermine conventional ideas. *The Alchemist* (1610) is a hyperactive comedy of deceit, pretence, rapid entrances and exits and a dupe locked in the toilet gagged with gingerbread. The company of tricksters, the 'venture tripartite' (1.1), as they call themselves, amass their customers' fees and gifts but fall out just as Lovewit returns to cash in on all their gains himself.

As Robert Smallwood observes, what is most intriguing is the lengths to which Jonson goes to suggest that the action of the play – originally performed in the indoor Blackfriars theatre – is happening at the same time and in the same place as the performance itself. Indeed, the play's own awareness of itself of a play which is itself playing a joke is central to the whole working of *The Alchemist.*

> An audience in a theatre in the autumn of 1610 pays money to pass what the Prologue promises will be two hours (and an interval), to watch three masters of pretence, in the autumn of 1610, take two hours (and an interval) to deprive a number of representative gulls of their money. Jonson's precision over the unity of time is clearly deliberate; it connects with his care over the unity of place to produce an important part of the play's overall effect ... Having promised us 'two short hours' entertainment in his Prologue, Jonson has Face tell Sir Epicure: 'Three hours hence, prepare you / To see projection [the final stage of the alchemical process]' (2.2). The incompatibility is part of the comic juxtaposition of the alchemist's and the actor's worlds of make-believe. If we fail to catch the joke we are being taken in as successfully as Sir Epicure. Theatrical self-consciousness reveals itself also in the series of illusion-breaking remarks scattered throughout.
>
> (Smallwood 1981: 147, 151)

As with *Volpone*, but by a different method, drawing the audience into the conspiracy or game of the play also works to compromise us morally. Our complicity, and our final applause for the victorious Face work to achieve Jonson's stated aim, not 'to grieve, but better men' (Prologue).

> The play exists under constant threat of imminent termination. The more we enjoy ourselves in watching it, the less welcome is this possibility and our desire that the play should stay alive thus draws us into immoral alliance with the efforts of Doll, Subtle, and above all Face to escape detection. ... In agreeing to become Face's guests we admit that we share the folly, lusts, and greed which our predecessors in his play, our fellow denizens of the Blackfriars, have revealed.
>
> (150, 160)

But Julie Sanders finds a more evident politics in the play. She argues that 'questions of republicanism' – in relation to audiences, commonwealths and the communal – are prevalent in this and other Jonson plays (Sanders 1998: 8). In opposition to what was becoming the dominant ideology of the country's rulers, there is no all-powerful, divinely justified monarch in the world of this play, but rather 'a community with all its attendant tensions, paradoxes and contradictions'. Furthermore, the hyperlocalized setting enables Jonson to make 'perhaps his most egalitarian (republican?) dramatic gesture' (Sanders 1998: 72). This emerges in Sanders's discussion of Doll.

Within the 'venture tripartite' there is political conflict for control between Face and Subtle, with Doll figured as their 'public thing', the *res publica*: she says pointedly 'Have yet some care of me, o' your republic' (1.1). But she acts as the mediator between the two, what Sanders calls 'the representative of the populace, the plebeian element in the oligarchical republic', the 'mixed state' seen in opposition to absolute monarchy. She is the most astute and perceptive character in the play, who 'knows the consequences of absolutism' and has a 'Machiavellian notion of the inbuilt decay of all political institutions' (73–75). She warns Face and Subtle of the risks they all run if the republican venture breaks down. But the two work brilliantly together: 'their relationship offers a kind of metaphor for performance'.

> [They] clearly lay considerable store by their partnership, or rather they have to, since in a strange way each is reliant upon the other ... Their lines spin off from one another; their exits and entrances are dependent upon each other's cues, and timing is a matter of implicit trust with all the door-openings and disguises which the plot entails. ... There is also the indisputable sense that once performance is set in motion a degree of control is sacrificed. Complete control is now qualified by the potential for audience interpretations; the clients provide various reasons why Face, Subtle and Doll must think on their feet. The analogy with the authorial position is clear; Jonson too in any performance sacrifices, both to audience and performers, part of his ability to determine the meaning and outcome of his plays.
>
> (78–79)

'There are absolutists in *The Alchemist*' – Sanders mentions the puritan Tribulation Wholesome and the monomaniacal Sir Epicure Mammon – 'but Ben Jonson is not one of them' (81). Rather, the effect of the play working in its many dimensions gives a model of a community where power has to be shared to some degree: in contemporary terms, a republic. The overlap in time and place between the world of the play and the co-ordinates of its real performance creates a localized self-recognizing community. The competitive, inter-reliant company of tricksters share their activities for mutual gain with that audience, who remain in on the joke. Just as the fraudsters adapt their performance to on-stage events, the play acknowledges its audience and their crucial role in the success of the enterprise. The author relinquishes the claim to total control. At the end of the play, when Face and Lovewit get all the money (and Lovewit the girl), 'the Blackfriars community has in effect been splintered by its collective efforts ... perhaps because such fissures are inherent in any given community'. When the audience rise to Face's call for self-knowing applause, it is 'democratic, egalitarian, republican applause' (88). It is the moment when all acknowledge their share in the common venture which no figure, divine or human, has dominated.

The Alchemist still finds and holds audiences today, but perhaps the most performed non-Shakespearean early modern play is **John Webster**'s *The*

Duchess of Malfi (1614). Its heroine's defiance of her brothers by secretly marrying her steward Antonio drives her twin brother Ferdinand to distraction by the idea that 'the royal blood of Aragon and Castile' should 'be thus attainted' (2.5). But it's the way in which Ferdinand obsesses luridly over the imagined details of his sister's sex life that has led critics since the 1920s to consider whether his impassioned and vengeful feelings have their origins in sexual jealousy, in his own thwarted incestuous desire.

Frank Whigham reads Ferdinand's fury – which culminates in lycanthropy – as being more political in origin, the result of the threat to his class position.

> [He is] a threatened aristocrat, frightened by the contamination of his supposedly ascriptive social rank, and obsessively preoccupied with its defence ... Ferdinand's incestuous inclination towards his sister [can be read] as a social posture, of extreme and paranoid compensation – a desperate expression of the desire to evade contamination by his inferiors ... [He sees] the sexual and the social, concerns with incest and with rank, status and blood, [as] concentric categories.
>
> (Whigham 1996: 190–91)

In an earlier essay Whigham put it like this.

> The news of the Duchess's liaison brings the social element firmly into view, for Ferdinand's fantasy leaps to the assumption of class-disparity. He imagines 'some strong-thigh'd bargeman; / Or one o'th'woodyard, that can quoit the sledge, / Or toss the bar' (2.5) ... and the debasement by occupation marks the intensity of the aversion. For him, [rivals] are mere labourers, well-equipped with poles and bars, false, and potent; by coupling with the Duchess they couple with him and contaminate him, taking his place.
>
> (In Kastan and Stallybrass edd. 1991: 268)

Indeed, as Linda Woodbridge observes, Ferdinand's fantasies seem focused on male body parts: there is more likely a displaced homosexual desire here. But, as Whigham argues, Ferdinand conflates the incest taboo with the sexual crossing of class boundaries, because his sister's marriage 'threatens to impose an awareness beyond his tolerance, of the human origin, and thus the mutability, of the elevation upon which he rests himself' (Whigham 1996: 197). The play exposes the ideology of a ruling aristocracy who see their class dominance as part of the unchangeable natural order.

Woodbridge, on the other hand, argues that '*all* sexuality troubles Ferdinand'. She sees him as a proponent of a particular Renaissance philosophy, Neoplatonism, which saw all the things of the body as what man (very much so in this case) should aspire above, in order to seek philosophical understanding and spiritual purity. Not to do so risked slipping back into the sub-human bestiality to which Ferdinand succumbs in the play's final act. Woodbridge persuasively suggests that

Ferdinand's fury towards his sister is caused by her heroic championing of the life of the body, and of desire itself as good, and indeed natural; and, in 'dying for her desire, the Duchess dies as a tragic hero'. She possesses a 'dogged sexiness – not to mention her cravings in pregnancy' that have 'troubled and intrigued audiences for four centuries'.

> In contrast to Ferdinand, the Duchess tells Antonio she is 'flesh and blood' (1.1), and her actions bear this out. She … 'vulturously' devours apricots (2.2), screams during childbirth (2.3), sprawls all over the bed when she sleeps, worries about grey hairs (3.2), and enjoys sex ('Alas, what pleasure can two lovers find in sleep!' [3.2]) … And the complete physical and spiritual humanity of the Duchess appears in the courage with which she faces torment and death.
>
> (In Liebler ed. 2002: 161–72)

Against those critics who find all early modern representations of female sexuality to be misogynistic, Woodbridge stresses the variety of contemporary views, including those who celebrated sexual pleasure within the 'companionate' marriage advocated by Protestants, a union between people who are, by nature, both body and soul.

> Philosophers taught that human dignity resided in the freedom to be either beast or angel. The best drama of the English Renaissance is built on the insight that the human condition consists of the necessity, and the opportunity to be both … Women have long been demonized as creatures of the senses, and it was risky for Webster to enlist a woman as a hero of desire. Just how risky it was appears in the number of readers who can't get beyond demonizing her for her desire, or at least claiming that Webster and his audiences did. But just as the view of *Othello* as a racist play founders on the stubborn fact that in an age when black characters were villains or served as comic relief, Shakespeare cast a black man as a tragic hero, so the view of *The Duchess of Malfi* as a cautionary tale about widows, gluttony and lust founders upon a similar, stubborn fact: Webster cast this sexy, desiring widow as a tragic hero.
>
> (182)

We end this chapter with another remarkable, versatile and resourceful woman, **Aphra Behn**, the first woman writer whom we could call professional. Her novel *Oroonoko*, about the black royal figure-turned-slave, has attracted much attention from both feminist and postcolonialist critics. Anne Fogarty sees the narrator and the narrative as conflicted.

> The chronicle of the life of Oroonoko is an equivocal one. Aiming to be a story of heroism, it turns into a register of loss … The female [narrator] does not deny otherness or shirk the reality of the racial, sexual and

> colonial conflicts which link the English community with that of the black slave. Yet Behn does not suggest that a feminization of history allows us a more balanced and inclusive account of events. Indeed, the problem for the narrator is that by assuming the role of historian she must also admit to her collusion with male coercive force. The text does violence to Oroonoko because it obliterates rather than celebrates him, making the narrator also part of the process whereby the African prince is transformed into the mutilated body of a European slave ... The narrator is torn between giving an account in the first-person singular of her experiences abroad – thus emphasizing the private intensity of her connection with Oroonoko – and producing a narrative in the first-person plural that stresses membership of the community of white female colonists in Surinam. On the one hand, her relationship with Oroonoko is personal and sympathetic, while on the other her admiring but distancing view of him is part of the collective response of a colonizing society to those it views as foreign.
>
> (In Plasa and Ring edd. 1994: 8–9)

Joyce Green MacDonald focuses on Oroonoco's bride Imoinda.

> Even within this absorption of black Africans by a white European narrative of slavery and the sexual and racial relations it dictates, Behn's Imoinda somehow confounds the construction of a seamless account ... The pregnant Imoinda initially resembles, but ultimately diverges from, the ideal of the English mother ... Her sexual history and her status as a sexually desiring subject, the active role she takes in fighting for her freedom by her husband's side, the alien origin traced in her very skin, mark Behn's production of her finally and only as Other than the white woman who tells her story. Imoinda's status as breeding stock in the minds of the planters is a plainly literal exhibition of how, for women in this period, reproduction has become the only means of production ... Behn recognizes gender difference within her representation of Africans, and also acknowledges the operations of gender within whiteness. As a white woman, Behn's narrator responds to the beauty and honourable qualities of Oroonoko and his African bride, Imoinda, and is curiously powerless to intervene in the public crisis of Oroonoko's capture and final, horrible public mutilation.
>
> (MacDonald 2002: 101–02)

Kate Aughterson, in the most recent of these contributions, argues that Behn's novel is both more radical and experimental than a novel like Defoe's *Robinson Crusoe* (which, since Ian Watt in 1957, has routinely been taken as initiating the 'rise of the novel'), not just in its bringing together the motifs of blackness and royalism but in its 'juxtaposition of a number of genres and discourse'. As Crusoe does, Behn's narrator claims 'both personal experience and eyewitness testimony'. Here's the opening gesture of the novel (Chapter 1).

> I do not pretend in giving you the history of this royal slave to entertain my reader with the adventures of a feigned hero … I was myself an eye-witness to a great part of what you will find here set down and what I could not be a witness of I received from the mouth of the chief actor in this history.

But Aughterson shows how, despite this insistence on 'truth' and 'reality', Behn deliberately stirs in 'elements of the exotic romance' and 'jarring discursive juxtapositions' into the narrative to provide interpretative challenges for the reader that go beyond the aims of a novelist like Defoe and the 18th century novel's 'evened out representational style and mode'. Aughterson says this. Her notion of how Behn's experimental fictions anticipate figures of modernity like Salman Rushdie is a reminder of why 'early modern' is a more appropriate label than the older term 'Renaissance' and is an appropriate last word for this chapter.

> These generic and discursive juxtapositions generate interpretative gaps into which the reader inserts herself: by thinking about the character of Oroonoko as both Westernized romance hero *and* black slave, the reader is forced to reflect on how we judge heroism and on political behaviour. By showing how slave traders literally disrupt the romance society, and that the values of oath-keeping in one discourse are meaningless in another, Behn suggests and displays a radical way in which the novel can use formal means to generate political meanings. Such a formal self-consciousness is absent from the novels celebrated by Watt and others as foundational: Behn is part of that alternative tradition through Sterne to Kundera and Rushdie who, in playing with genre and discourse, disrupt the notion of genre as a fixed model of representation and bourgeois identity formation.
>
> (In Aughterson and Philips ed. 2021: 28–30)

Works cited

Kate Aughterson and Deborah Philips edd., *Women Writers and Experimental Narratives* (Palgrave: 2021)

C.L. Barber intro., *Shakespeare's Sonnets* (Dell: 1960)

Francis Barker *et al.* edd., *1642: Literature and Politics in the Seventeenth Century* (Essex U.P.: 1981)

Francis Barker, *The Tremulous Private Body* (Methuen: 1984)

Ann Barton, *Ben Jonson, Dramatist* (Cambridge U.P.: 1984)

John Carey ed., *Andrew Marvell: Penguin Critical Anthology* (Penguin: 1969)

Rosalie Colie, *My Ecchoing Song: Andrew Marvell's Poetry of Criticism* (Princeton U.P.: 1970)

John Creaser, 'Volpone or the Mortifying of the Fox', *Essays in Criticism* Vol. 25, Issue 3: 1975.

Denis Danielson ed., *The Cambridge Companion to Milton* (Cambridge U.P.: 1999)

Thomas Docherty, *John Donne, Undone* (Methuen: 1986)

Jonathan Dollimore, *Radical Tragedy* (Harvester Press: 1984)

Robert Ellrodt, *Seven Metaphysical Poets* (Oxford U.P.: 1999)
William Empson, *Essays on Renaissance Literature*, ed. John Haffenden (Cambridge U.P.: 1993)
Jonathan Goldberg, *Voice Terminal Echo* (Methuen: 1986)
Stephen Greenblatt, *Renaissance Self-Fashioning* (Chicago U.P.: 1980)
Achsah Guiborry ed., *The Cambridge Companion to John Donne* (Cambridge U.P.: 2006)
Christopher Hill, *The World Turned Upside Down* (Penguin: 1975)
Christopher Hill, *Milton and the English Revolution* (Faber: 1977)
John Hollander, *The Work of Poetry* (Columbia U.P.: 1998)
John Holloway, *The Proud Knowledge* (Routledge & Kegan Paul: 1977)
Lorna Hutson intro., Richard Rowland ed., *'Volpone' and other Plays* (Penguin: 1998)
David Scott Kastan and Peter Stallybrass edd., *Staging the Renaissance: Reinterpretations of Elizabethan and Jacobean Drama* (Routledge: 1991)
Frank Kermode, *Shakespeare, Spenser, Donne* (Routledge & Kegan Paul: 1971)
Harry Levin, *Christopher Marlowe: The Overreacher* (Faber: 1961)
C.S. Lewis, *A Preface to Paradise Lost* (Oxford U.P.: 1942)
Naomi Conn Liebler ed., *The Female Tragic Heroine in English Renaissance Drama* (Palgrave: 2002)
David Loewenstein, *Milton: Paradise Lost* (Cambridge U.P.: 2004)
Joyce Green MacDonald, *Women and Race in Early Modern Texts* (Cambridge U.P.: 2002)
Arthur F. Marotti, *John Donne, Coterie Poet* (Wipf & Stock: 1986, 2008 ed.)
Philip Martin, *Shakespeare's Sonnets: Self, Love and Art* (Cambridge U.P.: 1972)
David Norbrook intro., H.R. Woudhuysen edd., *The Penguin Book of Renaissance Verse* (Penguin: 1993)
David Norbrook, *Writing the English Republic* (Cambridge U.P.: 2000)
Annabel Patterson, *Andrew Marvell* (Northcote House: 1994)
Carl Plasa and Betty Ring edd., *The Discourse of Slavery from Aphra Behn to Toni Morrison* (Routledge: 1994)
Claudine Raynaud ed., *La Poesie Metaphysique de John Donne* (Universite Francois Rabelais: 2002)
Christopher Ricks, *Milton's Grand Style* (Oxford U.P.: 1967)
Julie Sanders, *Ben Jonson's Theatrical Republics* (Macmillan: 1998)
Elaine Scarry, *Dreaming by the Book* (Farrar, Strauss and Giroux: 1999)
R.L. Smallwood, '"Here, in the Friars": Immediacy and Theatricality in *The Alchemist*', *The Review of English Studies* Vol. 32, Issue 126: May 1981
Margarita Stocker, *Paradise Lost: The Critics Debate* (Macmillan: 1988)
Frank Whigham, *Seizures of the Will in Early Modern English Drama* (Cambridge U.P.: 1996)
Raymond Williams, *Politics and Letters* (New Left Books: 1979)

4 Early romantic writings 1750–1800

Thomas Gray, William Blake, William Wordsworth

Romanticism was an international movement across the arts following and inspired by the 1789 French Revolution. This is Gabriel Josipovici in 1971, placing the proper initial stress on the political seeds of romanticism.

> Romanticism was first and foremost a movement of liberation – liberation from religious tradition, from political absolutism, from a hierarchical social system and from a universe conceived on the model of the exact sciences … What was important was the uniqueness of men and the uniqueness of each object in the world … There were moments [the romantics] felt … when life seems suddenly to reveal itself in all its mystery and terror … The function of art becomes that of exploring those areas of the mind and of the universe which lie beyond the confines of rational thought and of ordinary consciousness, and the hero of romantic art becomes none other than the artist himself.
>
> (Josipovici 1971: 180–81)

The Revolution, with its rallying calls to liberty, equality and fraternity, was based, then, on protests – against solidified class structures and deferential obedience to arbitrary authorities in politics and religion. It was also (among the poets, especially with Blake) in protest against the cruelties of early industrial capitalism with its exploitative working conditions cutting short so many lives, including those of children.

But romanticism should be seen neither as a monolithic nor neatly time-bounded phenomenon. Its roots extend backwards into the 18th century – with, as we'll see, poets like Gray and even Dr Johnson – and forwards into the later 19th – in the form of the subversive Emily Dickinson, whom we'll meet in Chapter 8. It contains, like other major movements and socio-cultural formations, contradictory energies and responses, as usefully illustrated in the title of Marilyn Butler's important book *Romantics, Rebels and Reactionaries*, as well as by the sense that a key text from the period, Mary Shelley's *Frankenstein* (which we'll meet in the next chapter), has been read as conflicted between radical and conservative responses to

DOI: 10.4324/9781003127567-5

the Revolution. We can also valuably put side by side representative but deeply divergent poems from the time as Blake's 'London' and Wordsworth's 'Westminster Bridge', and compare what Keats called Wordsworth's 'egotistical sublime' with Keats's own last Odes. The later and politically disillusioned Wordsworth has also been readily contrasted with his pro-Revolutionary early years. We'll see some of these contradictory and conflicted energies in what follows over this and the next chapter.

We saw in Chapter 3 that T.S. Eliot, arguing (with little historical evidence) for what he called a 'dissociation of sensibility' in the middle of the 17th century, had a decisive influence on the critical estimation of poets following his promotion of Donne and Marvell and his downgrading of, first, Milton and then Milton's great romantic (and some of the later Victorian) successors. Eliot was keen, for his own reasons (and his own poetry), to argue for the crucial role of impersonality that he felt was so damagingly violated by the romantic poets with their insistence on the unique imaginative creativity of the individualized self.

It wasn't until the 1960s that British romanticism, and Wordsworth in particular, were decisively re-assessed by – perhaps inevitably – leading American rather than British critics (with the notable British exceptions of John Jones, as we'll see below, and the brilliant chapter 'Sense in *The Prelude*' in William Empson's challenging 1951 masterpiece *The Structure of Complex Words*). These American critics were reacting against their erstwhile compatriot Eliot (who chose to become a royalist Anglo-Catholic Englishman), and they owed their allegiance instead to M.H. Abrams (a crucial book is his 1953 *The Mirror and the Lamp*, the illuminating lamp of romanticism being contrasted with the merely reflective mirror of the Enlightenment); later they were loosely grouped together as the instigators at Yale University from the 1970s of 'deconstruction'. This resulted in landmark studies of the romantic poets, particularly by Geoffrey Hartman (the most 'creative' reader among these theoretical critics) on Wordsworth, a poet he returned to throughout his career. Another of these Yale critics, Harold Bloom, started his controversial book *The Anxiety of Influence*, as we'll soon see, with the example of Wordsworth struggling against his 'Oedipal' father Milton, to find his own poetic identity.

Blake, at the start of this period, is the figure aslant from and in uneasy relations with the more idealizing and mystifying energies of romanticism (Eliot saw in Blake's songs the unpleasantness of great poetry) and Blake was championed from the 1940s by the demystifying myth-critic Northrop Frye and then properly assigned to the native tradition of radical dissent from the 1640s by British socialist critics like E.P. Thompson. At the other end of the period is another unclassifiable poet who stood apart from the trend, committed to telling the truth 'aslant', and who only much later, like Blake, came to be seen as radically enlarging our understanding of what poetry itself amounted to and what could be done with it. I mentioned Emily Dickinson above and you'll easily see later her connections with the equally radical, rule-breaking Blake, the two of them returning poetry to its roots in folk literature, children's rhymes and riddles.

But we start with **Thomas Gray**'s anthology favourite mid-18th century 'Elegy Written in a Country Churchyard' which gives me the chance, very soon, to give you William Empson again, at his amazing best (in his 1935 *Some Versions of Pastoral* – which contains, incidentally, the best criticism ever penned on the *Alice* books). Eliot, arguing from his assumption of a post-17th century dissociated sensibility (from which we have allegedly never recovered), tendentiously compared the 'Elegy' with Marvell's 'Coy Mistress' and claimed that the feeling in the Gray poem is cruder than in the Marvell poem. This was tendentious for several reasons. First, there are widely different generic conventions behind an elegy for the uncelebrated poor in a graveyard and a love-poem urging a young woman to have sex. Second, Marvell's poem (sounding, as Eliot knew, much more like Donne than his usual self – or like Hamlet bullying Ophelia in public) expresses, in a manner that would have appalled Gray, some of the crudest and most offensively misogynistic remarks to the woman (about, for instance, worms trying out her virginity in her grave) in a century not always known for its sexual delicacy towards women.

It was Dr Johnson who, only about thirty years after the poem was written, was the most influential early critic to celebrate the 'Elegy' (in his *Lives of the Poets*), a remarkable endorsement given his very harsh judgement of some of Gray's other poems, which he describes as 'glittering accumulations of ungraceful ornaments' and in which he accuses Gray of 'a kind of strutting dignity' and of being 'tall by walking on tiptoe'. But Johnson then turns to the 'Elegy' and we can almost hear his relief at being able to agree with the common critical consensus. In its miniature way this turn from what sounds almost like personal animosity towards breaches in neo-classical 'taste' to generous communitarian feeling is a proto-romantic moment itself. Johnson's mention of returning echoes of an originality that we all somehow know sounds pre-Wordsworthian: Wordsworth's greatest writing years are only a little more than ten years ahead, as we'll see. And in a famous letter of February 1817 Keats writes of how poetry should strike the reader as 'almost a remembrance'. Johnson says this.

> In the character of his 'Elegy' I rejoice to concur with the common reader; for by the common sense of readers uncorrupted with literary prejudices, after all the refinements of subtlety and the dogmatism of learning, must be finally decided all claim to poetical honours. The 'Churchyard' abounds with images which find a mirror in every mind, and with sentiments to which every bosom returns an echo. The four stanzas beginning 'Yet even these bones' are to me original: I have never seen the notions in any other place; yet he that reads them here persuades himself that he has always felt them.
>
> (In Cruttwell ed. 1968: 479–80)

A couple of years after this – and a couple of years before his own death – Johnson wrote an elegy himself, 'On the Death of Dr Robert Levet'. Levet was an untutored doctor who selflessly helped the suffering poor in whatever way he could, accepting small gifts (like gin) that were forced upon him in gratitude; Johnson gave him a home in his (rather haphazardly filled) home. The poem calls Levet 'obscurely wise' and 'of every friendless name the friend'. Do please read this poem. Patrick Cruttwell, editor of a fine collection of Johnson's work, says this, with the simplicity and force of critics at their best, faced with the best writing: 'For my own part, I can only say that I find it the most personally and directly moving elegy in the language' (569).

William Empson, 150 years after Johnson, also starts in ambivalence towards Gray. Teasing out the elegy's 'latent political ideas' he quotes the stanza:

> Full many a gem of purest ray serene
> The dark unfathomed caves of ocean bear;
> Full many a flower is born to blush unseen
> And waste its sweetness on the desert air.

After some very characteristic riffing on gems and flowers, Empson wonderfully broadens his analysis. (The extract that follows concludes with the end of Empson's chapter.)

> By comparing the social arrangement to nature, [Gray] makes it seem inevitable, which it was not, and gives it a dignity which was undeserved. Furthermore, a gem does not mind being in a cave and a flower prefers not to be picked; we feel that the [labouring] man is like the flower, as short-lived, natural and valuable, and this tricks us into feeling that he is better off without opportunities …
>
> And yet what is said is one of the permanent truths; it is only in degree that any improvement of society could prevent wastage of human powers; the waste even in a fortunate life, the isolation even of a life rich in intimacy, cannot but be felt deeply, and is the central feeling of tragedy … The poetic statements of human waste and limitations, whose function is to give strength to see life clearly and so adopt a fuller attitude towards it, usually bring in, or leave room for the reader to bring in, the whole set of pastoral ideas … They assume it is sometimes a good thing to stand apart from society as far as you can. They assume that some people are more delicate and complex than others, and that if people can keep this distinction from doing harm it is a good thing, though a small thing by comparison with our common humanity.
>
> (Empson 1935: 4–5, 20)

Terry Eagleton comments very well on this lovely passage in Empson and his attitude towards pastoral.

> For Empson the typically pastoral attitude is a more ambiguous one … Pastoral knows a moment of (potentially tragic) separation of mind from world, the cultivated from the simple, self-reflexivity from spontaneity; but it includes this moment within a richer, more complex relationship in

which it is recognised that ... the mind is after all a *part* of nature and not just its other ... and that even the intellectual – hard though it is sometimes to credit it – shares a common humanity with others, which ultimately overrides whatever demarcates him or her from them.

(Eagleton 1986: 159–60)

Nearly 40 years after Empson, another great British critic whom, like Empson, we met in Chapter 1, Raymond Williams, in effect the founder of what was later called cultural materialism, wrote in his masterpiece *The Country and the City* about Gray's 'Elegy' in relation to earlier and more complacent poems about the deserving poor. Williams, here as elsewhere in this extraordinary book, strikes a very personal note.

[Gray and other later poets show] only an extension of social sympathy, but it is interestingly marked by a radical change of tone. In the later poems, there is a sense of ineradicable melancholy, which we can show by contrast with the sense of settlement, even of satisfaction and self-satisfaction, in an earlier celebration of a humble condition, Herrick's 'A Thanksgiving' (1647).

Williams quotes some lines from the poem (in which Herrick thanks his Lord for his 'little house', 'humble roof' and 'low ... porch, as is my fate', while yet observing how 'the threshold of my door / Is worn by the poor'), and adds this.

As it happens, I first read this poem, as a child, under a roof and a porch probably lower than Herrick's, and I could then neither get the lines out of my mind nor feel other than angry about them. My father had brought it home ... from an evening class he was attending in the village. He had been asked (it is how values are taught) to learn it by heart; he asked me to see if he could. I remember looking and wondering who the poor were, and why they wore this threshold, if the poet's condition was indeed so low. I understand that better now. The poverty is seen ... by the former court poet, the royalist parson, deprived of his living in the Commonwealth ... But this was not the source of the anger, which came from a sense of the play at abasement, putting himself even lower than the porch and being so pleased about it ...

Gray's 'Elegy', with its churchyard setting, draws of course on a traditional commonplace – 'The paths of glory lead but to the grave' – but there is also a sustained and ambiguous celebration of 'the short and simple annals of the poor'. It is ambiguous because it at once ratifies this remote simplicity ... – 'the cool sequestered vale of life' – ... and admits, with an edge of protest, the social as opposed to the abstracted rural condition ... – [its] 'chill penury' – ... It cannot really be had both ways: the luck of the 'cool sequestered vale' and the acknowledged repression of 'chill penury'. But in this structure of feeling, temporarily, the ambiguities of the appeal to simplicity were held and mediated.

(Williams 1973: 92–95)

Here is a paragraph (in part) from Geoffrey Hartman on the 'Elegy' (from an essay on Wordsworth in 1965 to which we'll return later) to end this section on Gray.

> There is ... a general convergence of elegiac and nature poetry in the eighteenth century. Poems about place ... merge with meditations on death, so that landscape becomes dramatic in a quietly startling way ... Not only is the graveyard a major locus for the expression of nature sentiment, but Nature is herself a larger graveyard inscribed deeply with evidences of past life. This convergence of graveyard and nature ... is consecrated by the success of Gray's 'Elegy' in which the division between country-side and cemetery is hardly felt. We move with insidiously gradual steps from the one to the other; and Gray enters so strongly into the spirit of his poem that he imagines himself as one of the unhonoured dead rescued from anonymity only by his epitaph graved under a thorn. His poem ends, therefore, with an archaic image of itself – an actual inscription for which the whole elegy provides the setting, and this is nature in its most regular, ancient and oblivious form.
>
> (In Hillis and Bloom edd. 1965: 392–93)

From Gray to **William Blake** and early Wordsworth is less of a step and is closer in time than we might have thought. Patrick Cruttwell, quoted above, makes the point that there is continuity between the pungent and pithy anger about poverty in Johnson's early poem 'London' (1738, written in his late twenties) and Blake's 'London' (1794), from which, says Cruttwell, Johnson's poem is 'not so alien as one might think' (Cruttwell ed. 1968: 14).

The traditional comparison is to put Blake's 'London' next to Wordsworth's 'On Westminster Bridge' and the temptation (to which I have often succumbed in teaching) is to use the former to attack the latter, not altogether fairly because sonnets (the Wordsworth is one) bring all sorts of baggage with them regarding literary prestige and authority of utterance, whereas the Blake (despite its ferocity of despair, against which Wordsworth's tone is positively genial and satisfied) comes out of a much more folk-style tradition. It famously starts:

> I wander through each chartered street
> Near where the chartered Thames does flow,
> And mark in every face I meet
> Marks of weakness, marks of woe.
>
> In every cry of every man,
> In every infant's cry of fear,
> In every voice, in every ban,
> The mind-forged manacles I hear.

The pre-eminent Blake scholar, David Erdman, connects the poem to the revolutionary Thomas Paine and the perilous times for English radicals like Paine and Blake in the early 1790s, and he has important things to say about the evolution of the first two verses. I'll add that 'chartered' in the poem means licenced to conduct business (privatized and sometimes monopolized). Blake is also punning on the sense of mapped out (maps were originally assertions of ownership), like the fierce puns on 'mark', which include the sense of the poet cursed not only with the laser-like insight of having to read all the unhappiness on the faces of the city inhabitants but also having to inscribe it, to write it on their faces, like the mark of Cain, as he feels impelled to pace the streets. Erdman says this, in a fine essay called 'Infinite London'. (Part of a footnote is incorporated into the text.)

> In his first draft Blake wrote 'dirty street' and 'dirty Thames' as plain statement of fact … The change to 'chartered' (with an intermediate 'cheating') suggests agreement with (perhaps was even suggested by) Paine's condemnation of 'charters and corporations' in the second part of *The Rights of Man*, where Paine argues that … city charters, by annulling the rights of the majority, cheat the inhabitants and destroy the town's prosperity … Paine also [called] 'every chartered town … an aristocratic monopoly' in the first part [of the *Rights*]. Paine's work was circulated by shopkeepers chafing under corporation rule and weary, like Blake, of the 'cheating waves of chartered streams' of monopolized commerce.
>
> In the notebook fragment just quoted Blake speaks of shrinking 'at the little blasts of fear [t]hat the hireling blows into my ear', thus indicating that when he writes of the 'mind-forged manacles' in every cry of fear and every ban he is not saying simply that people are voluntarily forging manacles in their own minds. Hireling informers or mercenaries promote the fear; [Prime Minister] Pitt's proclamations are the bans, linked with an order to dragoons 'to assemble on Hounslow Heath' and 'be within one hour's march of the metropolis'. [Blake's] rejected reading, 'German forged links', points to several manacles forged ostensibly in the mind of Hanoverian [King] George: the Prussian manoeuvres on the heath, the British alliance with Prussia and Austria against France, and the landing of … Hanoverian mercenaries in England allegedly en route to battlefronts in France.
>
> (In O'Neill ed. 1970: 65–68)

E.P. Thompson, the great historian of the English working class, adds this to Erdman's analysis, taking us neatly back to Dr Johnson. (Part of a footnote is incorporated into the text.)

> 'Chartered' is more particularly associated with 'cheating' [the earlier version in the draft] … One might think of the monopolistic privileges of the East India Company, whose ships were so prominent in the commerce of the Thames, which applied in 1793 for twenty years' renewal of its

> charter, and which was under bitter attack in the reformers' press … No social historian can be surprised to find the banks of the Thames described as 'cheating' in the eighteenth century … The association of the banks of the Thames with commerce was already traditional when Samuel Johnson renewed it in his 'London' … On Thames-side already 'all are slaves to gold, / Where looks are merchandise, and smiles are sold'.
>
> (In Philips ed. 1979: 5–8)

Blake's 'dirty' and 'cheating' Thames certainly contrasts sharply with Wordsworth's 'river glideth at his own sweet will' in his 'Westminster Bridge'. I'll just add that Wordsworth has in effect been reprimanded, in an example of new-historicist criticism in its rather literalist guise, for calling the river Wye, in his 'Tintern Abbey', 'this delightful stream' when he would have known it was actually muddied and polluted by local iron-works.

Let's turn to another and very different poem in Blake's *Songs of Experience*, 'The Sick Rose'.

> O Rose, thou art sick!
> The invisible worm
> That flies in the night,
> In the howling storm,
>
> Has found out thy bed
> Of crimson joy
> And his dark secret love
> Does thy life destroy.

This, compared to 'London', is at once crystal clear and utterly opaque – and has, because of that, attracted a wide range of what are largely symbolic readings. Michael Riffaterre, in a bracing and scholarly stylistics analysis from 1973, starts from the point that readings by influential Blake critics like Harold Bloom and Kathleen Raine 'all aim outwards … find[ing] the meaning of the text in its relationship of its images to other texts'. Riffaterre instead argues that 'reading must be aimed inwards': the key words 'rose' and 'worm', for instance, matter less for what they symbolize and more for the polarity between them: 'their common significance cannot be derived from one without the other'.

> The rose therefore must contain a worm … The flower is not just the thing of beauty destined to future withering that it is singly. It is not a withering to be, but a withering in being, beauty as the latent destruction of itself, purity as the germ of impurity.
>
> (Riffaterre 1973: 40–41)

What the poem presents is a 'full actualisation of the binary opposition' (41). After his lengthy and very detailed unpicking of the various polarities that energize the poem (his essay really needs reading in full), Riffaterre says this about the 'chief characteristic of a poetic text'.

> While the text seems to progress from image to image, from episode to episode, it in fact keeps repeating the same information. The text progresses syntactically and lexically and it keeps adding meanings, but each step forward is actually a repetition of one significance. Each of these steps is only a transcodage of that significance from one means of expression to another. The significance, of course, is found in the structure first given in the text, with its network of binary oppositions and their transformations. Every subsequent transcodage is a variant of this structure. The text has been saying all along that *the rose is sick*. And the text is nothing more than an expansion of this matrix sentence which is … but a datum provided by the title itself … The poem is not a rehashing about a thing. The poem is a verbal derivation from a verbal group. Its object is not a rose and its parasite; its object is the phrase *the sick rose*, or rather the oxymoron formed by the phrase … the contradiction between *rose*, an exemplum that excludes adjectives such as *sick*, and its association with that very adjective. The message lies in this contradiction, as well as in the fact that it is repeated through forms of maximum efficacy: the text is exemplary throughout because it is composed solely of oppositions, of polarised polarities.
>
> (44)

Let's turn to an exemplary reading of 'The Sick Rose' as offered by Derek Attridge in his excellent short book *The Singularity of Literature* (2004). He starts by discussing the poem's uniqueness in its 'specific employment of the possibilities offered by the literary tradition and the wider cultural context'.

> [There is] the distinctive combination, for instance, of a nursery-rhyme-like rhythm with sexual imagery, or the exploitation of the genre of the apostrophe ['O Rose'], or the deployment of syntax to achieve an unrelenting onward drive that climaxes on a single powerful word.
>
> (Attridge 2004: 66)

Attridge turns to how any critical response to a poem is an attempt to realize and to convey the operation of its singularity: 'the reflex of that operation in my experience' which (done well) will generate 'in turn an event of singularity for the reader'. (In Chapter 2 we saw Michael Wood saying the equivalent about the effect of William Empson's critical response to *Macbeth* on readers.)

> For me, now, the poem's singularity arises in part from the combined experience, as the single syntactic unit unfolds and draws me on, of movements of enclosure and movements of opening. The sentence presents me with a series of words and phrases … on an uncontrollable journey through the resources of the culture and, though I can only guess at this, the

> unconscious. Word after word resonates through a variety of registers; to mention just a few, 'sick' (ill, sick with love, sick at heart), 'invisible' (ghostly, minute, immaterial, repressed, metaphysical) ... 'howling' (noise of wind, of grief, of terror, of animal rage or despair), 'crimson' (rose-red, intense, blood-like, sexual). The result of this opening out of meaning is that even a word like 'worm' acquires a density of suggestiveness that moves well beyond its apparent sense ... to archaic senses (serpent, snake, dragon) and figurative uses (... the gnawing of remorse) ... to myth (the Garden of Eden) ... and phallic suggestiveness ...
>
> The poem's occurrence as apostrophe is part of its singular happening, too. It positions the reader both as addresser and addressee: seeing the rose through the eyes of the speaker and sharing his or her undecidable, yet powerful, feelings about it (horror? gloating? pity? exultation?), and at the same time occupying the same place as the rose, indicted, exposed, destroyed.
>
> (68–69)

I'll just add another and very different way of reading 'The Sick Rose'.

The composer Benjamin Britten and the tenor Peter Pears left the UK for America at the start of the Second World War. They were lovers. In 1943 they returned to England and Britten (after a bout of measles) wrote for Pears (and the horn-player Dennis Brain) his 'Serenade for tenor, horn and strings'. Britten was 29. This sets to music a group of six poems, the third of which is Blake's 'The Sick Rose', which Britten called 'Elegy'. Do listen to this if you can, especially one of the two recordings featuring Pears. You'll be struck by the unearthly sound Britten conjures in the music for the horn that shapes and frames the movement. Some have heard in the sound of the horn in these passages a representation of the throbbing fever Britten suffered when ill. But for me much more immediately obvious is the evocation of the terrible 'music' of air-raid sirens. Britten and Pears avoided the Blitz of 1940 and 1941, lured – as I might be allowed to say – by the sirens of a 'secret love' in a New World of (as if Blakean) innocence. The Blake poem in 1943 is now being 'read' by Britten as an 'elegy' for an old European world 'destroyed' from within, and helplessly in lament, at once 'howling' about and serenading it. A serenade is an evening song – and serenades were traditionally sung under the windows of loved women. Britten's serenade, made vividly present through the plangent and weirdly sexless voice of his lover Pears, is in the setting of 'The Sick Rose' an unsettlingly 'secret', 'invisible' and – in effect – absent love song.

Let's turn to the early poems of **William Wordsworth** (which means the best of Wordsworth) and, first, to the most expressive and unsettling of his so-called 'Lucy' poems, about the death of an unknown, probably fictionalized, girl. (It was conventional to call real or imagined lost-loves 'Lucy'.) Like the other Wordsworth texts we'll be sampling, it was written in his late twenties and early thirties, from around 1798–1799 and up to about 1804.

A slumber did my spirit seal:
I had no human fears:
She seemed a thing that could not feel
The touch of earthly years.

No motion has she now, no force;
She neither hears nor sees;
Rolled round in earth's diurnal course,
With rocks, and stones, and trees.

Of the many very moving features of this poem, I want to mention the repeated 'and' in the three terms of the last line, as it allows me the opportunity to say something about Wordsworth in general. He was an inveterate reviser of his poems and, as he admitted himself, not always a successful one. His very long autobiographical poem *The Prelude* went through a complex history of revision but the two main texts are the long established 1850 edition (the year Wordsworth died) and the much earlier 1805 edition, not printed or widely read till the 1920s and 1930s but now more likely to be favoured by critics and editors. Here's the 1850 version of the opening lines.

O there is blessing in this gentle breeze,
A visitant that while he fans my cheek
Doth seem half-conscious of the joy he brings
From the green fields, and from yon azure sky.

There is something a bit artificial about the personification of the breeze (calling it – like the Thames above – 'he' and a 'visitant') and a bit self-consciously poetic and even archaic about 'doth' (like 'glideth' above) and 'yon' – and indeed 'azure'. Wordsworth certainly wrote those lines. But he originally wrote these, in November 1799.

O there is blessing in this gentle breeze
That blows from the green fields and from the clouds
And from the sky: it beats against my cheek,
And seems half-conscious of the joy it gives.

Fields and clouds and sky. Rocks and stones and trees. (Try reading both of those openings to friends without any explanation and see what they say.) Another Wordsworth passage in these great early years, part of the poem known as 'Tintern Abbey' which was the final poem in the landmark collection *Lyrical Ballads* put together by Wordsworth and Coleridge (1798–1802), has yet further repeated uses of 'and'. Wordsworth says he has felt a sense of the sublime 'Whose dwelling is the light of setting suns, / And the round ocean and the living air, / And the blue sky, and in the mind of man'. These 'ands' (though I sometimes wonder if in that extract there's one too many of them) suggest a mind working with marvellous and rapid fluidity, working by cumulative association rather than rational analysis. (The end of Keats's greatest and last ode, 'To Autumn', stretches three 'ands' across the last four lines, to very muted, almost unnoticeable and intensely moving effect – more on Keats in the next chapter. Those last lines of 'Autumn' may derive more from the end of Milton's 'Lycidas' than from Wordsworth and we'll see Wordsworth's relation with Milton below.)

J. Hillis Miller (who died in 2021), in a very close (deconstructive and also psychological) reading of 1979, analyses the language and form of 'A Slumber' in a way that will clearly remind you of what Riffaterre said about poetry in general. After a detailed account of the very many binary opposites in the poem (that include sharply divergent connotations of the word 'thing'), Miller says this.

> The invitation to interpret the poem in terms of oppositions is sustained in part by its syntactical and formal structure. Syntactically it is structured around words or phrases in apposition or opposition. The second line, for instance, repeats the first, and then lines three and four say it over again … Formally the poem is organised by the opposition between the first stanza and the second. Each stanza sets one line against the next, the first two against the last two: each also sets line one against line three and line two against line four, by way of the interlaced patters of rhymes … The bar or barrier or blank on the page between the two stanzas constitutes the major formal structuring principle of the poem. In the shift from past to present tense this bar opposes then to now, ignorance to knowledge … The 'I' of the first stanza … has disappeared entirely in the impersonal assertions of the second stanza. It is as though the speaker had lost his selfhood by waking to knowledge. He has become an anonymous impersonal wakefulness … This is the position of the survivor in all Wordsworth's work.
>
> (Miller 1979: 21–25)

We'll return to the idea of Wordsworth the survivor when we look at a beautiful short section of *The Prelude* that dates from this early period and is also centred on a dead child.

The structural opposition of the two stanzas discussed there by Miller (and in more detail than I have room for) was in one aspect anticipated in the late 1940s by the arch-New Critic Cleanth Brooks. (The New Critics, as we saw in Chapter 1, were sworn enemies of readings based on poets' intentions and fierce advocates of readings based instead around irony and formal tension.) He said this (in an essay later revised) about the two senses in which Lucy is insulated against the 'touch of earthly years', having noted (rather less subtly than Miller) that 'her unnatural slumber has waked him out of his'.

> In the first stanza, she 'could not feel / The touch of earthly years' because she seemed divine and immortal. But in the second stanza, now in her

> grave, she still does not feel 'the touch of earthly years', for, like the rocks and stones, she feels nothing at all. It is true that Wordsworth does not repeat the verb 'feels'; instead he writes 'She neither hears nor sees'. But the contrast, though not commented on directly by any device of verbal wit, is there nonetheless and is bound to make itself felt … The statement of the first stanza has been literally realised in the second, but its meaning has been ironically reversed.
>
> (Brooks 1948: 236–37)

It's widely agreed that Wordsworth's most distinguished, and most persistent, modern critic was Miller's friend and colleague Geoffrey Hartman (who died in 2016). Hartman used to say that Wordsworth pre-empts all later poets. He came to England as a Jewish refugee child (under a humanitarian scheme that the UK is now scandalously refusing to honour in its modern equivalence) and he openly acknowledged the early impact of Wordsworth when he found himself in the English countryside – as a survivor (to use Miller's word). Here, in the Introduction to his 1987 *The Unremarkable Wordsworth*, he pointedly quotes 'A Slumber'.

> The moment I was obliged to read him during high school in England, he reflected back my own sense of nature: rural nature, but more generally a world that felt as ancient and immemorial as 'rocks, and stones, and trees', that encompassed, inanimate yet animating, the mind in its earth-walks. But the discovery prompting me to write about him was that he could brood about himself in a way that nurtured rather than violated a 'culture of feeling'. No one before him had so naturally brought perception and consciousness together [and] … made us inherit unforgettably, after the Enlightenment, and in the dawn of the Industrial Revolution, a sense of 'unknown modes of being'.
>
> (Hartman 1987: xxv)

In a much earlier essay of 1965 Hartman has these very moving words to say about the 'Lucy' poems and 'English nature-feeling'. He notes along the way that Coleridge called 'A slumber' a 'sublime epitaph', to which Hartman adds that in the poem 'the casting of a lament in the form of an epitomised action [is] as if perfected from the Greek' – ancient Greek models of elegy, epitaph and epigram. In this same essay, Hartman also notes that Blake 'wrote his own Greek-style epitaph in "O Rose, thou art sick"'.

> It is in the 'Lucy' poems that the notion of spirit of place, and particularly *English* spirit of place, reaches its purest form … Lucy, living, is clearly a guardian spirit, not of one place but of all English places … while Lucy, dead, has all nature for her monument. The series is a deeply humanised version of the death of Pan, a lament on the decay of English nature-feeling. Wordsworth fears that the very spirit presiding over his poetry is

> ephemeral, and I think he refuses to distinguish between its death in him and its historical decline.
>
> (In Hillis and Bloom edd. 1965: 403–05)

Hartman (in 1987) notes that it is the 'commonplace' in Wordsworth that 'releases the "dread vibration"' and that his poetry is pre-eminently ghostly. (He detects in 'A slumber' ghostly puns on 'urn' and 'corse' (= corpse) in 'diurnal course' and the way the 'fears' / 'years' rhyme and the final 'trees' produce the ghostly anagram of 'tears'.)

> Under the words are ghostlier words, half-perceived figures or fragments that seem to be at once part of the lost object yet more living than what is present.
>
> (Hartman 1987: 29, 168)

This allows me to return to Miller, whose attentiveness to the language of 'A slumber' identifies an equivalent ghostliness that is expressed here very eloquently.

> The senses of the poem continually cross over the borders set up by the words if they are taken to refer to fixed 'things', whether material or subjective ... Each word in itself becomes the dwelling place of contradictory senses ... matched by the large-scale relation of going and coming between the two stanzas ... The tracing out of these differences within the same moves the attention away from the attempt to ground the poem in anything outside itself. It catches the reader within a movement in the text without any solid foundation in consciousness, in nature, or in spirit.
>
> (Miller 1979: 31)

In 1967 Paul de Man (with Miller and Hartman later the 'Yale deconstructors') gave a lecture on time and history in Wordsworth (the lecture was transcribed and published in 1987) that starts with recognizing how Hartman's early book on the poet (1964) was such an important breakthrough. A key part of this essay is on the early poem 'The Winander boy', from the same period as the 'Lucy' poems, later incorporated into *The Prelude* (whose first lines also date, as we saw, from this early period). This poem describes a boy gifted with the skill of using his mouth and hands to blow 'mimic hootings to the silent owls / That they might answer him'. And the owls 'would shout / Across the watery vale, and shout again, / Responsive to his call' in echoes that would be 'redoubled and redoubled'. But then sometimes there would be eerie silence.

> And when it chanced
> That pauses of deep silence mocked his skill,
> Then, sometimes, in that silence, while he hung
> Listening, a gentle shock of mild surprise
> Has carried far into his heart the voice

Of mountain torrents; or the visible scene
Would enter unawares into his mind
With all its solemn imagery, its rocks,
Its woods, and that uncertain Heaven, received
Into the bosom of the steady lake.

A line gap on the page (Miller's bar or barrier or blank?) then moves us to the last nine lines (of the original poem) that record how the boy died before 'full ten years old' and how the churchyard 'hangs / Upon a slope above the village school'.

And, there, along the bank, when I have passed
At evening, I believe that oftentimes
A full half-hour together I have stood
Mute – looking at the grave in which he lies.

De Man says this about how the boy responds to the silence that interrupts the echoes.

> We would have expected 'stood / Listening' instead of the unusual 'hung / Listening'. This word, 'hung' … reappears in the second part, when it is said that the graveyard … 'hangs / Upon a slope above the village school' … It is as if the solidity of earth were suddenly pulled away from under our feet and that we were left 'hanging' from the sky instead of standing on the ground.
>
> (de Man 1987: 7)

De Man notes that Wordsworth himself, in the preface to an 1815 edition of his poems, gives examples of the imaginative faculty working at its highest pitch in poetry of which those from Shakespeare and Milton describe, respectively, a samphire-gatherer seen as if hanging from the cliff and, in the Milton, a far-off fleet of ships that apparently 'hangs in the clouds'. Milton, says Wordsworth, 'dares to represent it as "hanging in the clouds"', and de Man adds this.

> This *daring* movement of the language, an act of pure mind, corresponds to the danger, the anxiety of the moment when the sudden silence leaves the boy *hanging* / listening … We now understand that the moment of silence … was in fact a prefiguration of [the boy's] death. The turning away of his mind from a responsive nature towards … [what] ultimately is called an 'uncertain Heaven' is … an orientation of his consciousness towards a pre-knowledge of his mortality.
>
> (8)

Reflecting on the fact that the earliest version of this poem has Wordsworth writing about himself as this boy, de Man notes that the two-part structure of the poem allows Wordsworth at the same time to look backward and to anticipate his own death: 'to be able to imagine … the consciousness of mortality, he can only represent death as something that happened to another person', allowing him to 'reflect on an event that is, in fact, unimaginable' (9).

A point I'd like to add about how the two parts of the poem work together is that, for me, the most moving feature in the description of the boy in the first part is the way, after all the uses of 'would', in the retrospective telling of the events that happened so often in this distant story ('they would shout', etc.), Wordsworth suddenly says that in the silence 'while he hung / Listening, a gentle shock of mild surprise / *Has carried* far into his heart the voice / Of mountain torrents; or the visible scene / *Would enter* unawares into his mind…'. The surprise change of tense in '*has carried*' ('would carry' is so expected) provides not only an increased sense of immediacy – the process happening – but also a vivid sense that the immediacy belongs to Wordsworth himself, that he is (as in the original version) indeed writing about himself. The poem then returning to 'would enter' makes the use of 'has' even more startling. But the 'has carried' also touchingly predicts the 'I have passed' and 'I have stood' of the second part (like the 'hung' / 'hangs' connection), weaving together at the syntactical level the relations between retrospection and anticipation that de Man explores so well.

In notes about his 'Immortality Ode' (1802–04), Wordsworth spoke about death in a way that connects directly with what de Man and Miller say about the poet only able to imagine (his) death in terms of it happening to someone else – the Winander boy or Lucy. Wordsworth says this.

> Nothing was more difficult for me in childhood than to admit the notion of death as a state applicable to my own being … I was [also] often unable to think of external things as having external existence, and I communed with all that I saw as something not apart from, but inherent in, my own immaterial nature. Many times while going to school have I grasped at a wall or tree to recall myself from this abyss of idealism to the reality. At the time I was afraid of such processes. In later periods of life I have deplored … a subjugation of an opposite character, and have rejoiced over the remembrances.
>
> (In Hayden ed. 1981: 978)

This is obscurely put but seems to mean that, whereas as a child he feared slipping away into pure immateriality, he now deplores such fears and welcomes remembering the sensations, though now they are only memories. Whatever, the dynamics outlined there, contrasting earlier and later periods of life, is structured into the 'Immortality Ode' which has, correspondingly, attracted differing readings about success and failure, losses and gains. The dynamics of loss and gain are also mirrored in the language of the poem that seamlessly weaves together the rhapsodic lyricisms of the shorter-lined parts (which almost ask to be sung or chanted: more below on one particular example) and the graver reflections on, for instance, how 'Shades of the prison-house begin to close / Upon the growing boy'.

Hartman, in his first book on Wordsworth of 1964, says very suggestively (he's talking about 'Tintern Abbey' but could be talking of the 'Immortality Ode'), that the 'calculus of gain and loss, of hope and doubt' is reproduced in the '*wave* effect of rhythm whose characteristic is that while there is internal acceleration, the feeling of climax is avoided … We can rarely tell, in fact, whether the "wave" is rising or falling' (in McMaster ed. 1972: 488–89).

I'd add that there's a miniature loss–gain dynamic in a strange shifting of tense in this great Ode, as I noted in 'The Winander boy' ('would shout' / 'has carried') but here in effect the opposite. Wordsworth writes of how birds 'sing a joyous song' and 'lambs bound' then adds: 'To me alone there came a thought of grief: / A timely utterance gave that thought relief, / And I again am strong'. It's as if the intruding grief and ability to relieve it are bracketed off in the past, the momentary loss safely inoculated by the dominant present tense of gain and re-gain.

Here's the famous ending of the Ode.

> Thanks to the human heart by which we live,
> Thanks to its tenderness, its joys, and fears,
> To me the meanest flower that blows can give
> Thoughts that do often lie too deep for tears.

(The 'fears' / 'tears' rhyme whose ghost Hartman sensed in 'A slumber'.)

A very different way of responding to the internally conflicted Ode was offered by Harold Bloom at the start of his 1973 controversial book *The Anxiety of Influence*, which I mentioned at the outset of this chapter and which (as you'll see) identifies a very different tragedy at issue. (The message from the Sphinx to Oedipus was, of course, that he'd kill his father. Bloom also mentions Prometheus who stole fire from the gods and who was taken as emblematic of heroic romantic humanism.)

Bloom sees the key conflict as that between Wordsworth setting out on his journey towards poetic identity and his need to overcome an Oedipal struggle with his poetic forbears, in his case Milton. Hartman pointed out that the form of Wordsworth's best early poems seems to be generated internally rather than inherited from the tradition but Bloom (another who pays tribute to Hartman) puts the emphasis on the tradition – in this case Milton – that, consciously or otherwise, Wordsworth is prompted by. He starts by mentioning Freud and sublimation, which, says Bloom, Freud 'recognized … as the highest human achievement'.

> Wordsworth too saw repetition or second chance as essential for development, and his ode admits that we can redirect our needs by substitution or sublimation. But the ode plangently also awakens into failure, and into a creative mind's protest against time's tyranny … [The ode] fights nature on

> nature's own ground, and suffers a great defeat, even as it retains its greater dream. That dream, in Wordsworth's ode, is shadowed by the anxiety of influence, due to the greatness of the precursor-poem, Milton's *Lycidas*, where the human refusal wholly to sublimate is even more rugged, despite the ostensible yielding to Christian teachings of sublimation …
>
> An implied anguish throughout this book is that romanticism, for all its glories, may have been a vast visionary tragedy, the self-baffled enterprise not of Prometheus but of blinded Oedipus, who did not know that the Sphinx was his Muse.
>
> (Bloom 1997: 9–10)

Before I end this discussion of early Wordsworth, I'll turn from Bloom's Oedipal tragedy to another kind of psychological struggle or crisis that has been identified in Wordsworth, a rather more domestic kind: this is the struggle against incestuous feelings between Wordsworth and his sister Dorothy (more on her in the next chapter) that F.W. Bateson in his controversial 1954 book argued was so formative to the development of the poetry. One can subscribe to the intensity of their mutual love without perhaps granting to its importance such a central psychic role in the poetry (as opposed to in their own domestic lives). But here is Bateson, on a more generalizing psychic struggle, and taking us back to Blake. (The claim made here for modernity against the tradition is echoed by John Holloway on Milton, which we saw in the last chapter.)

> So far from surrendering to the neurotic elements in his personality … Wordsworth's early life was one long desperate struggle against them … Wordsworth achieves greatness because his private struggles towards psychic integration have a representative quality. The poems generalise themselves, as they are read, into the reactions of the human individual fighting for its spiritual survival in a society that seems to have no place for it. And this makes him, with Blake, the first specifically modern poet … The earlier poets share with their audience both a belief in the literary tradition they inherited, and also an ultimate sense of obligation to the social order … Wordsworth and Blake did not accept either of these presuppositions. But Wordsworth's example was more important … because Wordsworth, or a part of him, would have *liked* to believe in a literary tradition and an inherited social order.
>
> (In McMaster ed. 1972: 387–88)

Bateson argues that Wordsworth's 'repudiation' of traditions was gradual, emerging strongly in his identification in *Lyrical Ballads* with figures 'at best only on the edge of organized society', and then becoming more submerged in the great poems of the new century which we've been looking at in this chapter. These are poems apparently 'less defiant' but actually 'more uncompromising' and due to what Bateson calls an egotism that 'is nearer to solipsism' that was formed in the crisis of the 'tragic discovery' of the brother and sister's passionate love for each other. The logic of Bateson's argument is that the Lucy poems, which we began with, are where Dorothy's 'symbolic death was recorded' as there could no longer be a place for her in her brother's 'poetic imagination' (388–90). I'll leave Bateson there.

I want to end this section on early Wordsworth by turning to a poet-critic, the great English poet Geoffrey Hill (who died very recently; more on Hill's poems much later in this book). But just before I do that, I want to highlight an outstanding English critic on Wordsworth, John Jones, whose *The Egotistical Sublime* came out (simultaneously with Bateson's book) as early as 1954, ten years before Hartman's first book. This contains some fine and subtle close reading of Wordsworth's language that ties up well with what we've seen excerpted above – and which leads helpfully to Hill's even more eloquent attention, thirty years later, to the words on the page.

Jones notes how four-syllable abstract nouns ending in '-ion' are very common in Wordsworth, usually occupying the fourth to seventh syllables in the pentameter (three examples in 'Tintern Abbey' alone): words like consummation, agitation, exultation and, says Jones, visitation, 'an important word in *The Prelude* [which] appears three times in the 1805 version of Book 1, and on each occasion it holds the middle of the line, immense, bare, a wind-like echoing'. Jones says this about another example.

> The famous sonnet that begins: 'It is a beauteous evening, calm and free, / The holy time is quiet as a Nun / Breathless with adoration ...' betrays [Wordsworth's] authorship in several ways. 'Adoration' is one sign. The simile is another, and the strange un-violence in which it relates very different natures, the woman and the hour. 'Holy' is certainly a kind of bond between them, but the essence of the thing is the unselfconscious movement from abstract to concrete ... 'Breathless', too, is characteristic of Wordsworth. There is unexpected tension and effort in the shift of stress to the first syllable, and the situation of the word allows its silent concentration to flood back through the line end pause. [Jones compares the lines in the 'Winander boy']: 'Then sometimes, in that silence, while he hung / Listening ...' Language takes time – time backwards as well as forwards.
>
> (In McMaster ed. 1972: 396–97)

Jones adds that Wordsworth used even longer words in strategic places, in phases like time's 'unimaginable touch', death's 'incommunicable sleep', sounds of 'undistinguishable motion' and, in 'Tintern Abbey', the 'weight / Of all this unintelligible world'.

> All these words arrest the movement of the sense ... and while they are going on they give the means of new awareness through release from the poem's time-scale. The murmured succession, the fearful patter, the prolonged striving, are different kinds of escape almost from language itself, to experience-worlds outside language.
>
> (397–98)

Little known among general readers and even among lovers (and students) of poetry, Geoffrey Hill was also a very learned and discriminating critic and in two separate chapters in his book *The Lords of Limit* (1984), chapters ostensibly about other writers and issues, Hill writes what are I think are some of the most suggestive and subtle – and moving – paragraphs about a fellow-poet I've read anywhere. Hill is writing about how any inquiry into the nature of rhythm in poetry always needs to account for the 'inertial drag of speech. Language gravitates and exerts a gravitational pull'. He turns to the great moment in the 'Immortality' ode between stanzas 8 and 9. Wordsworth is lamenting how age brings 'the inevitable yoke' and 'earthly freight' on to the soul 'full soon'.

> And custom lie upon thee with a weight,
> Heavy as frost, and deep almost as life!
>
> O joy! That in our embers
> Is something that doth live,
> That nature yet remembers
> What was so fugitive!

Hill says this about the last line of stanza 8.

> [It] is a weighted acknowledgement of custom's pressure; stanza eight is allowed to settle onto this line. However, the poet immediately breaks continuity, thrusts against the arrangement, the settlement, with a fresh time-signature … The break [between the stanzas], far from being an injury sustained, is a resistance proclaimed. If language is more than a vehicle for the transmission of axioms and concepts, rhythm is correspondingly more than a physiological motor. It is capable of registering, mimetically, deep shocks of recognition.
>
> (Hill 1984: 87)

Hill goes on to quote the poet Gerard Manley Hopkins (in a letter of 1886) who says that when Wordsworth wrote the ode 'human nature got another of those shocks … his insight was at its very deepest' – adding that the start of stanza 9 was the 'magical change' that conveyed the shock. Hill's comment on what Hopkins says is that Wordsworth saw 'rhythmically'. Faced (to paraphrase Hill) with the 'yoke' and 'freight' of the 'arrangement' and 'settlement' of custom, what Wordsworth has seen or foreseen rhythmically is (in Hill's words) 'the developing life-crisis of the nineteenth century', the shock to be suffered by so many in the years ahead under the settlements of industrial capitalism.

> In the Ode the shock … is redeemed by the silence between stanzas eight and nine and by the immediate, abrupt surge with which the 'joy' of

> nine's opening lines resists, pulls away from, the gravitational field of the closing lines of stanza eight. Wordsworth transfigures a fractured world.
>
> (87–88)

After further analysis Hill says this.

> The 'magical change' in the 'Immortality' Ode is perhaps the greatest moment in nineteenth-century English poetry.
>
> (97)

I vividly recall sitting bolt upright as if electrified by that last sentence when I first read Hill's book.

In the other chapter in Hill's book he engages briefly with Wordsworth's 'The Female Vagrant' (from *Lyrical Ballads*). The woman finishes her sad tale and the poem ends.

> She ceased, and weeping turned away,
> As if because her tale was at an end
> She wept; – because she had no more to say
> Of that perpetual weight which on her spirit lay.

And Hill's comments are, again, extraordinarily alert and enhancing for the reader.

> [Wordsworth] is indeed implying that words are 'in some degree mechanical' compared to the woman's actions and suffering. But in order to bring out the difference Wordsworth puts in a collateral weight of technical concentration that releases the sense of separateness: the drag of the long phrasing across the formalities of the verse, as if the pain would drag itself free from the constraint. In 'as if' and 'because', pedantically isolating her, we glimpse the remoteness of words from suffering and yet are made to recognise that these words are totally committed to her existence. They are her existence. Language here is not 'the outward sign' of a moral action; it is the moral action.
>
> (117)

Works cited

M.H. Abrams, *The Mirror and the Lamp* (Oxford U.P.: 1953)
Derek Attridge, *The Singularity of Literature* (Routledge: 2004)
Harold Bloom, *The Anxiety of Influence* (Oxford U.P.: 1997 ed.)
Cleanth Brooks, 'Irony and "Ironic" Poetry', *College English* Vol. 9, Issue 5: February 1948
Patrick Cruttwell ed., *Samuel Johnson: Selected Writings* (Penguin: 1968)

Paul de Man, 'Time and History in Wordsworth', *Diacritics* Vol. 17, Issue 4: Winter 1987
Terry Eagleton, *Against the Grain* (Verso: 1986)
William Empson, *Some Versions of Pastoral* (Chatto and Windus: 1935)
William Empson, *The Structure of Complex Words* (New Directions: 1951)
Geoffrey Hartman, *Wordsworth's Poetry 1784–1814* (Yale U.P.: 1964)
Geoffrey Hartman, *The Unremarkable Wordsworth* (Minnesota U.P.: 1987)
John O. Hayden ed., *Wordsworth: The Poems* (Yale U.P.: 1981)
Geoffrey Hill, *The Lords of Limit* (Oxford U.P.: 1984)
Frederick W. Hillis and Harold Bloom edd., *From Sensibility to Romanticism* (Oxford U.P.: 1965)
John Jones, *The Egotistical Sublime* (Chatto and Windus: 1954)
Gabriel Josipovici, *The World and the Book* (Macmillan: 1971)
Graham McMaster ed. *William Wordsworth: Penguin Critical Anthology* (Penguin: 1972)
J. Hillis Miller 'On Edge: The Crossways of Contemporary Criticism', *Bulletin of the American Academy of Arts and Sciences* Vol. 32, Issue 4: January 1979
Judith O'Neill ed., *Critics on Blake: Readings in Literary Criticism* (Miami U.P.: 1970)
M. Philips ed., *Interpreting Blake* (Cambridge U.P.: 1979)
Michael Riffaterre, 'The Self-Sufficient Text', *Diacritics* Vol. 3, Issue 3: Autumn 1973
Raymond Williams, *The Country and the City* (Chatto and Windus: 1973)

5 Later romantic writings 1790–1830

Dorothy Wordsworth, Jane Austen, Mary Shelley, John Keats

The focus in the last chapter was on what we call the first-generation romantics, especially Blake and Wordsworth. In this chapter I turn to the second-generation romantics whom conventional textbooks would identify especially as the poets Keats and Shelley. You'll find Keats towards the end of this chapter but the Shelley we'll be looking at here is not the poet Percy but his wife, the novelist Mary whose *Frankenstein* has, largely due to the impact of important feminist critics (who will be sampled here), been only relatively recently seen as the great and crucial romantic text that it is, crucial in particular as an intervention in post-Revolutionary political culture, even more so perhaps than the more explicitly political writings of her parents, Mary Wollstonecraft and William Godwin (both of whom we meet below).

And the other great romantic writer we'll look at in this chapter is also a woman and also controversially, and again only quite recently, seen as a key figure in romanticism (as opposed to the more traditional way of seeing her as a history-free and rather charming precursor of the Victorian novel), Jane Austen. Though born only a few years after Wordsworth (and Beethoven) her best novels were published when she was nearing 40. It's always worth remembering that the best of them all, *Emma* (1816), came out just a couple of years before *Frankenstein* (1818) – both anonymously and, though obviously so different, with surprisingly parallel elements of plot (the danger of playing God) and in both cases exhibiting uneasily conflicted cultural responses to the politics of the period. More on that below.

But I start with a third woman-writer as a way of connecting straight to the last chapter, a writer again, like Mary Shelley, much less celebrated at the time than her male counterpart: this is **Dorothy Wordsworth**, William's sister. Her journals and other personal writings were crucial to, and in a sense subsumed by, her brother's poetry. What modern critics, largely feminist, have insisted on is that Dorothy Wordsworth not only provided her brother with the raw observations of, and in, nature that he turned into poetry (he admitted as much, though not to the public) but that her writing represents a quite different strain in romanticism, one based in selfless and self-effacing transmission of

DOI: 10.4324/9781003127567-6

what she saw and heard rather than her brother's focus on what he felt about what he (or she on his behalf) saw and felt. (Another difference can be seen in her description of the daffodils that fed into his famous poem. She casually notices and notes people working; he edits out from the scene everyone apart from himself.) There's a connection here with Keats who famously distinguished his own poetry from what he called Wordsworth's 'egotistical sublime'.

Here are some examples of Dorothy's writings, certainly not intended for publication and noted down in effect as aide-memoirs for William. (The second item is quoted from his nephew Christopher's 1851 *Memoirs of William Wordsworth.*)

> [A birchtree is] yielding to the gust of wind, with all its tender twigs; the sun shone upon it, and it glanced in the wind like a flying sunshiny shower: it was a tree in shape, with stem and branches, but it was like a spirit of water.
>
> (In Woof ed. 2002: 40)

In Scotland she and William are warmed by a fire raised by a woman, 'scorching us into comfortable feelings', and she describes swallows in a ruin.

> Swallows that flew about restlessly, and flung their shadows upon the sun-bright walls of the old building: the shadows glanced and twinkled, interchanged and crossed each other, expanded and shrunk up, appeared and disappeared, at every instant – as I observed to W[illia]m and C[oleridge], seeming more like living things than the birds themselves.
>
> (*Memoirs* 1851: 1.212, 232)

Her Alfoxden journal (begun at the start of 1798) contains these astonishing words (from two entries) – astonishing because so modestly unassuming.

> After the wet dark days, the country seems more populous. It peoples itself in the sunbeams ... The absence of the singing of birds, the hum of insects, that noiseless noise that lives in the summer air.
>
> (In Woof ed. 2002: 141–42)

(This reminds me of Keats who, in his 'In drear nighted December', wrote of 'The feel of not to feel it' but that was ruinously changed by an early editor to this: 'To know the change and feel it'.)

Margaret Homans, in an important book about language and 19th century female experience, argues that, unlike Dorothy's, William's images of nature are 'killed into meaning ... [His] aim is not the preservation of images in itself ... but the pursuit of infinitude and eternity'. Dorothy's refusal to pursue such infinitude of meaning in what she sees undermines the male ego's coercive drive to transfigure the observed world, through sheer power of mind, into the ultimately meaningful realm of the symbolic, where nature is subdued to the human. Homans says this.

> Instead of the relation of symbolism … she presents nature gratuitously working in tandem with the human mind. Since she guarantees that she never imposes meaning upon nature, we trust that details that appear to be symbolic … are actually just the register of nature's free paralleling of human life … Her parallels have meaning only if nature has as full a value as the human experience.
>
> (Homans 1986: 51–54)

Aidan Day, in his book on romanticism on which I'm drawing, connects Homans with Meena Alexander's work on women in the period and her emphasis on community and nurture that she finds in Dorothy Wordsworth (and also in Mary Shelley).

> Women writers … often turned away from the abstractions and high sublimity of their male counterparts, to the concrete acts of nature and care … The visible world [in Dorothy's writings] gathers powers and luminosity precisely to the extent to which it is shorn of the overt hold of the self … The woman's sense of self [is] intrinsically bound up with the lives of others, rather than developed in exclusion from them. A striking correlative to such a sense of self is that the powerful counter-world of symbolism is then cast aside in favour of the actual.
>
> (Alexander 1989: 68, 88)

Here might be the place, before I turn to the three writers that form the core of this chapter, to share with you some critical observations from two great books about literature, women writers and the contexts of community. These are Nancy Armstrong's landmark 1989 *Desire and Domestic Fiction*, among the most thrilling and dazzling books of any kind I've read, and Marilyn Butler's deservedly influential 1981 book (mentioned in the last chapter) *Romantics, Rebels and Reactionaries*. Butler says this.

> Literature, like all art, like language, is a collective activity, powerfully conditioned by social forces, what needs to be and what may be said in a particular community at a given time … Authors are not the solitaries of the romantic myth, but citizens. Within any community tastes, opinions, values, the shaping stuff of art, are socially generated.
>
> (Butler 1981: 9–10)

Nancy Armstrong, drawing on the analyses of discourse and its relations with power offered in a series of books by Michel Foucault (whom we've already met), was concerned to show that the history and the rise of domestic fiction was inescapably and intimately connected with the history of sexuality and that the role of women, especially in writing, has been much more extensive and more central to cultural activity than usually admitted. Her great book starts – in a polemical first chapter – with three key propositions.

> First, that sexuality is a cultural construct and as such has a history; second, that written representations of the self allowed the modern individual to become an economic and psychological reality; and third, that the modern individual was first and foremost a woman. My argument traces the development of a specific female ideal in eighteenth and nineteenth century conduct books and educational treatises for women, as well as in domestic fiction … One cannot distinguish the production of the new female ideal either from the rise of the novel or from the rise of the new middle classes … Writing about the domestic woman afforded the means of contesting the dominant notion of sexuality that understood desirability in terms of the woman's claims to fortune and family name … Norms inscribed in the domestic woman … cut across the categories of status that maintained an earlier, patriarchal model of social relations. The entire surface of social experience [came] to mirror those kinds of writing – the novel prominent among them – which represented the existing field of social information as contrasting masculine and feminine spheres.
>
> (Armstrong 1989: 8–9)

Armstrong adds this hope for her book, very much in the spirit of Foucault. 'I would like it to demonstrate the degree to which modern culture depends on a form of power that works through language – and particularly the printed word – to constitute subjectivity' (25).

From the early 1970s there were groundbreaking critical efforts to locate **Jane Austen**'s novels in the contexts and debates of their period. While it's easy to see across Wordsworth's long writing life a clear shift from pre-Revolutionary impulses to deep disillusion in progress and a retreat to entrenched conservative ideas, in Jane Austen's much shorter career it's less a matter of change over time and more to do with – at least potentially – conflicted impulses represented in various ways in all the novels. But since the early 1970s until relatively recently the stress has been on Austen the 'anti-Jacobin' (anti-Revolutionary) writer.

Best known among these critics was Marilyn Butler's earlier *Jane Austen and the War of Ideas* (1975), though she had to an extent been anticipated by Alistair Duckworth's *The Improvement of the Estate* (1971), which is a nuanced analysis of Austen's allegiance to conservative values that balances Butler's perhaps more schematic insistence on the anti-Jacobin determinants that she finds throughout the novels. But prior to Duckworth and Butler came an extended essay by Graham Hough, 'Narrative and Dialogue in Jane Austen' (1970). Much more than Hough's modest title suggests, this essay argues for how the novels express (in David Lodge's words) 'the ideology of the English landed gentry … a peculiarly English ideology of social control, compromise and consensus' (Lodge ed. 1991: 23). Hough argues that, especially in the language of her dialogue and the moral judgements evoked (by characters like Mr Knightley or Edmund Bertram), Jane Austen points back from her own revolutionary age to the social and moral landscape of the mid-18th century and Dr Johnson.

> The world of which her novels present a corner was a world in convulsion, filled with wars, revolutions, the struggle for political liberty, black repression, miserable poverty and savage penal laws. To be sure, little of this came her way ... [But] her novels are firmly embedded in social reality. Money, position, marriage and personal relations are considered as facts, not elements in a fantasy ... In her work we never meet those occasions, almost endemic in nineteenth-century fiction, where we feel that the development of a character or a situation has been given a twist in response to novelistic convention ... Actions have their consequences; no one is let off by an illicit authorial tenderness; no one (with the possible exception of the Crawfords in *Mansfield Park*) is pursued by an unconscious authorial vendetta; judgements are minute and they are scrupulous.
>
> (In Lodge ed. 1991: 198–99)

Hough assesses the coherence of Jane Austen's vision and her novels as little or nothing to do with 'deep, unconscious roots of personality', as in Charlotte Bronte or even George Eliot, but a coherence springing from 'the will and the intelligence'. Hough reads the novels as 'powerful reinforcements of a particular class structure and of a moral structure adapted to support it. The reinforcement is powerful because the moral structure is a strong and coherent one' (200).

Raymond Williams's great *The Country and the City* (1973) that we met in the last chapter also has exemplary pages on Austen in her social and political contexts, but he identifies a more complex and provisional process than the more static picture presented by Hough. Despite the obvious importance in the plots of personal relationships, Williams says that what preoccupied Austen most of all was personal conduct, a 'testing and discovery of the standards that govern human behaviour', and that her understanding of conduct was sharpened and shaped by her awareness of change and mobility within her world of the landed gentry.

> It is no single, settled society: it is an active, complicated, sharply speculative process ... an acquisitive, high bourgeois society at the point of its most evident interlocking with an agrarian capitalism that is itself mediated by inherited titles and the making of family names ... The social confusions and contradictions of this complicated process are then the true source of many of the problems of human conduct and valuation, which the personal actions dramatize.
>
> (Williams 1973: 141–43)

Marilyn Butler very pertinently quotes the Victorian critic Richard Simpson who saw that conduct for Austen was a continuous process, a battle staged between (as Blake might have put it) contrary states of the psyche where Williams sees economic and social forces at work.

> She contemplates virtues, not as fixed quantities, or as definable qualities, but as continual struggles and conquests, as progressive states of mind,

> advancing by repulsing their contraries, or losing ground by being over-come … A character therefore unfolded itself to her as … a composite force, which could only exhibit what it was by exhibiting what it did.
>
> (Quoted in Justice ed. 2012: 392)

The most complete analysis of Jane Austen's chosen milieu, the English landed gentry, was offered the year after Butler's book by the sociologist and critic Terry Lovell in her conference paper, 'Jane Austen and Gentry Society' (1976). This is a landmark contribution to Austen studies. I'll excerpt two typically cogent and considered judgements in relation to the two best Austen novels to which this chapter now turns. These are *Mansfield Park* (1814), widely regarded as the most far-reaching but also most problematic of the novels, and *Emma* (that followed it two years later), the most dazzlingly brilliant in its formal and rhetorical techniques.

The problems that have been identified in *Mansfield Park* (which are, for some critics, more apparent than real) would include Fanny Price, a very unusually passive, reticent and (for some) prudish choice of heroine; the equally unusual antagonism shown by the novel (and its moral standard-bearers, Fanny and Edmund) towards the play *Lovers' Vows*, which is chosen for amateur theatricals at the centre of the novel's first phase; the startlingly different scenes set in Portsmouth; and the ways by which the novel chooses to deal with the undeniably attractive brother and sister Henry and Mary Crawford whose arrival from London generates the novel's main plot lines.

One added point about the unusual 'seriousness' of this novel is that it's made clear, if momentarily, that the wealth behind the grand house where nearly all the action takes place comes from one particular feature of the Antigua plantations owned by Sir Thomas. This occasioned a justly celebrated intervention into the normally becalmed waters of Austen criticism by the great Edward Said in his 1993 *Culture and Imperialism*, who pointed to the moment following Fanny's attempt to overcome her shyness with Sir Thomas by asking him about the slave-trade when, says Fanny later, 'there was such a dead silence' (Vol. 2, Ch. 3).

The conversation is, as it were, aborted. The silence is the default language of imperialism, which cannot be voiced otherwise or by other more privileged and less marginalized members of the family to whom the benefits of the slave-trade have accrued. That Jane Austen points to the slave-trade so unobtrusively and in effect so parenthetically merely draws our attention to how it must have been, if only in parenthetic consciousness, a conscious evil to her – as it was to Dr Johnson. Said's discussion really needs reading in full; his opening comment is that 'Antigua and Sir Thomas's trip there … is both incidental, referred to only in passing, and absolutely crucial to the action' (Said 1993: 106).

Terry Lovell says that Austen 'may be pessimistic about the ability of many people to achieve the highest possible good' but 'the characters that interest her, and us, are those that do have high potential … and whose failures are therefore worth condemning, or whose moral struggle is worth recording. The Crawfords present one of the most interesting cases.'

Lovell accepts neither the view of those (like Marilyn Butler) who condemn the Crawfords for their straightforward corrupting influence, nor of those critics who (like Graham Hough as noted above) see them as unfairly maligned by the author and Fanny (and the coercions of the plot).

> What is less frequently noted is the counterpoint between the Crawfords and Mansfield. If the Crawfords represent a threat to the moral order of Mansfield, it is because that order is weak and exposed; and Mansfield represents for the Crawfords the possibility of realising their own better natures.
>
> (In Barker et al. edd. 1977: 126)

Noting their awareness of Fanny's suffering and Mary's kind defending of her against Mrs Norris (Fanny's suffering under Mrs Norris is more than enough for many readers to acquit the novel of making her too tepid a heroine), as well as their recognition of Edmund's superiority to his siblings, Lovell suggests that the struggle that Austen dramatizes is between those attachments and the ones inherited from the Crawfords' own histories.

> Perhaps Jane Austen drew back from the slow process of re-generation which the Crawfords had begun under the guidance of Fanny and Edmund because of the imbalance between the two pairs … The moral threat which they represent for Mansfield is in the end greater than the moral power of Mansfield over the Crawfords. Jane Austen is wise to dismiss them rather than try and reform them.
>
> (126)

On *Emma*, Lovell makes broader and more general comments about Austen's ideological investment in the landed gentry and how she has been criticized for not writing novels more wholly committed to lives lived by figures like Miss Bates, lives which, says Lovell, must have been 'only too depressingly familiar to her' (129).

I'd add here that Graham Hough cites no less than three times the remarkable sentence about Miss Bates having 'no intellectual superiority to … frighten those who might hate her into outward respect' (Vol. 1, Ch. 3), calling it the comment of someone who has seen something that cannot be acquired from 'the society of right-minded and well-informed people', then as not irony but 'the flat statement of a devastating scepticism about the real motives of much ordinary social intercourse' and then (perhaps too sweepingly) as 'the one remark … [that] stands alone in *Emma*, unsupported by the rest of the book', a remark 'that expresses a shattering scepticism about this whole order of things' (in Lodge ed. 1991: 179, 180, 197). Perhaps 'stands alone' underplays what D.W. Harding, in a famously corrective essay from the 1940s, called the regulated hatred arguably shown by Austen towards her social world. Later critics say that Harding overplayed his hand (in understandable exasperation with the sentimental 'Jane-ites' who before him had for too long bathed the novels in mere adulation). Lovell says this.

> Emma's rudeness to Miss Bates is the turning point of the novel [and] she is roundly criticised for it by Knightley … But the rudeness of Emma and others is not the cause of Miss Bates' plight, and while 'kindness' may mitigate that plight, it is rooted in the structure of gentry society itself which offers such women no independent role … [Austen] instinctively avoids such dangerous territory, aware perhaps that the injunction to be kind to the Miss Bates of her world hardly measured up to their need and the indignity of their situation.
>
> (In Barker et al. edd. 1977: 129)

Lovell calls it wise of Austen to dismiss the Crawfords and instinctive of her to avoid a more probing and politically charged analysis of Miss Bates' plight; 'tactful' might be another word in both instances. As readers we must decide for ourselves. I'll return to Emma's cruelty to Miss Bates at the end of this section.

A challenging modern critical discussion of the 'problem' of the *Lovers' Vows* episode in *Mansfield Park* is offered by David Musselwhite in his little-known and admittedly uneven 1987 book *Partings Welded Together.* His approach to *Mansfield Park* (1815) is grounded in the immediate context of what can be seen as the edgiest of decades for England, from 1811 to 1819, with political disturbances and economic severities following the end of the Napoleonic wars in 1816, culminating in the Peterloo Massacre of 1819. These were years, says Musselwhite, when 'the possibility of a violent revolution In England was greater than at almost any other time and was contained, with ever increasing difficulty, by the resort to force alone'.

But instead of revolution 'what emerged was modern class society' (Musselwhite 1987: 31). This was achieved not just through the 'redirection of energies in the direction of parliamentary reform' but through the crucial cultural work played by 'the appropriation and containment of the popular appeal of egalitarian Jacobinism' (30). *Lovers' Vows*, Mrs Inchbald's translation of a German romantic play which was wildly popular on the London stage and elsewhere (including Bath where Jane Austen might well have seen it), was pre-eminently a text endorsing pro-revolutionary ideas about (in Marilyn Butler's words) 'the goodness of man, the legitimacy of his claims to equality, and the sanctity of his instincts as a guide to conduct' as well as championing 'intuition over conventions, indeed of sexual liberty over every type of restraint' (Butler 1975: 233–34).

Conventional accounts of the role of the play in the novel point to how Edmund, Mary, Henry and Maria 'are not adopting a pose, but … expressing their real feelings'. The stage roles 'imply not insincerity but liberation' (232), a liberation into the sexually compromising and authority-undermining corruption of Mansfield values, and defacement of the property itself, in the absence of its owner – which is why the play must be repudiated by the novel. But what Musselwhite – arguing that the characters of the novel actually derive from those in *Lovers' Vows*, rather than the usual assumption that they just happen to fit well together in the casting of the roles – insists on is that the novel, marking in Austen's career a new hard-headed determination to appeal to a new middle-class readership, appropriates the popular appeal of the play to such readers sympathetic to Jacobin ideas, in order to contain and neutralize such radical ideas. Here is Musselwhite on why the novel, having appropriated the play, condemns it.

> It is condemned not ... simply because it has a revolutionary message, but because it was so desperately needed. ... The new urban and industrial 'middling' classes were able to forge for themselves an identity and a consciousness only by modelling themselves upon and appropriating to themselves ... the popular democratic ... Jacobinism of the 'people'. The animus with which *Lovers' Vows* is condemned is due to that ... ideological consciousness that must at one and the same time acknowledge but disavow its debt to the revolutionary tradition.
>
> (Musselwhite 1987: 30)

Musselwhite develops his argument, perhaps rather tendentiously, in relation to the highly unusual Portsmouth chapters; enough to say here that the heterogeneity of the modes and styles of those chapters are an equivalent if complicated response to this assumed new and wider readership.

Before we leave *Mansfield Park*, I'll turn briefly to the great Vladimir Nabokov who lectured on the novel in his mid-century American years. I think he may have been the first to call the Portsmouth chapters 'positively Dickensian' in relation to the Price family household. In ways that anticipate D.A. Miller on Austen's style (more below), he locates that style 'at its best' in the description of Mrs Norris, before the ball scene (Vol. 2, Ch. 10), 'entirely taken up in fresh arranging and injuring the noble fire which the butler had prepared' (injuring!) and, as a passionate chess-player, he identifies what he calls the 'knight's move' to describe 'a sudden swerve from one or the other side on the board of Fanny's chequered emotions', as here, with the reactions to Sir Thomas leaving for Antigua (Vol. 1, Ch. 3).

> Fanny's relief, and her consciousness of it, were quite equal to her cousins', but a more tender nature suggested that her feelings were ungrateful, and [*knight's move*:] she really grieved because she could not grieve.
>
> (Nabokov 1980: 41, 56–57)

If *Emma* reflects the anxious post-revolutionary years in which, like *Mansfield Park,* it was written, it may be less a matter of the appropriation and containment of radical ideas in a specific text than in a more diffuse or structured way. There is clear tension between Emma's attempts to assert an equality of selfhood independent of others, her inclinations to trust to her intuitions and instincts rather than convention, her imaginative role as proxy-novelist – all of which are at least potentially to be valued – and the novel's counter-insistence on the futility and indeed the danger of these attempts.

There is radical feminist potential in Emma's wish to assert and exercise control, to be the subject of her own sentence, to be beyond and without men as sexual dominators – and a bitter irony in her having to discover that she has been, all along, the pawn in Frank Churchill's longer game, the object of his sentence. Politically, this is sharp as the novel obliquely associates Frank with Jacobin sympathies in his subversions of social protocols, like the Crawfords. (Emma, with unusual political vigour, accuses him of 'espionage' (Vol. 3, Ch. 10), a word used nowhere else in her novels and only recently imported into English from the French.) And the awarding of Jane Fairfax to Frank in marriage is itself a radical reversal of the anti-Jacobin treatment of equivalent characters such as Wickham, Willoughby and indeed Henry Crawford. Austen herself noted that one of the opinions about the book in her circle was that 'Frank Churchill [was] better treated than he deserved'. Another, very pertinent to our thoughts about her novels in the anxious post-revolutionary years was that it was wrong of her 'in such times as these, to draw such clergymen as Mr Collins and Mr Elton' (in Lodge ed. 1991: 34–35).

The diffusion of radical ideas may itself be a function of the most brilliantly sustained narrative feature of the novel, its recourse to – and in effect invention of – what later came to be called free indirect style. This is where the narrative is officially in standard third-person but adopts the thoughts, feelings and crucially the language of any character, with the result that the reader is always in danger of mistaking a character's thoughts and ideas for the author's.

What Jane Austen does with free indirect style in *Emma* is to restrict it – and to restrict the point of view generally in the novel – to Emma herself, who famously gets things so wrong. As Wayne Booth showed in the very influential pages of his landmark 1961 book *The Rhetoric of Fiction*, Austen has to negotiate the balancing act that Booth calls control of distance, between mystification (letting the reader make the same mistakes as Emma) and irony (allowing the reader the critical distance from Emma to read correctly).

D.A. Miller, perhaps Austen's most subtle modern reader, helps us understand the rhetorical as well as the political pressures operating to urge the potentially wayward (even pseudo-lesbian) Emma into the hetero-normative ending in marriage to Mr Knightley. Not only must she be corrected for being such a bad proxy-novelist but the reader is made to see that her bad novelistic match-making, what Miller calls her 'endless flirtation with a potentially infinite parade of possibilities' (Miller 1981: 15), is in effect positioned to empty the master-narrative (Emma as chosen by and for Mr Knightley in Austen's own 'good' match-making) of its ideological purposes, to naturalize and legitimize it.

In a broader sense the Emma–Knightley pairing is positioned as somehow more 'natural' than the Frank–Jane pairing, the latter marked as it is by secrecy and the suggestion of illicit desire that make it seem more akin to later 19th century romantic passions. If the Emma–Knightley pairing seems 'natural' it's both despite and because of the rhetorical force of their both becoming aware of their love through suddenly activated jealousy of their potential rivals, because of their love having (as it were) been dormant since Emma's childhood and, indeed, because of the (highly unusual) 16-year age gap between them – the latter then serving to endorse the paternalistic values underpinned by the entire novel. Mr Knightley is everyone's father because he has to be. There is a persistence in Austen's novels, more marked than perhaps any other motif, of the dangers of bad, inadequate, unthinking and even cruel parenting. Butler sharply notes that from the beginning Austen evidently sensed the threat to the traditional paternalism from within: 'the landed classes were much more likely to undo the old system for themselves than to have it overthrown by enemies' (Butler 1981: 100).

But for all that, the very last picture we have of the 'natural' state of the coming together of Emma and Mr Knightley in the confirmation of the latter's paternalistic role is comically undermined by the (on the face of it absurd) arrangement of Mr Knightley agreeing to move into Hartfield (until the death of Mr Woodhouse) rather than traditionally carrying off his bride into the patriarchal grandeur of Donwell. He in effect becomes a neutered child under female sway (Emma's and also that of her father who is like a tyrannical baby). It's a paradoxical and radical, even Jacobin and feminist confirmation of the power Emma has never wanted to concede, especially to men. Claudia L. Johnson put it like this in 1988.

> The conclusion which seemed tamely and placidly conservative thus takes an unexpected turn, as the guarantor of order himself cedes a considerable portion of the power which custom has allowed him to expect. In moving to Hartfield, Knightley is sharing *her* home, and … placing himself within her domain.
>
> (In Justice ed. 2012: 427)

In Miller's first book, *The Novel and Its Discontents* (1981), he presents a compelling case for another, more general and permanent tension, that in narrative fiction between closure and narratability: closure (as in the marriage of Emma and Knightley) can only work by abolishing (in a process of discontent) the possibilities of what could have narrated otherwise. Closure for Miller needs 'a suppression, a simplification, a sort of blindness', and is an act of make-believe that 'closure is possible', despite that belief being of 'self-betraying inadequacy'. For Miller 'what discontents the traditional novel is its own condition of possibility' (Miller 1981: 89, 265, 267).

If I can put it simply, narrative closure is guiltily aware of the coercions of having to exclude, or even expel, in order to reach closure. The guilt can be expressed, in novelists as sensitive to rhetorical processes as Jane Austen, in the note of anger or even rage struck as in the brutal future mapped out for Maria Bertram and Mrs Norris, expelled at the end of *Mansfield Park* to a distant part of the country, where 'shut up together with little society, on one side no affection, on the other no judgment, it may be reasonably supposed that their tempers became their mutual punishment' (Vol. 3, Ch. 17). This is not so much the regulated hatred that Harding claimed Austen felt against her society as, more rhetorically far-reaching, rage against the coercive compulsions of narrative itself. Rhetorically, if not in simple political terms, Jane Austen's novels are deeply radical.

Miller also has an especially fine discussion of free indirect style in his (more discursive) later book *Jane Austen, or the Secret of Style* (2003). He draws attention to the unprecedented transition between two chapters (the end of Vol. 2, Ch. 2 and the beginning of Vol. 2, Ch. 3). Emma, determined to think better of Jane Fairfax, is trying to extract some information from her about Frank. This proves exasperatingly unsuccessful and Chapter 2 ends with the words 'Emma could not forgive her'. Then there's the chapter break. Then Chapter 3 begins with the words 'Emma could not forgive her'. Miller says this.

> During the chapter break, what had been the indirect and impersonal *performance* of Emma's consciousness has become the mere matter-of-fact *notation* of that thought ... What generates the first 'Emma could not forgive her' is Emma's own affective consciousness, intimately accessed and ironically inflected by its free indirect narrative performance. What generates the second 'Emma could not forgive her' is pure narration, a detached consciousness to which Emma's own has ceased to contribute, having been reduced to a little bit of information useful to the plot ... It is as though the narration is trying, and failing, to pull away from the attraction of free indirect style ... But in the course of shaking off its secret, severed identification with Emma, it has produced a cloud of dust that only resettles on it, as the tell-tale residue of that same identification. It seems as hard for Jane Austen to relinquish her identificatory [emotional investment in] Emma, or to cool it down into an even more detached form, as it is for Emma to relinquish her grudge against Jane Fairfax.
>
> (Miller 2003: 64–66)

In 1984 Adena Rosmarin, in a provocative article on 'Misreading *Emma*', complained about what she called 'the consensual blandness' of 20th century Austen criticism, as well as its tendency to what she calls 'the subtlety and persistence of ... denigration' in its 'notion of diminutive greatness', as found in such critics as Butler and Hough (in Lodge 1991: 237; she seems unaware of Miller's 1981 *Discontents* book). Her focus, like Wayne Booth's but in a much more elaborated way, is on the reader's necessary involvement in, and often unknowingly involved collusion with, the instabilities and subversions of Austen's irony which – in what she calls a 'dance of bewildering complexity' (222) – lead us through processes of interpretive revision and reassessment. Free indirect style is one obvious source of this irony but Rosmarin makes a more complex case.

I'll end this section on Jane Austen by sampling her account of how we are involved and implicated in the great Box Hill scene, where Emma is so famously cruel to Miss Bates, and its painful aftermath. Rosmarin says of Miss Bates's frequent monologues that they are 'strategically devious' for the reader.

> However amusing, they irritate Emma, and partly because we tend to feel as she feels, partly because they are as they are, they also irritate us – so much so, in fact, that we are manouvered into subscribing to Emma's insult on Box Hill … [After Mr Knightley's reproaches], because our need to recollect and be tutored has become as great as Emma's, her guilt becomes ours, and in the page upon page of elaborately detailed remorse that follows we are denied the luxury of distance … The insult is so well prepared by our growing irritation, so irresistibly invited by Miss Bates' own remark, and so well camouflaged by its brevity and the surrounding pages of verbal play that we are distracted from both Miss Bates' pain and the implications of our distraction.
>
> (229–30)

The insult is prefaced with what must be Jane Austen's most brilliant short paragraph: 'Emma could not resist' (Vol. 3, Ch. 7). And, of course, nor can the reader.

We saw above that a Victorian critic noted that for Jane Austen virtue was a matter of struggle and conquest, of advancing or losing ground. At one particularly fraught point in *Emma*, after the Elton/Harriet/Emma debacle, it's said that 'their being fixed, so absolutely fixed … was bad for each, for all three. Not one of them had the power of removal or of effecting any material change in society' (Vol. 1, Ch. 17). In both cases this is, potentially, the language of social change and the need for it. There's also in *Emma* a probable ironic glance at two of the most radical of the pro-Revolutionary pamphlets of the period, *The Rights of Man* (1791) and *A Vindication of the Rights of Woman* (1792), when it's observed that 'a private dance, without sitting down to supper, was pronounced an infamous fraud upon the rights of men and women' (Vol. 2, Ch. 11). Those were the pamphlets by Thomas Paine and Mary Wollstonecraft, **Mary Shelley**'s mother.

Frankenstein, as also mentioned above, shares with *Emma* an implicitly conservative warning about the dangers of playing God, in Emma's case by in effect creating Harriet who then, like Shelley's Creature, turns against its maker when Harriet aspires, with 'elevation', to marry Mr Knightley – and words like aspire and elevation are muted echoes of Milton's Eve in *Paradise Lost* which, of course, is explicitly evoked in *Frankenstein* from the title page onwards.

But if *Emma* and *Mansfield Park* show a refracted or muted engagement in post-revolutionary politics, with perhaps conflicted ideas and instincts as suggested above, *Frankenstein* is a major intervention in the debates of the time, especially in the wake of the pamphlet wars that pitted radicals like Paine and both of Mary Shelley's parents against (especially) Edmund Burke (whose writings about improvement, according to Alistair Duckworth whom we met briefly above, influenced Jane Austen). This way of looking at *Frankenstein*, as a text richly involved in contrary ways of reading the Revolution, was powerfully argued in Chris Baldick's excellent book *In Frankenstein's Shadow* (1987).

Baldick shows how what he calls 'the politics of monstrosity' – monsters turning on their makers – was involved on both sides of the debate. Burke, in his hugely influential *Reflections on the Revolution in France* (1790), which led to Paine and Wollstonecraft's replies, writes about 'the spirit of innovation, which soon was turned against those who fostered it, and ended in their ruin' and (quoting a French report) describing military democracy as 'a species of political monster, which has always ended by devouring those who have produced it'. In a later pamphlet he calls France a 'monster of a state', 'the mother of monsters' and a 'cannibal republic' (in Baldick 1987: 18). He attacks the Revolutionaries in France as not only cannibals but (in Baldick's words) as 'sorcerers, alchemists, and fanatical scientists' (the wording there is clearly very relevant to the plot of Mary's novel).

Burke's opponents answer the charge of monstrosity head-on, as Paine does here, as he targets the aristocratic rule of primogeniture (only the first-born male child inherits) that so distorts child–parent relations.

> In a family of six children, five are ... begotten to be devoured. They are thrown to the cannibal for prey, and the natural parent prepares the unnatural repast ... To restore, therefore, parents to their children, and children to their parents – relations to each other, and man to society – and to exterminate the monster Aristocracy, root and branch – the French constitution has destroyed the law of primogenitureship. Here then lies the monster; and Mr Burke, if he pleases, may write its epitaph.
>
> (20)

As Baldick puts it 'Burke announces the birth of the monster child Democracy, while Paine records the death of the monster parent Aristocracy'. Paine calls Monarchy the 'sort of breathing automaton' (!) that is now laid to rest as humanity is remade: 'the present generation will appear to the future as the Adam of a new world' (21).

In a few acute words that cut to the heart of her daughter's novel Mary Wollstonecraft, in another reply to Burke in 1794, says that 'people are rendered ferocious through misery' (23) and her father William Godwin, in his 1793 *Enquiry Concerning Political Justice*, which influenced the early Wordsworth among many others, says that the old system of aristocratic feudalism 'was a ferocious monster, devouring, wherever it came, all that humanity regards with attachment and love' (24). It's precisely attachment and love that Shelley's Creature is systematically and cruelly deprived of, above all by his parent, and so desperately seeks.

The relevance of all this to *Frankenstein* in the light of the well-known biographical details of Mary's life, especially the intricate connections between birth and death in the early deaths of her children, with her guilt over her own birth in effect causing her mother's death, and yet more guilt over her elopement with Percy causing her father to disown and reject her, will need no emphasis. It's easy to see how the conflicting terms of the debate as just outlined feed into the conflicted nature of the novel, though readers will decide, as you need to decide, how to assess the balance between the two sides as it plays out in your own reading. Baldick puts it like this.

> The monster is derived from the lurid imagery of Burke's counter-revolutionary polemics, but manages at the same time to voice the opposing views of Mary Wollstonecraft and others, indicting the prevailing system from the standpoint of the oppressed and outcast ... Read from the Burkean position ... the novel seems to warn against the recklessness of [trying] to construct a new body politic. But read from the position of Paine, Wollstonecraft, or Godwin, it seems to suggest that the violence of the oppressed springs from frustration with the neglect and injustice of their social 'parent'.
>
> (54–55)

For Baldick, Shelley responds to the Creature with an uneasy mix of 'fearful revulsion and cautious sympathy' – an 'anxious liberalism' (55) – but for me her sympathy outweighs her fear and revulsion, especially so whenever the Creature's eloquence (always much more marked and more genuinely 'human' than his maker's) is allowed to express itself, as in his wishes to be part of a wider communality, 'linked to the chain of existence ... from which I am excluded ... in forced solitude' (Ch. 17), having been rejected by his parent as well as by his chosen foster family and refused in his desire for a partner. (In a sign of Shelley's conflicted feelings as they developed over time, her later 1831 revision significantly retreats from some of the more radical emphases of the 1818 original.)

To make a link to the next part of this chapter where the focus is on feminist readings of *Frankenstein*, I'll say a little about Frankenstein rather than the Creature. For me, and in a quite unprecedented way for its time, the novel – as if casually and accidentally – presents an acute portrait of a man who is terrified of women, especially of sex with women, and who overcompensates for this in sex-substituting acts of creation and destructive rejection. In turn the novel, through Walton, overcompensates by re-creating the inadequate Frankenstein as a gloriously god-like figure in a network of male–male bondings. The analysis, which surfaces at astonishing moments like his pre-Freudian dream after the Creature is made – embracing Elizabeth he finds her transformed into his mother's mouldering corpse – is of an obsessive loner, incapable of heterosexual love, his anxieties displaced onto the Creature's utter loneliness and solitude, so movingly capable of the love denied to him by his maker.

Feminist readings of the novel have, very broadly, approached it in three ways. The first focuses on Shelley as the marginalized and silenced teenage woman out-performing and out-lasting the much more famous and older men (including the rock-star Byron) in the original ghost-story writing 'competition' – though Percy then exerted male power over her by rewriting much of the novel to make it more ornately literary (as what survives of her manuscript reveals). The second stresses the importance of Frankenstein usurping the female role in giving birth (a related point to playing God, as mentioned above). The third sees the Creature as 19th century woman herself, denied a full role in culture and society, in effect a half-formed or incomplete creature. Let's turn to some influential feminist readings that have moved the debate on further.

Ellen Moers in 1976 notes the crucial importance of Frankenstein rejecting in horror and fleeing from the new-born Creature after (as you'll recall) it stands by his bed expecting love. Moers says this is where the novel is at its 'most feminine'.

> In the motif of revulsion against newborn life, and the drama of guilt, dread and flight … *Frankenstein* seems to be distinctly a woman's myth-making on the subject of birth precisely because its emphasis is not upon what precedes birth, not upon birth itself, but upon what follows birth: the trauma of the after-birth.
>
> (In Hunter ed. 1996: 218)

Moers connects that moment, as well as Frankenstein's early wish to 'bestow animation upon lifeless matter', with the 17-year-old Mary's journal record following her baby daughter's death.

> Dream that my little baby came to life again, that it had only been cold, and that we rubbed it before the fire, and it lived. Awake and find no baby. I think about the little thing all day.
>
> (222)

Connecting Frankenstein's usurping of the female role, by giving birth, with Mary writing the novel, Barbara Johnson in 1982 says this.

> In order to prove herself worthy of her parentage, Mary, paradoxically enough, must thus usurp the parental role and succeed in giving birth to *herself* on paper. Her declaration of existence as a writer must therefore figuratively repeat the matricide that her physical birth all too literally entailed … What her book suggests is that what is at stake behind … female fear of success is nothing less than the fear of somehow effecting the death of one's own parents.
>
> (249)

Mary Poovey, in 1984, turned the focus on to what the novel suggests about desire and imagination, in contrast to standard Romantic doctrine and more in line with 18th century moralists (like Dr Johnson) – as well as (I'd add) with both Dorothy Wordsworth and Jane Austen.

> Mary Shelley characterises innate desire not as neutral or benevolent but as quintessentially egotistical … She sees imagination as an appetite that can and must be regulated – specifically, by the give-and-take of domestic relationships. If it is aroused but is not controlled by human society, it will project itself into the natural world, becoming voracious in its search for objects to conquer and consume … to turn back on itself, to mark all external objects as its own.
>
> (253–54)

This may simply be described as Frankenstein's rejection of the feminine in his psyche, to console and support the male egotistical drive to control. This is made even more clear when, in an act of violently destructive rape and 'passion', he tears to pieces the female body of the half-made Creature which he'd promised to make. Anne Mellor puts this very well in 1988, in terms like those I've used above.

> What Victor Frankenstein truly fears is female sexuality as such. A woman who is sexually liberated, free to choose her own life, her own sexual partner (by force, if necessary). And to propagate at will, can only appear monstrously ugly to [him], for she defies that sexist aesthetic that insists that women be small, delicate, modest, passive, and sexually pleasing – but available only to their lawful husbands.
>
> (279)

If I can put it like this: punishing the Creature for desiring the equality and mutuality of empowered love from the female that he denies in himself, Frankenstein compounds the cruelty of the offence by ensuring that at least this woman will remain a half-formed thing.

That Mary Shelley so unerringly understood, and then dramatized, early 19th century power relations between the genders seems to me perhaps the most far-reaching achievement of later romanticism. (For the 1931 film of the novel, see Chapter 1 of this book.)

Frankenstein was published in 1818, the year towards the end of which **John Keats** embarked, though he couldn't have known it, on the astonishing twelve months in which he wrote all his greatest poems, famously the great odes, of which the 'Nightingale' ode and 'To Autumn' are the very best and at the same time the most startlingly different from each other. I have explored the implications of these differences elsewhere (Jacobs 2020: 130–39), arguing that 'Nightingale', with its debt to *Hamlet*, is a mini proto-realist novel while 'Autumn' has the tone-free voicelessness and the sealed space of poem as mere form of proto-modernism. Anyway, so much has been written about the seemingly miraculous way these poems seem to bear out the myth of the solitary genius somehow outside his own social and cultural moment, especially given the agonizing way his very short life came to an end, that it's not easy to look at Keats as politically involved in the tensions and debates of his time. It's easier to focus on the personal, as has proved so tempting – not least for filmmakers – over Keats's doomed love for Fanny Brawne, with the bitter accusations and cruel jealousies revealed in his letters to her as well as in the astonishing poem, probably his last, 'This living hand', to which I'll return at the close of this chapter.

But before we turn to the political in Keats, we'll sample his most brilliant close-reading critics, both from the 1960s, John Bayley in 1962 (in what was originally a British Academy lecture) and John Jones from his superb 1969 book *John Keats's Dream of Truth* (in the last chapter we looked at Jones on Wordsworth). For Bayley, Keats's genius was 'unmisgiving', always prepared to risk vulgarity, and at its best in the richer earlier poems rather than ambitious projects like *Hyperion*.

> The earth reveals the rift of ore; it turns what might appear mean and embarrassing into what is rich and *disconcerting*: for at his most characteristic Keats always disconcerts … Keats is most fully his poetic self, most wholly involved in what he is writing, when he is … on the edge of 'badness' … *Hyperion* is, so to speak, not bad enough, too full of hard-worn decorum.
>
> (Bayley 1962: 98–105)

John Jones writes with subtle discrimination on types of blushing in Keats. He quotes from the early long poem *Endymion* on a cheek 'so fair and smooth; / O let it blush so ever! let it soothe / My madness! let it mantle rosy-warm / With the tinge of love' and connects this with the generosity of Keats's respect for an 'object's freedom' just when it proves 'ripe for tasting'. This is criticism as heightened imaginative work at its most exciting.

> In urging 'let it mantle rosy-warm' Keats apprehends something alive on its own, self-charged, a separate and secret centre … This life-fostering fancy of his spills over into the many attempts to guess admiringly not just at phases of other lives but at their latent principles … Blushing joins with glowing and flushing, with smothering and stifling and obscure inner pressures, with floating and heaviness and aching and languor – a central knot of conditions which hover on the verge of namelessness, all hard worked by him and all striving to mature an account of how one feels into a revelation of what one is.
>
> (Jones 1969: 144)

A breakthrough study of the neglected issue of Keats's political involvement is Nicholas Roe's 1997 book *John Keats and the Culture of Dissent*. This is explicitly set against the reactionary reading of Keats and of romantic poetry in general influentially set out by Jerome McGann in his 1983 book *The Romantic Ideology* which talked of 'displacement efforts', 'escape trails' and the evasive pursuit of 'states of harmony and reconciliation' (McGann 1983: 133–34). Answering McGann in 1989, Daniel Watkins argues that Keats's poetry was always 'haunted by politics'.

> His complex and turbulent poetic articulation and reworking of traditional poetic topics, of myth and legends, and of contemporary and past history and politics are signs of intense anxiety … the historical anxiety of an age threatened by economic collapse, by the militarization of culture, bad harvests, staggeringly high unemployment, and by a fear both of bourgeois, industrial triumph and of a return to feudalism.
>
> (Watkins 1989: 22–23)

Nicholas Roe starts from this sense of Keats as the poet of 'a nation and culture in crisis … registering the distress caused by contemporary social, political, and economic upheavals'.

> This is a dangerous Keats: a poet who embodied and gave voice to the anxieties and insecurities of his times; a poet thus capable of challenging and unsettling the preoccupations of his readers; a poet whom the establishment would be obliged to silence.
>
> (Roe 1997: 7)

Roe crucially traces the 'enduring and malign influence on later approaches to his life and work' to the 'vigorous campaign to suppress John Keats, carried out in Tory journals of the day' (a premonition, I'm tempted to add, of today's 'culture wars' played out against those labelled 'woke' in the rabidly Tory press in England, to distract attention from the government's disastrous actions or inactions). The target in the attacks in *Blackwood's Edinburgh Magazine* in 1817 and 1818 were on what was identified mockingly as the 'Cockney School' and, beyond the specified target of Keats's first two volumes of poetry which were roundly ridiculed, the real danger to these Tory critics were radical thinkers like Leigh Hunt and William Hazlitt with whom Keats was associated.

What's interesting in terms of our discussion above about Mary Shelley, and her analysis of Frankenstein's denial and fear of the feminine, is that the young Keats was attacked not just for being ill-educated (the school he attended had a high tolerance of religious dissent) or lower-class – he was called 'an uneducated and flimsy stripling … a boy of pretty abilities' – but in terms of being insufficiently male, with a 'feminine' intellect, capable only of the kind of writing scribbled by 'farm servants … unmarried ladies [and] superannuated governess[es]' (10–16). 'Mankin' was a regular name used for Keats (he was just five feet tall; the word also suggests sexual inadequacy) and Byron, with lordly disdain, accused him of 'frigging his imagination'. In terms of the ill-educated charge, Roe very pertinently quotes Shelley's mother Mary Wollstonecraft (in her *Rights of Woman*) on women's 'disorderly' education.

> The cultivation of the understanding is always subordinate to the acquirement of some corporeal accomplishment; even when enervated by

> confinement and false notions of modesty ... education thus gives this appearance of weakness to females.
>
> (11)

This is why the attacks focused at once on Keats being uneducated and effeminate, his poetry exhibiting the symptoms of 'malady' and 'violent fit[s]', weakly feminine ailments. In a more explicitly political attack Keats, Hunt and Hazlitt were said to be supporters of the 'unsettled' party, the word that Roe says was 'closely associated with the Jacobin revolution' (19–20).

Keats himself, in a long letter to his brother and sister in September 1819 (after the great odes had been written and after the Peterloo massacre), gives a brief sketch of how 'civilised countries become gradually more enlightened'.

> The French revolution ... put a stop to the rapid progress of free sentiments in England; and gave our Court hopes of turning back to the despotism of the 16th century. They have made a handle of this event in every way to undermine our freedom. They spread a horrid superstition against all innovation and improvement. The present struggle in England is to destroy this superstition. What has roused them to do it is their distresses ... This is no contest between Whig and Tory – but between right and wrong.
>
> (In Cox ed. 2009: 365–66)

What a recent editor of Keats's letters, Grant Scott, said in 2002 needs emphasis against the old myth of Keats as solitary genius detached from society as well as history. Keats always saw the connection between writing poetry and the world of suffering and misfortune. He said in a letter that he was 'ambitious of doing the world some good' and, adds Scott, 'he meant through his poetry'. What the letters make so clear is Keats's commitment to sociability and camaraderie. Scott says this.

> Although literary critics have recently stressed the political aspect of Keats's life and thought, it is important to remember that Keats himself felt that 'the first political duty that a man ought to have a mind to is the happiness of his friends' ... Such camaraderie advocates the 'gregarious advance of intellect' ... And he signs off his final letter to Charles Brown by admitting that he 'always made an awkward bow', as if even in the end he was trying to close the gap between letter and life, write a gesture that would place him for one last moment in the physical presence of his friend.
>
> (557–59)

What Jack Stillinger said in 1971 about the great poems of the final year – from 'The Eve of St Agnes' to 'To Autumn' – closely correlates to what has been emphasized above. The danger is always to lose touch with the world's realities, to deny or forget that pleasure and pain are inseparable, to dream too trustingly in the visionary imagination. Stillinger says this about the 'Grecian Urn' and 'Nightingale' odes.

> In each poem the speaker begins as dreamer, hoodwinked with the idea that he can unperplex bliss from its neighbour pain, that he can find an anodyne to the ills of the flesh by joining the timeless life pictured on an urn, or by fading away into the forest with a bird. In each case the result is an awareness that spells are but made to break: the speaker recognises the falseness of the dream, the shortcomings of the ideal he has created, and he returns to the mortal world ... If the major concern of these poems is the conflict between actuality and the ideal, the result is not rejection of the actual, but rather a facing-up to it that amounts, in the total view, to affirmation.
>
> (613–14)

Helen Vendler's famous 1983 book on Keats's odes (which draws on critics we met in the previous chapter like John Jones and Geoffrey Hartman) disputes what she calls the 'up-down' shape that Stillinger and others see in all the odes. She argues instead that each ode has a different shape (and utilizes the five senses differently), a shape appropriate to the view of art explored in each and culminating in the Autumn ode in what Vendler calls a 'form of structural polyphony' in which several forms, 'each one autonomous, each one pregnant with meaning', overlap (Vendler 1983: 12). Vendler sees the odes as a single project.

> I began to see the odes as a single long and heroic imaginative effort, in which Keats examined ... his own acute questions about the conditions for creativity, the forms art can take ... the hierarchy of genres within poetry, the relation of art to the order of nature, and the relation of art to human life and death.
>
> (6)

In 2008, a book on Keats was published that Jack Stillinger called 'certainly the best book ever written about Keats (and I've read all the others) and may well be the best book anybody has written on any writer'. This is Stanley Plumly's *Posthumous Keats*. Plumly sets next to each other the central stanza of 'Nightingale' ('I cannot see what flowers are at my feet') and the opening stanza of 'Autumn' ('Season of mists and mellow fruitfulness') and says this.

> Late spring evening turning blue dusk into dark in the one instance; early autumn early in the day warming toward afternoon and sunset in the other instance. Both examples share ... the bower consciousness of an intimacy with the domesticated natural world ... the abundance of what will become – in a breath, in a thought – emptiness, absence, fled, soft-dying, gone. With Keats, it is sometimes difficult to choose between the falling dark and the fallen day as the richest moment of lost time. At his best, in the odes, time is not only suspended but extended to an edge, to where the running-over almost spills.
>
> (Plumly 2008: 344)

In the same passage Plumly develops what Vendler saw about Keats's self-examining art. This is a beautifully expressed way of thinking about romanticism as we near the end of these two chapters.

> Keats is arguably the first lyric poet to make a matter of the art of the poem as its ultimate subject, and the first to treat the transformation of that subject not simply as ironic but tragic ... Poetry is beauty only to the extent and power of its truth, its tragic sense of itself as a made and perishing thing.
>
> (345)

But I'd like to end with Keats's last poem (I'm sure of that, others aren't). Here is 'This living hand'. It has been much argued over in relation to when and why it was written, arguments that have got nowhere. I present a case for its history elsewhere (Jacobs 2020: 139–41).

> This living hand, now warm and capable
> Of earnest grasping, would, if it were cold
> And in the icy silence of the tomb,
> So haunt thy days and chill thy dreaming nights
> That thou wouldst wish thine own heart dry of blood
> So in my veins red life might stream again,
> And thou be conscience-calmed – see here it is –
> I hold it towards you.

The very literary, lapidary movement of the first lines reflects the knowledge Keats has that wishing Fanny might pacify her conscience by giving him life at the expense of her own is melodramatic, but in the amazing last nine words syntax and punctuation collapse, rhythm (the grave pentameter) becomes speech, 'thou' becomes 'you' and the poem in effect disappears, becomes a voice speaking, a hand offered.

Paul de Man, in the famous Introduction to a Keats selection of 1966, says this. I've always (since I met it in 1970) treasured this, and shared it with generations of students, as quite marvellous. De Man says that Keats offers his hand 'as the victim who defies another to take away from him the weight of his own death'.

> Romantic literature, at its highest moments, encompasses the greatest degree of generality in an experience that never loses contact with the individual self in which it originates ... Nowadays, we are less than ever capable of philosophical generality rooted in genuine self-insight, while our sense of selfhood hardly ever rises above self-justification ... For the great romantics, consciousness of self was the first and necessary step towards moral judgment. Keats's last poems reveal that he reached the same insight; the fact that he arrived at it by a negative route may make him all the more significant for us.
>
> (In de Man ed. 1966: xxxiii–xxxiv)

Works cited

Meena Alexander, *Women in Romanticism* (Macmillan: 1989)
Nancy Armstrong, *Desire and Domestic Fiction* (Oxford U.P.: 1989)
Chris Baldick, *In Frankenstein's Shadow* (Oxford U.P.: 1987)
Francis Barker *et al.* edd., *Literature, Society and the Sociology of Literature* (Essex U.P.: 1977)
John Bayley, 'Keats and Reality', *Proceedings of the British Academy* XLVIII: 1962
Wayne Booth, *The Rhetoric of Fiction* (Chicago U.P.: 1983 (1961))
Marilyn Butler, *Jane Austen and the War of Ideas* (Oxford U.P.: 1975)
Marilyn Butler, *Romantics, Rebels and Reactionaries* (Oxford U.P.: 1981)
Geoffrey N. Cox ed., *Keats's Poetry and Prose* (Norton: 2009)
Aidan Day, *Romanticism* (Routledge: 1996)
Paul de Man ed., *Introduction: Selected Poetry of John Keats* (Signet Books: 1966)
Alistair Duckworth, *The Improvement of the Estate* (Johns Hopkins U.P.: 1971)
Margaret Homans, *Bearing the Word: Language and Female Experience in Nineteenth Century Women's Writing* (Chicago U.P.: 1986)
J. Paul Hunter ed., *Mary Shelley: Frankenstein* (Norton: 1996)
Richard Jacobs, *Literature in Our Lives* (Routledge: 2020)
John Jones, *John Keats's Dream of Truth* (Chatto and Windus: 1969)
George Justice ed., *Jane Austen: Emma* (Norton: 2012)
David Lodge ed., *Jane Austen: Emma, A Casebook* (Macmillan: 1991)
Jerome McGann, *The Romantic Ideology* (Chicago U.P.: 1983)
D.A. Miller, *The Novel and Its Discontents* (Princeton U.P.: 1981)
D.A. Miller, *Jane Austen, or the Secret of Style* (Princeton U.P.: 2003)
David Musselwhite, *Partings Welded Together* (Methuen: 1987)
Vladimir Nabokov, *Lectures on Literature* (Harcourt: 1980)
Stanley Plumly, *Posthumous Keats* (Norton: 2008)
Nicholas Roe, *John Keats and the Culture of Dissent* (Oxford U.P.: 1997)
Edward Said, *Culture and Imperialism* (Chatto and Windus: 1993)
Helen Vendler, *The Odes of John Keats* (Harvard U.P.: 1983)
Daniel P. Watkins, *Keats's Poetry and the Politics of the Imagination* (Fairleigh Dickinson U.P.: 1989)
Raymond Williams, *The Country and the City* (Chatto and Windus: 1973)
Pamela Woof ed., *Dorothy Wordsworth: The Grasmere and Alfoxden Journals* (Oxford U.P.: 2002)

6 Realist fiction in England and America 1840–70

Nathaniel Hawthorne, Edgar Allen Poe, Herman Melville, Charlotte and Emily Bronte, Charles Dickens

A few words to start about what we mean as realism in fiction, sometimes called classic realism. This is from Catherine Belsey's very influential *Critical Practice* of 1980. She starts with the opening of George Eliot's *Middlemarch*, regularly described as the greatest English novel, one that exemplifies more than any other the extraordinary power of realism in the novel (more on Eliot in the next chapter). The first sentence is this: 'Miss Brooke had that kind of beauty which seems to be thrown into relief by poor dress.' Belsey says this.

> The opening sentence [draws on] a shared body of knowledge, 'that kind of beauty which [Belsey adds: 'as we all recognise'] seems to be thrown into relief by poor dress'. The phrase lends the authority of an apparent familiarity to the image constructed ... The experience of reading a realist text is ultimately reassuring, however harrowing the events of the story, because the world evoked in the fiction, its patterns of cause and effect, of social relationships and moral values, largely confirm the patterns of the world we seem to know ... The term [realism] is useful in distinguishing between those forms which tend to efface their own textuality, their existence as discourse, and those which explicitly draw attention to it. Realism offers itself as transparent.
>
> (Belsey 1980: 50–51)

But sometimes it doesn't work, sometimes we don't 'all recognise' what we are assumed to: I once read of a lecturer who, on sharing that famous opening sentence from *Middlemarch* with her class, got an immediate response from one student who said, 'Right, that tells me clearly enough that this book isn't including or talking to me'.

Realism's aim is to hide its artifice from the reader as consumer, positioned as passively and uncritically absorbing the text – and comfortably agreeing with the world as transparently revealed by the text as 'the way things are'. Most of you will know that this is what critics call ideology. Classic realism, in this

DOI: 10.4324/9781003127567-7

account, calls its readers into a kind of politically neutered space where the text agrees with its readers' world view while it just happens to be simultaneously creating that view in its pages. (For remarks on ideology and the early realist novel, see Chapter 1 of this book.)

Not many years after the Victorian period officially began in 1832, two American writers of genius wrote works which, in retrospect, we can see as radically subverting and destabilizing classic-realism as just outlined, the very notion of the solidly knowable and comfortably readable Victorian realist novel, the project which got underway by the middle of the century. I'm referring here (very selectively, of course) to **Nathaniel Hawthorne**'s short story 'The Minister's Black Veil' (1835) and his novel *The Scarlet Letter* (1850) and **Edgar Allan Poe**'s short story 'The Man of the Crowd' (1840). I'll also refer here to Hawthorne's brilliantly and differently subversive story 'The Birthmark' (1846). And once the Bronte sisters and Dickens were published or publishing, another American writer of genius, **Herman Melville**, capped his predecessor's subversions of fictional convention by publishing, in the wake of, and perhaps partly because of, the public failure of his epic *Moby Dick*, what must be the most startling affront to the very nature of the readable (let alone realist) text, 'Bartleby' (1856).

These American texts point to something that may be emphasized at the start of this chapter devoted to some famous milestones of 19th century realist fiction, especially in a book about critical responses to texts, as these texts not only defy the very urge to interpret that is intrinsic to realism itself but are clearly designed to do just that. Needless to say, these texts have attracted legions of critical interpretations. In the case of the Poe story, this has meant readings by luminaries like the symbolist poet Baudelaire, who translated Poe and saw alienated city-life in the story, and the great Marxist cultural critic Walter Benjamin (whom we also met in Chapter 1) who saw the embryonic birth of crime fiction that Poe inaugurated a few years later in his Dupin detective stories, stories that in turn anticipate, among others, Dickens's Inspector Bucket in *Bleak House*. (Actually, for me, Poe's story in effect evacuates or parodies all that constitutes crime fiction.) But however ingenious such readings have been, they seem destined to fail in the face of the texts' internal refusal to 'mean' or at least (in the case of *The Scarlet Letter*) their dramatization of the arbitrary nature of the meaning-making process.

If the leading figures of late 20th century 'postmodernist' fiction have been American writers (as we'll see in the last chapter of this book), especially at the time when the novel in the UK was largely formulaic, tired and often rather obviously looking to be turned into film scripts, it's somehow fitting that before the British-Victorian novel got solidly underway these American writers were quietly undermining the fictional enterprise of realism itself.

The 'Minister's Black Veil' and 'Man of the Crowd' stories at the start of this period of American subversion are unsettling dramatizations of the urge to interpret. The reader reads of these urges – of Hooper's parishioners who variously believe their minister's veil must or might be hiding guilt for some crime or (more wildly) his communion with the devil or (more prosaically) mental disease; of the narrator's desperate (diseased?) stalking of the man in the crowd (or is it the other way round?), equally desperately suggesting (again) that some obscurely terrible crime is somehow or somewhere involved – and at the same time the reader in effect finds him or herself engaged on a search for meaning in a parallel process.

But both texts insist that the act of interpretation is in effect just clutching at straws – like the lawyer at the end of 'Bartleby' who tentatively offers a rumour he has heard that may help 'explain' Bartleby – but the lawyer doesn't really believe that at all, unlike Hooper's parishioners or Poe's perhaps definitely unreliable narrator, who says himself that he may or may not have glimpsed suspicious items in the man's clothing. We are left with the words of these texts gesturing into silence, signifiers remaining blank, refusing to attach themselves to solidly signified meaning.

They also, in Poe's case, merely gesture both forwards and backwards to other words on the page, the words of Dickens, the story borrowing as it does from Dickens's early Boz sketches and then perhaps prompting Dickens to borrow the double-stalking for the Headstone/Wrayburn doubling in *Our Mutual Friend* (that doubling is explored below). I'd add that the textual ancestor to the Poe story that means most to me is Blake's 'London', a poem he couldn't have known, that we explored in Chapter 4 of this book. But silence seeps backwards from these two extraordinary texts, unravelling them. 'Bartleby' (which also shadows or parodies Dickens) ends – also – with the lawyer silencing himself. And crying.

A few more words about 'Bartleby'. Miller aptly brought the story together with 'The Minister's Black Veil' (in 1991), pointing out that Bartleby's signature refusal – 'I would prefer not to' – has the 'performative effect' equivalent to Hooper's silent adoption of the veil.

> In both cases, once by an act of language, once by an act outside language, language is brought to a stop, rendered powerless ... Like Bartleby's phrase, with its conditional 'should', its gently indecisive 'prefer', both inhibiting the 'not' from being the negative of some positive and thereby something we can make part of some dialectical reasoning, *The Minister's Black Veil* is neither positive or negative. It is patiently neutral. It says neither yes or no to whatever hypotheses about it the reader proposes.
>
> (In Person ed. 2005: 711, 717)

'Patiently neutral' applies well not just to Bartleby himself but the text's patiently putting up with the babble of critical readings that, as Dan McCall says in his book *The Silence of Bartleby*, are little more than intrusions into the young man's privacy.

'Bartleby' sets out conventionally enough with a cast of minor characters straight out of Dickens, with their nicknames and their complementary character traits, and then complicates this with showing the elderly lawyer on a surprising journey in which he, in effect, grows up to feel, for the first time, rich sympathy for a suffering human being, and then crosses, or cuts the ground beneath, these methods of characterization with the presentation, or rather the absenting of characterization, in the form of the utterly unknowable Bartleby himself. Suffering he may, sufficient to humanize the elderly lawyer, but suffering how and why? Silence. Again, we're left just with words.

That Melville's words, as well as Bartleby's few utterances (counted by Elizabeth Hardwick as 37 short lines in a 16,000-word story), are wildly comic in a text that otherwise seems to gesture (but not seriously?) at the ghost-story as well as (more seriously but bafflingly obscurely) at tragedy, is just another radical subversion of reader expectations. It is impossible not to laugh at Melville's scrupulous adverbs here – '"I prefer not to", he respectfully and slowly said, and mildly disappeared' – or, when asked by the lawyer to be 'a little reasonable', to laugh at both the reply and the impossible description of its mode of delivery, here: '"At present I would prefer not to be a little reasonable", was his mildly cadaverous reply.' This is language on the edge of novelistic propriety, ready to collapse at its own absurdities.

Also subversive is the way the text populates its field with its cast of characters and then immediately depopulates it (the opposite of what classic realism does with its richly peopled pages throughout extended novelistic time), leaving just the lawyer and Bartleby on a blank canvas. And then leaving the lawyer, at Bartleby's death, alone with an 'explanation' he doesn't believe in. And then his tears.

Let's turn to Hawthorne's 'The Birthmark' and *The Scarlet Letter* to make a related point about early American subversions and that is that the two texts are also very radical interventions in sexual politics, strikingly feminist or pre-feminist. That the novel is also explicitly about adultery gives me the chance to start this chapter a second time with some prefatory remarks from Tony Tanner's classic critical work *Adultery and the Novel* as he shows how crucial the adulterous woman (always the woman, of course, in terms of identification and punishment) is to the functioning of narrative in classic-realist novels.

Both 'The Birthmark' and *The Scarlet Letter* are about signs and the reading of signs – that is, they are about reading. In the one case the sign is a pre-existing and arbitrary, apparently meaningless sign that nature has inscribed (in blood) upon a beautiful woman's body; in the other case society, in the form of a punitive Puritan community, has itself ordered the inscription (in lettering on clothing) of a sign, with a very intentional and intentionally unambiguous meaning, upon another beautiful woman's body. In the one case, the coercion (by a man) is to force a reading upon the woman's sign; in the other, the woman who wears the sign herself has the effect (without any intention) of reading the coercive (male) sign otherwise. Judith Fetterley wrote strongly about 'The Birthmark' in 1978, reacting against conventional Christian readings of the mark on Georgiana's cheek as the symbol of original sin, whereas for Fetterley (as I've always thought) the mark is the visible sign of her – of women's – sexuality itself.

> *The Birthmark* provides a brilliant analysis of the sexual politics of idealization and a brilliant exposure of the mechanisms whereby hatred can be disguised as love, neurosis can be disguised as science, murder can be disguised as idealization, and success can be disguised as failure ... Hawthorne is writing a story about the sickness of men, not a story about the flawed and imperfect nature of women ... [Aylmer's] revulsion for Georgiana has its root in part in a jealousy of the power which her sexuality represents and a frustration in the face of its impenetrable mystery ... man's jealousy of woman's having something he does not.
>
> (In Person ed. 2005: 719–22)

That is very relevant to the brilliantly assured novel *The Scarlet Letter*. So let me turn briefly to Tony Tanner on adultery in the European novel, in the Introduction to his landmark study of 1979.

> Although the 18th and [early] 19th century novel may be said to move toward marriage ... it often gains its particular narrative urgency from an energy that threatens to contravene that stability of the family on which society depends ... To put it at its most succinct – contracts *create* transgressions; the two are inseparable, and the one would have no meaning without the other ... It is the unstable triangularity of adultery, rather than the static symmetry of marriage, that is the generative form of Western literature as we know it ... If society depends for its existence on certain rules governing what may be combined and what should be kept separate, then adultery ... offers an attack on those rules, revealing them to be arbitrary rather than absolute. In this way, the adulterous woman becomes the 'gap' in society that gradually extends through it. In attempting to ostracize her, society moves towards ostracizing itself.
>
> (Tanner 2019: online)

That generative triangularity we will return to when we look at Dickens's *Our Mutual Friend* with the critical help of Eve Sedgwick and, behind her as well as Tanner's work, René Girard (in his 1960s study *Desire, Deceit and the Novel*). I'll also return to Tanner on adultery in the next chapter when we look at James's *The Portrait of a Lady* (where adultery is, notoriously, refused).

In the light of those remarks about the narrative need for the very notion of adultery we can turn to Hawthorne's novel to notice its radically subversive treatment of the subject, its series of refusals, as embodied by Hester herself and also by the narrative.

Hester refuses to disclose who is the father of her child Pearl. She refuses to carry out the punishment for adultery – wearing the embroidered A on her dress – in the expected drab Puritan style but instead makes the sign herself 'with so much fertility and gorgeous luxuriance of fancy', the effect 'enclosing her in a sphere' (Ch. 2). Rather than signs of shame the letter and the precious and cherished Pearl together signify the defiantly unfallen woman and even her autonomous sexuality. She also refuses to be 'fallen' in another subtly intimated way. The narrator says that it's 'marvellous' that Hester, rather than submit to the coercions of signification by being the ultimate symbol of 'woman's frailty', 'the figure, the body, the reality of sin' – that is, by re-embodying the biblical Eve – she refused to flee to England 'with the world before her' (Milton's words about Eve, with Adam, at the end of *Paradise Lost*), choosing instead to stay and, later, to minister to her community (Ch. 5).

In an even more remarkable loosening of the ties between the sign and its intended signification, her A is never allowed to settle definitively upon the meaning Adulterer but, in her ministering to women in need, it attracts other meanings like Able, Admirable and Angel. Gabriel Josipovici put it like this in 1971.

> It is even suggested that the letter on her breast is a sort of nun's cross, the sign of her good work in the town among the poor and sick, and near the close of the book we learn of the Indians who have come out of the forest … and who 'fastened their snake-like eyes on Hester's bosom, conceiving, perhaps, that the wearer of this brilliantly-embroidered badge must needs be a personage of high dignity among her people' [Ch. 22]. In other words the letter forms part of a conventional, not a natural, language, and how we read it depends on what assumptions we bring to it, what language-game we are playing.
>
> (Josipovici 1971: 169)

Nina Baym (who in 2004 ruefully admitted that she'd been swimming against the tide since the 1970s in arguing for Hawthorne as feminist) put the issue in the broad context of American literature in her Introduction to the novel.

> The conflict between repressive societies and defiant individuals is everywhere in American literature. Hawthorne's version is unique because he has created a *mother* as the defiant outcast. Hester's values are strikingly different from those usually associated with the American rebel-hero, who is always on the road, rejecting his own past as well as any and all social obligations. The community has rejected Hester, but she stands for another idea of community – a more nurturing, flexible, less judgmental community. A matriarchy, in contrast to the legalistic patriarchy of the Puritan elders.
>
> (In Baym ed. 2003: xxiii)

Hester's defiantly possessive motherhood is certainly in sharp contrast with later adulterous mothers like Emma Bovary and her immediate descendent Kate Chopin's Edna Pontellier, who are very much not mother-women (more on Kate Chopin in Chapter 8).

Just as radical is a moment at the very end of the novel, which perhaps has not received due attention. This is a radical turn in conventional third-person narrative technique. In the long penultimate paragraph we learn of how Hester comforted the many women who came to her in their varying kinds of distress, as (in a marvellous phrase) with 'the dreary burden of a heart unyielded, because unvalued and unsought', comforting them with her belief that one day 'a new truth would be revealed, in order to establish the whole relation between man and woman on a surer ground of mutual happiness' and, though not herself, the 'apostle of the coming revelation must be a woman'. Three lines later the final paragraph begins 'So said Hester Prynne ...' (Ch. 24). But it was not Hester but the male narrator who 'said' the previous paragraph. The effect, quite wonderfully, is a merging of male narrator and female protagonist, or rather a submerging and willing submission of the former into the latter, an emblem of male–female union in the mutuality which Hester's hopes have just looked forward to.

In the first important book of modern feminist criticism, Virginia Woolf's 1929 classic *A Room of One's Own*, Woolf reads Jane Eyre's passionate demand for the recognition of women's faculties and feelings – 'I shall be called discontented. I could not help it ... but women feel just as men feel; they need exercise for their faculties and a field for their efforts as much as their brothers do' (Ch. 12) – and, though finding that **Charlotte Bronte**, speaking through Jane, needed to 'write in a rage where she should write calmly', she saw very clearly how the 'discontent' was a direct result of the constrictions under which women writers lived.

> Anger was tampering with the integrity of Charlotte Bronte the novelist ... She remembered that she had been starved of her proper due of experience – she had been made to stagnate in a parsonage mending stockings when she wanted to wander free over the world. Her imagination swerved from indignation and we feel it swerve ... We [also] feel the influence of fear in it; just as we constantly feel an acidity which is the result of oppression, a buried suffering smouldering beneath her passion, a rancour which contracts those books, splendid as they are, with a spasm of pain.
>
> (Woolf 1929: 55–58)

The rage which Woolf identified is re-identified in Sandra Gilbert and Susan Gubar's landmark study *The Madwoman in the Attic* (1979) in Jane herself. Two years before the book, Gilbert published the article *Plain Jane's Progress* (1977), which is an earlier version of the book's relevant chapter, and I turn to it now. Among the very many insights offered there is the crucial one that Bertha is not only Jane's dark 'other' or alter-ego but that, in her actions through the novel, she in effect acts out Jane's suppressed rage, her 'ire' (to pun on Jane's name. The pun is also on heir. Bertha sets fire to Thornfield and throws herself into the air to her death). The passage that Woolf found too close to 'rage' Gilbert calls a 'rational desire for liberty' and 'as logical as anything in an essay by, say, [Mary] Wollstonecraft'. On the other hand, the 'bad animal who was first locked up in the red room is, we sense, still lurking somewhere, behind a dark door, waiting for a chance to get free' (in Newman ed. 1996: 483).

Gilbert traces the series of actions in which Bertha – 'the angry aspect of the orphan child, the ferocious secret self Jane has been trying to repress' – enacts what Jane wishes to but can't.

> Jane Eyre secretly wants to tear the [wedding] garment up, Bertha does it for her. Fearing the inexorable 'bridal day', Jane would like to put it off. Bertha does that for her too ... Jane's feelings of 'hunger, rebellion, and rage' ... were accompanied by Bertha's 'eccentric murmurs' ... Jane's profound desire to destroy Thornfield, the symbol of Rochester's mastery and of her own servitude, will be acted out by Bertha, who burns down the house and destroys *herself* in the process, as if she were an agent of Jane's desire as well as her own ... Bertha not only acts *for* Jane, she also acts like Jane. The imprisoned Bertha, running 'backwards and forwards' on all fours, for instance, recalls not only Jane ... whose sole relief from mental pain was to pace 'backwards and forwards' in the third storey, but also that 'bad animal' who was ten-year-old Jane, imprisoned in the red room, howling and mad.
>
> (In Newman ed. 1996: 492–93)

Gayatri Spivak famously brought together *Jane Eyre* with *Frankenstein* and with Jean Rhys's *Wide Sargasso Sea* (where Bertha is of course recuperated and given sympathetic life and a voice), in terms of women's writing and imperialism, in an influential article from 1985 (later revised but quoted from the original here). Rather than see Bertha as a psychological double, Spivak sees her as racially demonized. She asks how it is that Jane moves from her initial place in what Spivak calls the 'counter-family' (with the Reeds as the 'legal' family) to her position as legalized family with the Riverses and then with Rochester. She answers that is through 'the active ideology of imperialism', through the Bertha story.

She focuses on the extraordinary (and suspiciously capitalized) passage in which Rochester, telling Jane about his unhappy married union with Bertha in the West Indies, and (I'd add) telling Jane this self-aggrandizing story as part of his strategy to gain over Jane's doubts, said that one night he felt 'a wind fresh from Europe' purifying the 'fiery' Indian storm, and heard 'Hope' and 'Wisdom' urging him to leave and 'live again' in Europe, because 'you have done all that God and Humanity require of you' (Ch. 10). Spivak says this, after also looking at Jane's earlier first sighting of Bertha as 'beast or ... strange wild animal' (Ch. 26).

> The figure of Bertha Mason [is] produced by the axiomatics of imperialism. Through Bertha Mason, the white Jamaican Creole, Bronte renders the human/animal frontier as acceptably indeterminate, so that a good greater than the letter of the Law can be broached ... [In the passage quoted] Bronte presents the imperative for a shift beyond the Law as divine injunction rather than human motive ... We might say that this is

> the register not of mere marriage or sexual reproduction but of Europe and its not-yet-human Other [with] the field of imperial conquest here inscribed as [fiery] Hell ... It is the unquestioned ideology of imperialist axiomatics, then, that conditions Jane's move from the counter-family set to the set of the family [as sanctioned] in law.
>
> (In Richter ed. 2007: 1840)

I'll add that though Jean Rhys's *Wide Sargasso Sea* is indeed a crucial postcolonial intervention and answering-back to Bronte's ideologically conditioned and (in sharp contrast with Jane's early feminist thoughts we looked at with Virginia Woolf) decidedly unsympathetic representation of Bertha, Rhys's *Good Morning, Midnight* (1939) contains an earlier and remarkably concentrated postcolonial version of Bertha.

This is in a narrative within a narrative within a narrative at the novel's centre (Part 2), the second narrative told by a French painter about living earlier in London and being interrupted by a drunk woman outside his door. She's from Martinique, is what the painter calls 'half-negro', and she's kept on the top floor of the house by a man who brought her from the West Indies via Paris. She is so hated and abused by everyone that she hasn't left the house for two years, except at night, and except for that day when she ventured out only to be called dirty and smelly by a little girl. So she drinks a bottle of whisky and collapses outside the painter's door. He listens to her story, which he can't wholly understand as she speaks partly in English as well as French, gives her more whisky, and sends her away. Rhys's protagonist Sasha is telling the novel's main first-person narrative, and neither she nor the painter show even limited understanding of, let alone sympathy for, the unnamed woman from Martinique whose postcolonial story, like Bertha's, is never directly told and remains unavailable to the reader. And, unlike Bertha, the painter's narrative anecdote is the last we hear of her.

To move from *Jane Eyre* to *Wuthering Heights*, published by Charlotte's sister **Emily Bronte** in the same year, is something of a culture-shock – as it must have been for its first readers, though they seem to have been more exercised by trying to guess the gender of the pseudonymous authors. (One American reviewer advised reading *Jane Eyre* and burning *Wuthering Heights*, advice which at least keeps things simple.) The opening pages of the two novels could hardly be more different. Charlotte makes sure the reader is consolingly and comfortably aligned with the young Jane as she reads her book and feels, as we do in such moments, the sense of isolated but self-assured uniqueness in the family unit. Emily throws us into the confused and baffled uncertainties faced by the awkwardly narrating Lockwood, a figure at an oblique angle and as if excluded from his own narrative, comically unaware of the pathos he elicits in the reader. If Charlotte's novel seems firmly in the classic-realist tradition, Emily's suggests the experiments and discontinuities of modernism. Terry Eagleton put the differences very well in his 1975 study of the sisters' novels when he identifies the ideologically contending currents in such novels as 'romance' and 'realism'.

> *Wuthering Heights* achieves its coherence of vision from an exhausting confrontation of contending forces, whereas Charlotte's kind of totality depends upon a pragmatic integration of them ... We are almost never at a loss what to think about a Charlotte character, which could hardly be said of *Wuthering Heights* ... The narrative techniques of [that] novel are deliberately framed to preserve [its] ambivalences; those of Charlotte Bronte allow us fairly direct access to a single, transparent, controlling consciousness which maintains its dominance even when its bearer [like Jane] is in practice subdued and subordinated ... Charlotte's novels ... exploit fiction and fable to smooth the jagged edges of real conflict ...; *Wuthering Heights*, on the other hand, confronts the tragic truth that the passion and the society it presents are not fundamentally reconcilable – that there remains at the deepest level an ineradicable contradiction between them which refuses to be unlocked.
>
> (Eagleton 1998: 50–51)

Nancy Armstrong (in her excellent *Desire and Domestic Fiction* excerpted in the last chapter) writes with typical brilliance about both the Bronte novels.

> The Brontes call up the ghosts of the history of sexuality to represent a domain of passion that seems to well up in opposition to the contemporary conventions of courtship and kinship relations. To be internalized and made safe for polite readers, historically earlier sexual practices are discovered in dreams, hallucinations, and unfulfilled wishes that conflict with the conduct of sexual relationships in the present. In the hands of the Brontes ... the history of sexuality becomes the stuff of individual neuroses.
>
> (Armstrong 1989: 204)

One remarkable feature of *Wuthering Heights*, in which it differs very sharply from *Jane Eyre*, was identified back in 1949 by Derek Traversi (later revised for a more general chapter on the Brontes in 1958, excerpted here). That is the way the novel conveys a permanent haunting by death. Before I turn to Traversi, I'd say that this is not just about the many deaths that the novel registers (some in paradoxical casualness) or even the larger pattern suggested by the child Heathcliff being found starving in Liverpool at the novel's outset (Eagleton among others suggests the likelihood of his being an abandoned victim of Irish famine) and the adult Heathcliff in effect dying of hunger strike at the end (as, incidentally, does Bartleby), but a more generalized sense of Freud's death-wish, the desire of the organism to just stop. (We'll meet this later in relation to the narrative theorist Peter Brooks on *Great Expectations*.) Here's Traversi on the novel as a tragedy (in effect Shakespearian, though the word is not used).

> The presence of death is felt intensely in *Wuthering Heights*, at times as something against which the protagonists react with all the force of their passionate energies, and at times as a profoundly evocative intuition of peace. The two attitudes ned to be seen in relation to one another ...

> When Nelly Dean, after Mr Earnshaw's death, hears the children comforting each other ... 'pictur[ing] heaven so beautifully as they did' ... the next sentence comes as the intrusion of a more real and more truly tragic experience, as unexpected as it is profoundly moving in its simplicity: 'While I sobbed and listened, I could not help wishing we were all there *safe* together' [Ch. 5; Traversi's italics]. The end of Heathcliff, too, stands in the closest relation to a tragedy in which ... the exclusive fulfilment of passion and the self-destruction which inevitably accompanies it, are inextricably fused ... 'My soul's bliss kills my body, but does not satisfy itself' [Ch. 34]. The phrase is [animated by] the consuming desire for a completeness unattainable in time but implied by temporal experience.
>
> (In Ford ed. 1958: 271–72)

Traversi's emphasis on how consciousness of death – or to put it more generally, of loss – pulses through the novel, as it does through the strikingly similar poetry of Emily Dickinson (who steeped herself in Bronte, especially in her poems which – though in their more obviously romantic and ballad-like way – anticipate Dickinson's). For Dickinson, to be conscious is to be conscious of loss. There's no other adequate way of conceptualizing the Cathy/Heathcliff relationship than to sense it (to feel it) as constructed by and constituted in loss, formed and deformed across a wounding series of losses and separations, as well as grounded in their need to be each other's mother, the loss of mother being at the novel's psychic heart.

Teaching the novel, I used to point to Cathy's diary account in Chapter 3 of Hindley's prohibitions forbidding the two children to sit, eat and play together, and we would wonder if trauma may have caused Cathy to omit to record the most painful of those separations. The evidence comes 100 pages later in Chapter 12 when Cathy muses to Nelly about the 'separation that Hindley had ordered between me, and Heathcliff – I was laid alone for the first time'. So the children were forbidden to sleep together and the wording clearly suggests a child separated, for the first, traumatic time, from the mother's bed.

Miller put this characteristically well in 1982 (though he doesn't make the connection with the diary entry), tracing the idea back to the impossibility of not just storytelling but language itself to express what lies beyond and behind expression, where (to paraphrase Dickinson's words) the heart freighted down most heavily with loss cannot move at all. Miller notes that we never see the two children sleeping together in a union 'prior to sexual differentiation'.

> This union was prior to any sense of separate selfhood, prior even to language, figurative or conceptual, which might express that union. As soon as Cathy can say, 'I *am* Heathcliff', or 'My love for Heathcliff resembles the eternal rocks beneath' [Ch. 9], they are already divided. This division has always already occurred as soon as there is consciousness and the possibility of retrospective storytelling. Storytelling is always after the fact, and it is always constructed over a loss.
>
> (In Allott ed. 1992: 231)

But I want to say that, for me, the most incisive as well as the most eloquent critical contribution to the understanding of the Cathy/Heathcliff relationship, with its roots in the intensities of childhood and in mother-loss, comes in Stevie Davies's 1988 study. She points out that the cry 'I *am* Heathcliff' has worked on generations of readers who 'as if drugged or entranced' can only imperfectly understand such 'beautiful, vagrant speech-patterns' with their 'frank, uncensored outbursts of raw egotism'.

> *Wuthering Heights* is a unique act of search for a language which will capsize the boundaries and thresholds between self and other: a magical language which will somehow empower the creative persona to conjure that dissolution of borders into being; to run time back into itself so that early security and potency may be retrieved ... Deep in its own experience of lack, absence and loss, the psyche in *Wuthering Heights* perceives a spiritual home identifiable with the mother ... The children's refusal of control in *Wuthering Heights* is also a mute demand for the embrace that gathers the child in to himself, providing the limit to his ire and destructiveness ... [But] the means of such embrace (the mother) is almost wholly absent from the text ... The motherless author of *Wuthering Heights* releases the voices of her characters as a universal cry of need. The novel records both the potency of that need and its absolute failure to register or to obtain the satisfaction of a reply.
>
> (In Stoneman ed. 1993: 164–65, 171–72)

To turn to **Charles Dickens** and to his orphans, we might first connect the recurrence in his novels of lost children with the return to myths and fairy-tales. Harry Levin put it well in 1966. (In passing, he refers to Mircea Eliade's claim that the 'real spiritual function of the 19th century novel' was to act as the 'great repository of degraded myths'.)

> The most powerful writers gain much of their power by being mythmakers, gifted – although they sometimes do not know it – at catching and crystallizing popular fantasies. Thus Dickens's novels enthrall us again and again by taking us back, recurrently and obsessively, to the old folktale about the Babes in the Woods. Oliver Twist, Little Nell, David Copperfield, Esther Summerson, Pip, and his other waifs have to cope with the wicked witches of sullen bureaucracy and greedy industrialism.
>
> (Levin 1966: 29)

One of the most moving chapters in *Bleak House* is when Esther and Mr Jarndyce seek out the orphaned children of Neckett, the sheriff's officer. They find two young children locked up alone, in cold poverty, while the older sister (aged 13) is out making some little money to sustain the three of them, by washing. This girl, Charley, returns to meet the visitors who are profoundly affected by the children's situation, by the two children's dependence on Charley and by Charley herself who (Esther says to us) is 'so young and yet with an air of age and steadiness that sat so strangely on the childish figure'. Jarndyce speaks with Charley 'half playfully, yet all the more compassionately and mournfully'. He asks her: '"And how do you live, Charley? O! Charley," said my guardian, turning his face away for a moment, "how do you live?"' (Ch. 15).

As it happens this scene has elicited two particularly eloquent critical responses which I turn to now. These are, first, in Nabokov's lecture on the novel to American undergraduates (we met his lecture on *Mansfield Park* in the previous chapter) and, in 1966 and much less predictably, in Steven Marcus's study of Victorian pornography. Nabokov very sharply connects this scene with the immediately preceding chapter in which Skimpole, who likes to refer to himself as a child, lightly muses on his release from debt because of Neckett's death. Dickens says that Charley's fingers are 'wrinkled with washing' and adds 'but for this, she might have been a child, playing at washing, and imitating a poor working-woman'. Nabokov says: 'So Skimpole is a vile parody of a child, whereas this little girl is a pathetic imitator of an adult woman'. And he says this about the charge of sentimentality that some might level at this scene.

> Dickens's great art should not be mistaken for a cockney version of the seat of emotion – it is the real thing, keen, subtle, specialised compassion, with a grading and merging of melting shades, with the very accent of profound pity in the words uttered, and with an artist's choice of the most visible, most audible, most tangible epithets.
>
> (Nabokov 1980: 86–87)

Steven Marcus's landmark study of Victorian pornography, *The Other Victorians*, devotes much space to a detailed account of the frankly hair-raising anonymous mid-century *My Secret Life*, an enormous and explicit retelling of the author's sexual encounters with countless girls and women, usually working-class. One vivid section concerns a young teenage girl called Kitty. After paying her for sex he casually asks her about her life. She has siblings who are often in the lodgings alone and she pays for food through prostituting herself to men like the narrator. Marcus makes the connection with the 'immediately relevant novelistic counterpart' in Dickens and adds this, in what I take to be the most moving thing of its kind I've read.

> The chief difference between the two episodes is that Charley … has made a different choice than Kitty … There can be no doubt that both choices were made all the time in Victorian England, and in the pages of *My Secret Life* Kitty exists for us in a fully human way – her reality is not to be denied. But her humanity is of a different kind than that of Charley … and this difference is itself the result of the difference in consciousness between Dickens and the author of *My Secret Life* … The scene [in *Bleak House*] dramatizes Dickens's consciousness – and his readers' as well – that these children are members of ourselves, that their humanity belongs to ours,

> that we are their society … The author of *My Secret Life* … regards Kitty with interest, amusement, and pleasure … He sees nothing degrading or dehumanising in her selling herself. In this he is wrong. Yet it adds considerably to our understanding of the Victorian novel if we read it against such scenes as those represented in *My Secret Life*, if we understand that the Victorian novelists were aware of such scenes, and that their great project, taken as a whole, was directed dialectically against what such scenes meant.
>
> (Marcus 1966: 107–09)

Miller's 1971 Introduction to the then Penguin edition would have been many readers' first encounter with this critic. Among many fine insights, Miller says that, 'as everyone knows, [Dickens] finds England in a bad way' and that 'someone must be to blame'. I'd add that perhaps Miller is echoing Carlyle's famous opening to his 1839 book *Chartism*, which I'll quickly slip in here as so Dickensian in its anger and energy.

> A feeling very generally exists that the condition and disposition of the working classes is a rather ominous matter at present: that something ought to be said, something ought to be done, in regard to it … To us individually this matter appears, and has for many years appeared, to be the most ominous of all practical matters whatever; a matter in regard to which if something be not done, something will *do* itself one day, in a fashion that will please nobody.
>
> (In Ford ed. 1958: 169)

Miller continues like this about the England of *Bleak House*.

> It is in a state dangerously close to ultimate disorder or decay. The energy which gave the social system its initial impetus seems about to run down. Entropy approaches a maximum … There must be steps to take to save England before it blows up, like the springing of a mine, or catches fire, like Krook, or falls into fragments like the house in Tom-all-Alone's, or resolves into dust, which awaits all men and all social systems … In spite of Dickens's generous rage against injustice, selfishness and procrastination, the evil he so brilliantly identifies is irremediable. It is inseparable from language and from the organisation of men into society … Everyone in *Bleak House* is, like Jo, made to 'move on', in one form or another of the displacement which separates so many of the characters of *Bleak House* from themselves … As in all Dickens's work, there is at the centre of *Bleak House* a tension between belief in some extra-human source of value, a stable centre outside the shadows of the human game, and on the other hand the shade of a suspicion that there may be no such centre, that all systems of interpretation may be fictions.
>
> (Intro. Miller 1971: 13–32)

I'd put it this way. The novel, in a proto-modernist way, ensures the reader persist in the pursuit of interpretations, equivalent to those pursued by the characters (and by Esther as the alternative narrator), with the ironic goal of destabilizing the very nature of the interpretive act, even of reading itself. Miller says that the novel is 'deliberately constructed by Dickens to make the reader a bad detective' (20). Or as David Musselwhite puts it in his *Partings Welded Together*: '*Bleak House* is, then, a dreadful prison – a prison house of language, a prison house of the soul, a prison house of genius' (Musselwhite 1987: 225).

Perhaps the novel's solely 'free' figure, with her wonderfully named birds (a proto-modernist demonstration of the arbitrary nature of language), is the 'mad' Miss Flyte. These names are at once random and an accurate and exhaustive account of the socio-legal world of the novel (Ch. 14).

> Hope, Joy, Youth, Peace, Rest, Life, Dust, Ashes, Waste, Want, Ruin, Despair, Madness, Death, Cunning, Folly, Words, Wigs, Rags, Sheepskin, Plunder, Precedent, Jargon, Gammon, and Spinach.

Musselwhite says these birds 'take flight in the dusk of the novel – a winging into the darkness of the variegated and volatile moods of our existence ... the sheer insanity that might save us' (225). I'm reminded of the end of Melville's 'Bartleby', written shortly after *Bleak House* (and, in its miniature way, parodying it with an uncannily duplicating law-copyist who is and isn't like Nemo, is and isn't 'loony' and who flatly refuses all interpretation) where we hear about 'dead letters' that never reach their destination. 'On errands of life, these letters speed to death.'

Great Expectations is the subject of a particularly powerful and influential chapter in what many would agree is the most important modern book on narrative, Peter Brooks's great *Reading for the Plot* (1992). This is a richly illuminating application of ideas based on Freud's 'Beyond the Pleasure Principle' to the dynamics of narrative and the ways by which narrative is structured. The battle that Freud identified between the pleasure principle and the death-drive is what Brooks sees as underpinning the way narratives at once seek, and delay their drive to reach, closure (the quiescence of death), a delaying through the gratifications of the divergences and bindings together of plot – especially through repetition-compulsions and the returns of the repressed.

Brooks's analysis of *Great Expectations* is too elaborate to do more than briefly sample here, as in his opening point about the novel's narrative searching for its own beginning. Pip's life (says Brooks) in effect starts 'in search of plot. Pip when we first see him is himself in search of the authority ... that would define and justify – authorise – the plot of his ensuing life' (Brooks 1992: 115). I'd add that Pip's beginnings of consciousness, as he stands among the gravestones and feels his first impression of 'the identity of things' is uncannily duplicated much later in Magwitch's retro-autobiographical narrative in Chapter 42 – 'I first became aware of myself', etc. – and that both of these primal narratives owe a perhaps unconscious debt to the Creature's autobiographical account of becoming aware of himself in the world in *Frankenstein*. That novel is explicitly evoked when Magwitch stages his return as if from the dead into Pip's life in London, the scene well described by Brooks as one that 'decisively re-enacts both a return of the repressed and a return to the primal moment of childhood' (127).

But it's Brooks's analysis of the end of Pip's search for meaning and authority that is most tellingly illuminating and most revealing of the radically unusual nature of what Dickens does in this novel. What is so odd is that having at last discovered Estella's true parents (having, in effect, taken over and mastered the authorial role of the detective as well as having out-mastered his Oedipal father Jaggers in that detective-role), he can't put the information to any use. In a more typical Dickens novel Pip would have deployed the knowledge to win and marry Estella. But the knowledge is in effect redundant. Brooks calls it 'radically unusable … offer[ing] no comfort and no true illumination … It produces no authority for the plot of life' (135). Brooks says this (after noting that, in his analysis, the vexed question of which of the two endings should be preferred is now 'somewhat arbitrary and unimportant': I much prefer the original with the last and saddest of misrecognitions when Estella thinks the child with Pip is his).

> As at the start of the novel we had the impression of a life not yet subject to plot … so at the end we have the impression of a life that has outlived plot, renounced plot, been cured of it: life that is left over … It is with the image of a life bereft of plot, of movement and desire, that the novel most appropriately leaves us. Indeed, we have at the end what could appropriately be called a 'cure' from plot, in Pip's recognition of the general forfeiture of plotting, his renunciation of any attempt to direct his life.
>
> (136–38)

Steven Connor makes very good and related points in his 1985 book on Dickens.

> *Great Expectations* displays progressively Pip's alienation from himself. The [main] revelations of the book … are revelations of Pip's marginality in his own life … Pip is forced to recognise that not only are the objects of his desire unobtainable, but also that his desires are not even really his own. Rather, he is acting out the desires of others, or their desires are acting through him. It is Magwitch's desire that Pip should become a gentleman, and Miss Havisham's desire that he should love and be abandoned by Estella.
>
> (Connor 1985: 138)

On that last point Brooks very pertinently remarks, about the 'generalised breakdown of plots … an evident subversion and futilization of the very concept of plot' in the novel, that Miss Havisham's plot over-reaches into failure. The plot 'turned Estella into so heartless a creature that she cannot even experience emotional recognition of her benefactress' – the word 'creature' there making me think again of this novel as feeding off (here in a more complicated way) *Frankenstein* (Brooks 1992: 135–36).

I'd add to Brooks and Connor that Pip's absence from his own desire for Estella, its sense of belonging elsewhere, may have a textual source in it literally being at least partly derived from the Cathy/Heathcliff love in *Wuthering Heights*, many close verbal echoes of which emerge in Pip's speeches to Estella – just as, more generally, the painful family situation of the child Pip seems to draw on that suffered by the child Jane Eyre, as Dickens's Orlick (sort of acting out Pip's rage) is perhaps rather unconvincingly drawn from Bertha (who acts out Jane's). Pip's love can seem as artificially felt as it is artificially constructed, though I'd be keen to add that artificially created love can easily be as wounding as any other, if not more so. Below we'll look at the low-energy treatment of Pip's male–male rivalry with Drummle compared to the incandescent equivalent in *Our Mutual Friend* to which we'll be turning now. With the very possible debts to *Frankenstein* as well – to say nothing of the overt borrowings from *Hamlet* – one is faced with the fact that this most carefully planned of Dickens's novels is his most intertextually dependent.

This is my cue to give more space to Edward Said who wrote brilliantly about the performance of *Hamlet* starring (if that's the word) Wopsle that Pip and Herbert go to see in Chapter 31. This wildly comic account of a travesty of the play accompanied by vociferous audience heckling ('On the question whether 'twas nobler in the mind to suffer, some roared yes, and some no, and some inclining to both opinions said "toss up for it"') leads Said to relate what happens in this scene to what a critic in the deconstruction school, like Jacques Derrida, would say is susceptible to all texts and all readings of texts.

> Shakespeare's play, its text, is there offstage, and what happens onstage is a result of the text's imperfect or insufficient power to command this particular performance … [Dickens's] narrative somehow manages to portray *Hamlet* and *Hamlet*-travestied, together, not so much only as montage but as criticism, opening the venerated masterpiece to its own vulnerability … [and its] unprotected consequence, which is that each time it is performed the performance is a substitute for the original, and so on to infinity … The text commands and indeed permits, invents, all its misinterpretations and misreadings, which are functions of the text.
>
> (Said 1983: 198–99)

More than any other Dickens novel, *Our Mutual Friend* – his last complete novel – demonstrates with peculiar clarity René Girard's ideas about desire and identification that we met in Chapter 1. While common sense would suggest that desire leads to identification Girard argued the opposite: that identification precedes desire, that we identify with another's desire before desiring and that the most urgent trigger for such desire is identification with a rival's desire when the desired object is the third party, marking out a triangulation of psychic energy. Tracing this back to primitive cultures he argued further that male–male relations underpin the commodification and exchange of a woman, a counter in the economy of the culture.

Building brilliantly on such ideas, Eve Sedgwick's 1985 book *Between Men* was a breakthrough study of a range of texts and showed how, even (especially) in novels of apparently normative heterosexual relations, it is actually the relations between men (which she calls homosocial and that she shows can take a variety of expressions on a spectrum of feelings) that form the inner narrative that propels the plot. Nowhere in Dickens is this clearer than in the triangulated story of Bradley Headstone, Lizzie Hexam and Eugene Wrayburn, in which the Headstone/Wrayburn relations are acutely explored and felt. (That Dickens emotionally, and partly guiltily, saw parts of himself in both men only intensifies the analysis.) At the same time another pair of homosocial male–male bondings, with again Lizzie at the centre, are played out, more obviously homoerotic though also less intensely energized, between Headstone and Lizzie's brother Charley (twice Headstone physically grips the boy in very odd non-embraces), and between Eugene and his close friend Mortimer Lightwood (who airily say they love each other). In all three cases issues of education are richly entangled in the mix of difficult feelings and energies. For me, as for many others, Bradley Headstone is the single most disturbingly realized characterization in Dickens, drawing (as suggested above) on some guilty and deeply buried feelings on Dickens's part.

Sedgwick notes that the importance of dust, rubbish and (by extension) excrement, and their relations with capital, has been obvious to most critics of the novel but, she adds, at the expense of not noticing the importance of anality. She explores another doubling in the plot as well as the Headstone/Wrayburn doubling, and that is the doubling between Headstone and the man who becomes his nemesis, Rogue Riderhood. Both doublings culminate in violently murderous attacks that Sedgwick reads as anal rape. Here she is.

> Sphincter domination is Bradley Headstone's only mode of grappling for the power that is continually flowing away from him … It only succeeds in grappling more closely to him men who have already been drawn into a fascinated mirroring relation to him … His initial, hating terror of Lizzie was a terror of, as he kept putting it, being 'drawn' from himself, having his accumulated value sucked from him down the great void of her illiteracy and powerlessness. … He is [the] man who, fearing to entrust his relations with patriarchy to a powerless counter, a woman, can himself only be used as a woman, and valued as a woman, by the men with whom he comes into narcissistic relation.
>
> (Sedgwick 1985: 169–70)

Compared to the forcefield generated by the Headstone/Wrayburn doubling (to say nothing of its culmination), the more typical male–male rivalry of, say, the Pip/Drummle relations in *Great Expectations* seems very low-powered. In a strong account of both these novels Brian Cheadle puts it very well.

> The aggressive 'maleness' which feeds off libidinal energy is fettered: Pip and Drummle are allowed to lock themselves in their later combat for Estella only by squaring up in straining immobility for the direct warmth of the fire, like a pair of sumo hearth-dogs.
>
> (In Jordan ed. 2001: 81)

Cheadle shows how much more potent in the novel's unconscious is the anxiety thrown up by the Magwitch story, particularly at the end of the novel's first part where (to stay with the idea of male–male violence) Magwitch attacks Compeyson before he's recaptured and rowed out to be transported to the colonies (the novel thus preparing to expiate the Victorian colonial guilt in Magwitch's 'success').

> The import is all the more intense in that the climax of the hunt, Magwitch grappling with Compeyson in a grotesque version of a ruffianly assault on a gentleman, taps into the primal bourgeois fears of lower-class violence and of losing class. The plot pivots on the expunging of Magwitch … [and] a brutal suppression of the 'low'.
>
> (78)

This central Victorian pre-occupation to suppress the low also contains its opposite, what Cheadle calls the 'hankering for the low', and this emerges with worrying clarity in Jaggers's bodily control of his housekeeper Molly, Magwitch's wife and Estella's mother. I'd add that Molly is, and she seemingly has to be, 'tamed' (as is Mrs Joe by Orlick), in line with what is clearly Dickens's constitutional fear of strong or unclassifiable women – like Miss Wade in *Little Dorritt* and Rosa Dartle in *David Copperfield.* Cheadle says this.

> Molly [is] the murderess whom Jaggers forces into domestic dutifulness in a weird parody of the angel in the house. Jaggers's obsessive disciplining of her has an intense erotic charge. With equal measures of sadism and an epicure's delight in a prize specimen he displays the power of the arm with which she had strangled a rival.
>
> (83–84)

Typical of Cheadle's understanding of the way Dickens intuitively explores these undercurrents of suppression, control and aggressiveness in libidinal energies is his reading of Eugene Wrayburn's suppressed motives in relation to the Lizzie/Headstone triangulation, which we can add to the passage from Eve Sedgwick we looked at above.

> As his relationship with Lizzie develops, Eugene subliminally channels repressed guilt into a self-destructive impulse, which takes the form of goading Bradley Headstone to murder him … If Eugene discovers an eroticised need to feed off Bradley's unrestrained energies, the impulse is

> yet resolutely deathward, and working against his overt will-to-power over Lizzie.
>
> (89)

Cheadle is right to recognize that one of the most profound insights into Dickens's mind was offered (in the casual way he regularly offered such insights) by John Bayley in 1962 (writing on *Oliver Twist*. Immodestly, I'll just say that I highlighted this quotation from Bayley forty years ago. We met Bayley on Keats in the last chapter).

> No novelist has profited more richly than Dickens from not examining what went on in his own mind. His genius avoids itself like a sleepwalker avoiding an open window … [Unlike] the author being perfectly aware what he is up to, Dickens presents the nightmare of what we are and what we want in its most elemental and undifferentiated form. All unknowing, he does not let us escape from the ignominy of our fascinations, because he does not try to escape from them himself.
>
> (In Price ed. 1967: 83–84)

Perhaps the simplest way of distinguishing between the genius of Dickens and the genius of George Eliot is to say that nobody would ever think of saying that about George Eliot, to whom I now turn for the next chapter.

Works cited

Miriam Allott ed., *Emily Bronte: Wuthering Heights, A Casebook* (Macmillan: 1992)
Nancy Armstrong, *Desire and Domestic Fiction* (Oxford U.P.: 1989)
Nina Baym ed., *Hawthorne: The Scarlet Letter* (Penguin: 2003)
Catherine Belsey, *Critical Practice* (Methuen: 1980)
Peter Brooks, *Reading for the Plot* (Harvard U.P.: 1992)
Steven Connor, *Charles Dickens* (Blackwell: 1985)
Terry Eagleton, *The Eagleton Reader*, ed. Stephen Regan (Blackwell: 1998)
Boris Ford ed., *From Dickens to Hardy* (Penguin: 1958)
René Girard, *Desire, Deceit and the Novel*, trs. Yvonne Freccero (Johns Hopkins U.P.: 1966)
John O. Jordan ed., *The Cambridge Companion to Charles Dickens* (Cambridge U.P.: 2001)
Gabriel Josipovici, *The World and the Book* (Macmillan: 1971)
Harry Levin, *Refractions* (Oxford U.P.: 1966)
Steven Marcus, *The Other Victorians* (Basic Books: 1966)
Dan McCall, *The Silence of Bartleby* (Cornell U.P.: 1989)
J. Hillis Miller intro., *Charles Dickens: Bleak House* (Penguin: 1971)
David Musselwhite, *Partings Welded Together* (Methuen: 1987)
Vladimir Nabokov, *Lectures on Literature* (Harcourt: 1980)
Beth Newman ed., *Charlotte Bronte: Jane Eyre* (Bedford/St. Martin's: 1996)
Leland S. Person ed., *Hawthorne: The Scarlet Letter and Other Writings* (Norton: 2005)
Martin Price ed., *Dickens: A Collection of Critical Essays* (Prentice-Hall: 1967)
David H. Richter ed., *The Critical Tradition* (Bedford/St. Martin's: 2007)

Edward Said, *The World, the Text, and the Critic* (Harvard U.P.: 1983)
Eve Sedgwick, *Between Men* (Columbia U.P.: 1985)
Patsy Stoneman ed., *Wuthering Heights: New Casebooks* (Macmillan: 1993)
Tony Tanner, *Adultery in the Novel* (Johns Hopkins U.P.: 2019) [originally published 1979]
Virginia Woolf, *A Room of One's Own* (Hogarth Press: 1929)

7 Realism towards modernism

English and American fiction 1870–1900

George Eliot, Henry James, Oscar Wilde, Herman Melville, Joseph Conrad

In 1980, the novelist A.S. Byatt celebrated **George Eliot** in a powerful introduction to *Middlemarch*. This seems a good place to start.

> I was in my late twenties when I began teaching *Middlemarch*, and I taught it with passion because I perceived it was about the growth, use and inevitable failure and frustration of all human energy … George Eliot was, I suppose, the great English novelist of ideas … She took human thought, as well as human passion, as her proper subject – *ideas*, such as thoughts on 'progress', on the nature of 'culture', on the growth and decay of society and societies, are as much actors in her work as the men and women who contemplate the ideas, partially understand them or unknowingly exhibit them … She had no real heir as 'novelist of ideas' in England: Lawrence's 'ideas' are comparatively simple and strident, Forster's timid, and less comprehensive and forceful than hers. Her heirs were abroad – Proust in France, Mann in Germany … She was European, not little English, her roots were Dante, Shakespeare, Goethe, Balzac, not just, as Leavis's Great Tradition implies, Jane Austen … And I, as a woman writer, am grateful that she stands there … She made a world, in which intellect and passion, day-to-day cares and movements of whole societies cohere and disintegrate. She offered us scope, not certainties.
>
> (Intro. Byatt 1980: online ed.)

A dozen or so years before Byatt, Mark Schorer examined the structure of *Middlemarch*, finding the interplay between the world of ideals and the world of facts.

> Over and over, George Eliot reminds us of what she calls the 'entanglements' of human action: 'anyone watching keenly the stealthy convergence of human lots, sees a slow preparation of effects from one life to another, which tells like a calculated irony on the indifference or the frozen stare which we look at our unintroduced neighbour' [Ch. 11] … It is through the great

DOI: 10.4324/9781003127567-8

> scenes of the book … where 'choice' and 'circumstance', or, if you wish, idealism and fact, love and money – where these become 'enmeshed', where the plot gradually closes down on the characters, that the book derives its real movement and life. At the same time, there is a larger, different kind of movement … an opening and closing, *serial* movement, from social idealism to social fact – the breadth of aspiration versus the breadth of the community; a widening scene and tempered values.
>
> (In Hardy ed. 2013: 14–15)

When the 19-year-old Dorothea is on her honeymoon in Rome, just married to Casaubon in his mid-forties, she's found by Ladislaw weeping with despair at her complete isolation from her new husband who reads all day, every day at the Vatican. Ladislaw is 'struck mute for a few moments' and the narrator adds that he feels inclined to laugh at his older cousin as 'a bat of erudition' (Ch. 21). Rosemary Ashton, the leading George Eliot critic and scholar, explains the odd phrase as one that Eliot would have found in an early number of the medical journal *The Lancet* (attacking the enemies of medical reformers like the novel's Lydgate) and adds that the novel, so characteristically of Eliot at her best, 'gets us to look at the world from Casaubon's point of view'. This article, appropriately, is in a recent number of *The Lancet.*

> When describing the Casaubons' return from Rome, the narrator deliberately – and strikingly – corrects her own perspective: 'One morning, some weeks after her arrival at Lowick, Dorothea – but why always Dorothea? Was her point of view the only possible one with regard to this marriage?' Though her authorial fellow-feeling remains largely with Dorothea, Eliot insists that we accept our connection with her dejected husband. 'He had an intense consciousness within him, and was spiritually a-hungered like the rest of us' [Ch. 29] … Like Charlotte Bronte's Jane Eyre, the young women in Eliot's novels protest at their restricted possibilities in life … However, Eliot also engages the reader's imagination and sympathy for the men who are often partly responsible for women's limited lives.
>
> (Ashton 2019: 1799)

Peggy Johnstone, in a systematic 1994 psychoanalytic analysis of Eliot's novels, sees both Dorothea and Rosamond as arrested in development, Dorothea in what Eliot calls her 'childlike ideas about marriage', which involve wanting a husband as 'a sort of father' (Ch. 1), suggesting not just avoidance of her own adult sexuality but delayed sexual development. This is perhaps symbolized in Dorothea's indifference to her share of her mother's jewels. When she learns that Sir James Cheetham is in love with her, Eliot says 'her revulsion was so strong and painful … She thought with disgust about it' (Ch. 4), which to many readers will sound like a premonition of ideas associated much more elaborately with Gwendolen in *Daniel Deronda,* about which more below.

Behind this sense of arrested development is, according to Johnstone, a stifled, fearful and even murderous anger, as suggested when – at the nadir of her failed marriage with Casaubon and just before his death – it's said that, after a long struggle with her conscience between her duty to herself and to him, she decided 'she could not smite the stricken soul that entreated hers' (Ch. 48). This is itself a variation on the wonderfully interiorized examination of how Harriet Bulstrode, knowing the truth about how her husband caused the death of the blackmailing Raffles, decides her duty is to stay and support him.

Johnstone finds stronger evidence of 'failed development', and of rage, in Eliot's equivalently searching analysis of Rosamond, parentally over-indulged (like Gwendolen), an 'infantine' woman who actually rather dislikes men, with her preening self-regard and need for control suggesting 'pathological narcissism' (again, in a less detailed presentation than with Gwendolen) and feeding off the vulnerability of Lydgate in a relationship in which they both 'serve as extensions of one another's fantasies'. Johnstone says this.

> Eliot's portrayal of Rosamond suggests that her need to dominate Lydgate is the result of her own incomplete self-development. Prepared by her upbringing and education to expect self-completion through marriage ... [she] feels humiliated by her husband's financial difficulties ... The narcissistic rage that follows from her own sense of inadequacy, then, is at the root of her brutality towards Lydgate.
>
> (Johnstone 1994: 138–41)

That Gwendolen Harleth, in *Daniel Deronda*, lends herself to the kind of diagnosed narcissism as outlined by Johnstone in her book, is unsurprising, given the moment early in the novel when she is seen kissing her reflection in a mirror. But seeing Gwendolen as narcissistic has been given a quite new and much enriched grounding in what has become an important article on Gwendolen and her psychological history, as can be reconstructed from subtly placed hints in the narrative. This is the 2007 article by Margaret Reimer, 'The Spoiled Child: What Happened to Gwendolen Harleth', the first phrase of which is of course Eliot's title for the opening book of the novel.

Eliot's portrayal of Gwendolen has long been considered one of the most profound achievements of the Victorian novel and I devote space to it here in accordance with that.

Gwendolen is the 'spoiled child' in more than the usual sense. What Reimer insists on, and in a detailed reading finds evidence for, is that Gwendolen was sexually abused in childhood – spoilt – by her stepfather Captain Davilow, whom Eliot calls 'the unlovable step-father whom she had been acquainted with the greater part of her life while her frocks were short' (Ch. 3) and that as a result 'her sexuality lies frozen within her' (Reimer 2007: 37). As she says herself to her mother: 'I shall never love anybody. I can't love people ... I can't bear anyone to be very near me but you' (Ch. 7). A very revealing moment is when, back in England from Leubronn, Eliot says that for Gwendolen 'men were hateful. Yes, men were hateful. Those few words were filled out with very vivid memories' (Ch. 21).

It is a sign of Reimer's argument being admitted to the mainstream of Eliot criticism that in K.M. Newton's Introduction to the 2014 Oxford World's Classics edition her article is referenced under a comment saying that Gwendolen 'may have suffered sexual abuse as a child', a comment coming shortly after her strangling of her sister's canary is judged as suggesting 'childhood trauma' (intro. Newton 2014: ix–xi).

I'll turn to Reimer in her own words shortly but will just say now that much of the evidence (for instance, Gwendolen's pathological responses to any overt or even suggested sign of physical approaches by men, or her fear of sleeping alone) only really finds its point and clarity in retrospect, especially from where we would expect Gwendolen to be at her most unintentionally revealing, in her distraught confessional monologue to Deronda at Genoa, after Grandcourt drowns. Eliot would be a lesser novelist if the 'clues' had been of equal weight and transparency, or available simply through a linear passage through the book, and the reader's experience would also have been the less intense and rewarding. She knows what narrative theorists know, that as we read on we are also reading (if not literally turning back the pages) retroactively and retrospectively.

Let's turn to Reimer's account, sampled here in summary.

> [Gwendolen's] experience of incest at the hands of her stepfather … reverberates in the numerous allusions to the 'spoiled child' and the 'little white bed' … the virginal childhood refuge that was supposed to keep [her] safe … and arranged 'when possible … in her mamma's room' [Ch. 3] … It culminates in her violent fit of hysteria on her wedding night when she is overwhelmed by 'the insistent penetration of suppressed experience, mixing the expectation of a triumph with the dread of a crisis' [Ch. 31] … An obvious sign of Gwendolen's early sexual abuse is her violent reaction to a man's touch, even from gentle Rex … With Rex's advances Gwendolen suddenly becomes aware of how repelled she is by any sign of physical love-making. 'But now the life of passion had begun negatively in her' states the text suggestively [Ch. 7] … Eliot's choice of vocabulary bristles with suggestions of victimisation and abuse: Gwendolen is … convinced that 'people have come near me only to blight me' [Ch. 21]; she vows 'not to let people interfere with me anymore as they have done' [Ch. 3] … Her mother 'had always been in an apologetic state of mind for the evils brought on her by a stepfather' [Ch. 3].
>
> (Reimer 2007: 33–50)

In Chapter 56, at Genoa after the drowning and under the burden of feeling guilty for it, Gwendolen, speaking to Deronda with 'low-toned eagerness', says this about the start of the fatal boat trip.

> And then we got away – out of the port – into the deep – and everything was still – and we never looked at each other, only he spoke to order me – and the very light about me seemed to hold me a prisoner and force me to sit as I did. It came over me that when I was a child I used to fancy sailing away into a world where people were not forced to live with any one they did not like – I did not like my father-in-law to come home. And now, I thought, just the opposite had come to me. I had stepped into a boat, and my life was a sailing and sailing away – gliding on and no help – always into solitude with *him*, away from deliverance.

A few seconds later, speaking 'more hurriedly, and in more of a whisper', Gwendolen recounts the drowning itself, after she fails to throw the rope to Grandcourt: 'I was leaping away from myself – I would have saved him then. I was leaping from my crime, and there it was – close to me as I fell – there was the dead face – dead, dead.'

The conflation of husband and the figure she calls 'father-in-law' is a conflation subtly underlined by the italicized '*him*', as if the 'solitude' (paradoxically it's a solitude because of her being with him) and impossibility of 'deliverance' from it attach to both men. The dead face of Grandcourt in the water evokes the dead face and the figure fleeing from it in the locked cabinet that appalled her and induced hysteria much earlier in the novel, that earlier pictured dead face being easy to identify with her stepfather's. These doublings have been much commented on though I can't find any comment as to why Gwendolen calls her stepfather her father-in-law. Presumably the two terms were less sharply distinguished than now but 'father-in-law', in grotesquely superimposing stepfather with husband's father, allows for the idea that in Gwendolen's psyche her stepfather was in effect the precursor of, as if the symbolic father of Grandcourt.

The memory of dreading her stepfather coming home surfaces precisely where it does as she feels the exact equivalence on the boat as a 'prisoner' forced to 'sit as I did' which in turn allows us to read Davilow's abuse, in which he forced the child to sit – or lie – where he ordered her to, as equivalent to what can be easily imagined as the sadistic sexual abuse, in effect rape, exacted in their marriage by Grandcourt and enjoyed by him yet more in his knowledge of her fear of resisting him. The two abuses act as codes to read each other (as I'll argue about Mira Lapidoth's narrative). And in 'leaping away from myself' she is the figure fleeing from the dead face (in the cabinet) at the same time as forced to return to it as Grandcourt in the sea.

The abuse that has formed as well as scarred Gwendolen is later and distressingly paralleled in her sexual degradation at Grandcourt's hands. As Newton says about this nexus of ideas: 'though Eliot was always a psychological novelist … the classic Victorian novel is moving into new territory' (Newton 2014: ix). I'd add that it's as if she's taking some of the more lurid tropes of the gothic (incest, varieties of abuse and cruelty) and recuperating them in the cause of a realism that anticipates psychoanalysis.

I want to move briefly to another way of authenticating the case for the incestuous abuse being the dark thread of the novel and that means moving to larger matters of form. It is perhaps the most brilliant aspect of the novel that the abuse of Gwendolen as a child is both absent from the surface of the text in literal form but made present by being realized overtly but elsewhere, analogically or as if in displaced form. I mean that the unnarrated 'secret' of the abuse of Gwendolen by her stepfather is narrated as another story, as literal narration, in the form of Mira Lapidoth's story (in Chapter 20) of how she was abused – differently but equivalently – by her father. The two abusive fathers are also subtly linked in that they both steal and sell precious family jewellery, jewels and sexuality being themselves connected as we saw with Dorothea. Mrs Davilow pointedly says that 'all my best ornaments were taken from me long ago' (Ch. 24).

Mira's story is Gwendolen's story displaced, translated, realized and voiced 'otherwise' – and we know from Genoa that voicing the story of her abuse is precisely what Gwendolen can't do. The story of Mira's abuse is the literal or allowable and narratable version of the story of Gwendolen's abuse, Eliot's way of making the latter spectrally visible and readable despite its unreadable invisibility in the 'official' novel. Mira's abuse is both more and less literal than Gwendolen's, more because it undoubtedly happens at the surface of the narrative (her father nearly selling her into prostitution), less because she escapes the actual threatened sexual degradation (unlike Flaubert's Rosanette, in *Sentimental Education*, seven years earlier, whose story of being sold by her mother into abuse might have been a model for Eliot). The story of Mira's abuse brings into a shadowy, as if glimpsed, half-light the abuse Gwendolen suffered as a child, in silence.

And as Gwendolen hears from Daniel the news of his impending marriage to Mira, she needs the clasp of his hands in order 'to dispel a horrible vision': and she submits 'like a half-soothed child, making an effort to speak, which was hindered by struggling sobs', evoking (at last almost explicitly) the mother at the little white bed ministering to the benightmared and abused child (Ch. 69). What Eliot does with the usual techniques and conventions of revelation and discovery within narrative in these two related ways of telling by not telling the story of Gwendolen's abuse is very radical.

A larger issue of form in the novel is, of course, the more overtly doubled stories of Gwendolen and of Deronda (notoriously discussed by F.R. Leavis as we'll see shortly). This makes the novel more complex and more innovative than *Middlemarch* where, as Mark Shrorer saw, the entanglements of an enlarged community is, though superbly rich in connections and wonderfully realized, a single or unitary world narrated in a correspondingly unitary way. *Daniel Deronda*'s two worlds and two ways of narrating and realizing those worlds – though no less wonderfully rich in connections and entanglements between the two – is a novelistic innovation of startling import. A very helpful way of responding to this is offered by K.M. Newton in his discussion of the roles played by realism and romance in the novel.

> A notable feature of the novel is the greater emphasis on probability rather than fact … Probabilities govern the characters' thinking about their lives and hopes. Both Gwendolen and Deronda, by being particularly conscious of probability, as a result feel they exist in a world that is unpredictable. The shift in thinking about the world and reality, with its emphasis on probabilities rather than 'facts' or likelihood, inevitably leads to the heigh-tening of a sense of instability … *Daniel Deronda* is an implied critique of conventional realism on the grounds that such a conception of realism undermines itself by the restrictions and exclusions that have to be in place to give it credibility, such as rejecting the improbable … Rather than using conventional realism to try to make the improbable believable, in the Jewish part of the novel conventional realism is, to a considerable extent, set aside in a plot that obviously draws on romance and even fairy tale. Much criticism of the Jewish part of the novel has been based on the assumption that there is a mismatch with the canons of conventional rea-lism. But recognising the limitations of these canons and not adhering to them fully does not mean that empiricism is set aside but only that the real is mediated through aspects of the style and some of the devices associated with romance narrative.
>
> (Newton 2014: xxiv–xxv)

What Newton says about criticism of the Jewish part of the novel leads me, inevitably, to F.R. Leavis and his discussion of the novel in his *The Great Tradition* (1948), a book that – like the critical judgements of T.S. Eliot – had an enormous (and not altogether benign) influence at the time and for a considerable period afterwards. This is the book that restricts its 'great tradition' of the novel to Eliot, James and Conrad and (as we saw A.S. Byatt mention above) gestures towards including Austen at one end and Lawrence at the other, consigning Dickens and the Brontes (and many others) to the margins.

Leavis argued that George Eliot was both at her best and her worst in *Daniel Deronda*, the worst being what he (astonishingly) called the astonishing badness of the 'bad' half of the book about Daniel and his Jewishness, and the best being the 'good' half about Gwendolen, which Leavis seriously thought (at least for a time) should be packaged and sold separately as a novel to be called *Gwendolen Harleth*. (In which case, of course, there'd be no Mira story at all.)

Leavis himself was also at his best and his worst in the chapter where he elaborately discusses *Deronda* in comparison to **Henry James**'s *The Portrait of a Lady*. The worst of Leavis (bullying, doctrinaire, insensitive) is about the 'bad' Jewish part of the book. The best of Leavis is his comparative analysis of the novels and his assessment of the superiority of Eliot's novel to James's, though it's true that Leavis overstates the debt James owed to Eliot, in his over-asserted belief that Isabel and Osmond are modelled on Gwendolen and Grandcourt.

Leavis (to paraphrase him here) called James's presentation of Isabel Archer, compared to Eliot's of Gwendolen, partial as well as indulgent, with less spe-cificity and much excluding and simplifying. James is accused of idealizing and

Isabel's peculiar impressiveness is said to be determined by her *not* being thoroughly known. James's lack of explicitness and indirectness is called evasive and equivocal. In his sharpest accusation Leavis says that the evasiveness in *The Portrait* has the effect of partly emptying the novel of its moral substance.

That last charge may be a Leavisite moment too far (one of hundreds) and there may be less urgency than he feels to evaluate so sharply between two great novels and novelists. After all, I'm thinking of the greatest of all dialogue scenes in these novels – scenes which somehow defy the very notion of the novelistic and even the literary: as between Grandcourt and Lydia in *Daniel Deronda*, between Madame Merle and Osmond in *The Portrait* and, perhaps especially, between Dorothea and Rosamond in *Middlemarch*. But many might feel how much more terrifyingly realized and more inwardly felt – and more tactfully mediated – Eliot presents the Gwendolen story compared to James with the Isabel story.

Evasive is the word that might also apply to James's treatment, or rather his avoidance, of the issue of Isabel's dead child and her feelings about that, absent even from her great night-time retrospective analysis of the (otherwise unnarrated) three years of her marriage (Ch. 42), a very celebratedly realized chapter which, I almost hesitate to add, perhaps foregrounds James's brilliance at analysis more than his understanding of Isabel's self-analysis. Millicent Bell put it more sharply in 1991, calling it 'a denial of presentation, a sleight of hand to cover the wide gap ... as memory it is peculiarly unevocative of specific past action' (in Gorra ed. 2018: 603). The effect of Isabel's mind slipping between generalized perceptions allows James to 'own' the chapter at least as much as she owns it, in his presentation of her thoughts mediated by what he thinks as-if on her behalf, or of his thoughts presented as hers.

Leavis's charge of evasiveness comes to a head, again notoriously so, in James's handling of the ending and Isabel's extraordinary decision to return to Italy and what she knows will be a life-sentence of profound unhappiness and almost certain and vindictive abuse with Osmond. She says herself that her return will cause not 'the scene of a moment; it will be a scene of the rest of my life' (Ch. 53). She runs away, almost literally, from the insight that 'she had never been loved before' and the ensuing and frankly sexualized plea from Caspar Goodwood to choose (adulterous) happiness with him instead (Ch. 55). This has, quite rightly, exercised and worried readers and, of course, critics.

James rewrote the ending to remove what he realized was, even by his standards, a situation too opaque, indefinite and unsettled – and in particular too available to be read as Isabel planning to accept Caspar Goodwood and leave her marriage. So that Isabel will return to Rome and that Henrietta Stackpole's reassurance of Caspar is merely 'cheap comfort' is, in the revised ending, clear enough (Ch. 55). Everything else is uncertain.

Does Isabel act from an ethical-moral faith in marriage as sanctified contract, a generalised moral commitment to her words and promises, obedience (if injured obedience) to her husband's word, a conventional belief in what 'good' women can and can't do, from unrecognized psychological and/or sexual issues, with fear of both sex and of loss of control somewhere in the mix? And if fear of sex is meant to be in the mix, the fear may attach itself at least as convincingly to James as to Isabel, as first suggested (I think) by Dorothea Krook in 1962 when she connected James's revulsion towards sexual passion to his feelings about his dead young cousin Minny Temple, feelings that included – in Krook's words – 'a holding back … a refusal to share her suffering … and [his] own imperfect capacity for love' (in Buitenhuis ed. 1968: 105).

Tanner, in *Adultery and the Novel* (and using here Leavis's word 'evasive'), describes Isabel as caught between the 'conceptually magnificent form' of marriage that Osmond had evoked, what Caspar correctly calls the 'ghastly form' of what awaits her back in Rome, and the 'cynicism of forms' (represented by the Countess Gemini) of partners just playing the marriage game for the sake, precisely, of form. (I'd add that the latter, in an innocent form, seems acceptable to James in the form of the elderly Touchetts.)

> Isabel is thus caught in an impossible crisis of forms, which is one reason why the ending seems so ambiguous or mystifying or evasive to many readers. But in running from … Caspar's kiss … Isabel is avoiding … the absolute annihilation of forms that [adultery] would imply for her.
>
> (Tanner 2019: online)

But for me much the best account of the ending, a richly contextualized, subtle and balanced reading, is by Tessa Hadley in 2002. She resists the kind of vindictive or retributive reading based on the notion that James wants Isabel punished, noting pertinently that such a reading didn't occur to the original reviewers. As it happens, Leavis accuses Isabel of 'extremely unintelligent obstinacy' in preferring her vision of Osmond over everyone else's and Hadley adds that Leavis 'seems to think James does not punish Isabel *enough*' (in Gorra ed. 2018: 616). Hadley, instead, contemplating Isabel's dilemma, picks up Tanner's remark that it's the 'tension between law and sympathy which holds the great bourgeois novel together' and she adds this, about the precursor Eliot novels.

> The 'solutions', or resolutions, for Dorothea Casaubon and Gwendolen Grandcourt (and for that matter for Jane Eyre) come from offstage, in the form of convenient demises; but we already know from something in the texture of *The Portrait of a Lady* … that James is pressing the development of the tradition to a new point where that kind of formal manipulation will not answer.
>
> (614)

And of the ending itself Hadley say this, very movingly.

> Isabel, having been plunged dizzyingly under the surface by her discoveries about her husband and by Caspar's kiss, scrambles back out onto the dry

> land of her belief in herself, leaving us with the sensation of an opaque and not entirely fulfilling ending … Isabel has taken the first steps out onto a bridge which as yet only reaches into the air and has no dry land the other side to come down on … James has accurately recorded the inbuilt constraints, the double binds, in a 'good' woman's psychology … but he has not found another voice for his woman yet. She thinks and feels beyond the conventional, but she cannot say or act: he cannot imagine it for her. She does not have a language to override what 'seems right', nor to say yes to that erotic that opens up for her late, and frighteningly.
>
> (626)

Just before Isabel leaves Rome for England she has one last and very painful exchange with Osmond's daughter Pansy. This reaches its most moving moment – for me more moving than anything else in the novel, more than the comparatively melodramatic scene at Ralph's deathbed – when Isabel, her heart beating fast, says to Pansy 'Will you come away with me now?' When they part, they 'held each other a moment in a silent embrace, like two sisters'. This silent picture is enough to express the impossibility (but why should it be impossible?) of these two women finding some novelistic space (in the words that Isabel considers much earlier in the novel) to 'be able to live to' themselves, sisters 'perfectly possible to be happy' without men – in effect outside narrative or at least outside what James is able to narrate. But it's the ten words exchanged between Pansy and Isabel, leading up to the impossible glimpse of them leaving Rome together, that sound the most achingly vacant depths of the Isabel that troubles me more than anything.

> 'You're not happy, Mrs Osmond', said Pansy.
> 'Not very. But it doesn't matter.'
>
> (Ch. 52)

Almost twenty years after the original version of *The Portrait*, and shortly after the brilliant *What Maisie Knew*, James published his deeply worrying short masterpiece *The Turn of the Screw*, like *Maisie* a novel centred on what James clearly knew would be tendentious, children and adult sexuality. In both sharp distinction from and some paralleling with *The Portrait, Turn of the Screw* ends, again notoriously, with one absolutely certain thing, what Shoshana Felman, in an extract from her great long study of the novel, named as 'A Child Is Killed in *The Turn of the Screw*' (more below): Miles's dead body in the governess's grasp. As if definitively the opposite of evasive, that appallingly and obstinately dead child nonetheless leads on, but (like in *The Portrait*) not broached and certainly not answered in the novel, to some very disturbing speculations that may or may not account for that death. The novel just stops (Ch. 24) – 'his little heart, dispossessed, had stopped' (but dispossessed how and of what?) – making no attempt to return to the extraordinarily elaborate framing with which James shaped the novel's opening. So the shock to the readers of the death is duplicated or underpinned by the refusal to satisfy the readerly expectation of framings being set back in place, tidily reversing their establishment at the start.

About the interwoven framings of the opening I'll say this. The way the story is handed on, in its spoken and written forms, is like a neurotic or obsessive process, one marked by muted and incomplete suggestion, half-formed and unspoken desire (between the governess and Douglas, between Douglas and the narrator), and the idea of handing something on in an obscure chain of desire, as something between a love gift and a taint or curse, is also reproduced within the story, indeed at its climax, when we hear of how Miles was asked to leave his school.

The story that reaches us through these mutedly desiring intermediaries may be one in which the governess is embarked (her image is of being at the helm of the boat) on her own illusionary, delusionary, displaced desires and finding them everywhere apart from in her repressed self, but the reader is very challengingly caught up in the same process, trying to create meaning out of a chain of teasingly suggestive signs, and forced, like the governess, in effect to write the story ourselves in order to make it readable – scaring the wits out of ourselves as we do.

This uncanny text has, predictably, attracted some very distinguished critics from the 1930s onwards. (I draw here gratefully on the Norton edition of 1999.) Edmund Wilson, the first to identify the governess rather than actual ghosts as the source of the darkness, said this in 1934.

> *The Turn of the Screw*, then … would be a masterpiece – not as a ghost story, there are a great many better ones of the ordinary kind – but as a study of morbid psychology … It belongs with *Moby Dick* and the *Alice* books to a small group of fairy tales whose symbols exert a peculiar power by reason of the fact that they have behind them, whether or not the authors are aware of it, a profound grasp of subconscious processes.
>
> (In Esch and Warren edd. 1999: 172)

In 1959 Maurice Blanchot noted that, after finding the embryo of the story in an anecdote he was told, James needed an outsider-narrator to activate the plot. Blanchot here, and Todorov in the next extract, move beyond the either/or choice of Wilson to open out on to discussions of narrative's ambivalence in the face of the urge towards elucidation itself – which is where the chapters on the 'realist' novel in this book (this and the previous one) began, in early American 'unreadable' stories by Hawthorne, Poe and Melville.

> The *plot*, this narrator who is the essence of the story, an alien essence admittedly, a presence seeking to penetrate the heart of the story where she is an intruder, an outsider forcing her way in, distorting the mystery, perhaps creating it, perhaps discovering it, but certainly breaking in, destroying it and only revealing the ambiguity which conceals it. … The plot … is quite simply James's talent, the art of stalking a secret … which is

> not only a real secret – some event, thought or fact which might come to light … but something which evades elucidation because it belongs to a realm beyond light.
>
> (188)

And in 1970, Tzvetan Todorov (the crucially influential narrative theorist) identified the stages in what he called 'fantastic' narratives whereby an event proceeding from (what might be) the supernatural provokes a reaction of 'hesitation' and the textualized fantastic. But this can be a problem in texts like James's.

> Nonetheless the text may emphasise the fantastic (ie, the reaction) so strongly that we can no longer distinguish the supernatural which has provoked it: the reaction makes it impossible to grasp the action, instead of leading us back to it … In other words … if the insistence on the perception is too strong, we no longer perceive the object itself … In *Turn of the Screw* … perception constitutes a screen rather than removes one.
>
> (195–96)

Soshana Feldman's lengthy 1977 study of this story is a masterly psychoanalytic analysis of the ways in which an uncanny text seems to offer strategies of mastery at the same time as unmasking such illusionary efforts to master – and Feldman teases out many bewildering facets of the very word 'master' (and mast: at the helm, and the little wooden mast that Flora, meaningfully or not, screws into the toy ship), including the absent-present master of Bly, the governess's employer. Feldman answers, for instance, Edmund Wilson's attempt to master the governess's sexually repressed madness by saying that he fails to see that madness in the novel is uncanny precisely as it 'cannot be situated'. He is bound to fail to 'situate himself outside it'. This is because (Feldman perhaps here developing Todorov) James imposes the governess's point of view on the reader 'as the rhetorical condition of our perception of the story' (233).

Feldman is excerpted in a number of volumes. Here she is (from a different edition of the novel), to end this section, on Miles's death, as mentioned above, at the hands of the governess, in her grasp (mastering him).

> When Miles dies, what is … radically and unredeemably divided is at once the unity of meaning and the unity of its possessor: the governess. The attempt to master meaning … can reach its goal only at the cost … or an irreversible 'separation' … Meaning's *possession* is itself ironically transformed into the radical *dispossession* of its possessor. At its final, climactic point, the attempt at grasping meaning and at closing the reading process with a definitive interpretation in effect discovers – and comprehends – only death … As a reader, the governess plays the role of the detective … Not knowing what the crime really consists of, the governess-detective finally ends up committing it herself … The detective process, or reading process, turns out to be … nothing less than a peculiarly and uncannily

effective weapon. The story of meaning as such (or of consciousness) thus turns out to be the uncanny story of the crime of its own detection.

(In Beidler ed. 1995: 203–05)

If Feldman's analysis suggests that the story in effect parodies the detective story, it's even more obvious that it engages with, perhaps parodically, the gothic with its grandly haunted houses and doubled Others – here with Miss Jessel doubling the governess and Peter Quint the employer – as well as its dark and forbidden desires, clustered in whatever versions of love that impel the governess's actions and inactions.

Nearly all of that would also apply to another sort of haunted, sort of gothic, illicit desire-driven story, **Oscar Wilde**'s *The Picture of Dorian Gray*. Here the gothic formula of the picture itself is used to allow for the text's reticence at naming the gay desire that threads the three male protagonists together, for if Dickens splits himself into Headstone and Wrayburn, Wilde divides himself into Dorian, Lord Henry and Basil. The picture's gothic 'presence' also helps to avoid explicit details about the (obvious but absent) sexual nature of Dorian's activities, on the one hand, in the 'dreadful places' of the East End of London and, on the other, in his apparent but never defined influence, even fatal influence, over young aristocratic men. Joseph Bristow puts it like this, about the 'fatal' friendship with young men that Basil urges Dorian to explain, moments before his murder.

> The cause of such disgrace remains nowhere – and yet everywhere – to be seen. Like the picture … the narrative that enshrines him both conceals and reveals the nature of the 'friendship' that has such fatal effects … Even if the narrative provides an extremely rich repertoire of coded allusions that [figuratively suggest] homoeroticism, at no point does the story make Dorian's desire for other men [or boys] indubitably visible. Indeed, by using a picture to portray the young man's unseen sins, the narrative foregrounds the idea that representations may hide as much as disclose the truth.
>
> (In Raby ed. 1997: 211)

The reticence over gay desire and gay actions is partly a result of the rewriting processes and the editorial changes that can be traced from manuscript to magazine version to the final novel, whereby textual evidence was quietly made less overt and more sexually guarded. For instance, an editor removed reference in the manuscript to Dorian being driven away 'in horror' from the managers of those 'dreadful places' who 'had to be appeased by monstrous bribes'. (See Gillespie ed. 2007: 270. As it happens, I don't think I'm alone in much preferring the far shorter magazine version.)

But the novel, of course, was still available to be used against Wilde in his first court case as evidence of advocating 'unnatural desire'. Edward Carson quoted from the magazine version but oddly failed to quote what Wilde later cut out, Basil saying to Dorian that 'somehow I had never loved a woman' (250). What Carson might also have added (if he'd been a more alert reader) was the way the novel covertly supports its coded homoeroticism in its treatment of women which is, in the case of Sibyl Vane, crudely and patronizingly manipulative and, in the case of Lord Henry's wife, downright cruel. In effect, the novel dispenses with women while ostensibly including them. Melville's 'Bartleby' pointedly excludes women.

That is my cue to turn to Eve Sedgwick, whom we met in relation to Dickens's *Our Mutual Friend*. This is from her *Epistemology of the Closet* (1990). She explains that, planning her new book, she tried to settle on a representative text for her ensuing argument and found herself 'circling round a text of 1891'.

> [This text] has provided a durable and potent physical icon for gay male desire. It tells the story of a young Englishman famous for an extreme beauty ... If the gorgeous youth gives his name to the book and stamps his bodily image on it, the narrative is nonetheless more properly the story of a male triangle: a second, older man is tortured by a desire for the youth for which he can find no direct mode of expression, and a third man, emblem of suavity and the world, presides over the dispensation of discursive authority as the beautiful youth murders the tortured lover and is himself, in turn, by the novel's end ritually killed.
>
> But maybe, I thought, one such text would offer an insufficient basis for cultural hypothesis. Might I pick two? It isn't yet commonplace to read *Dorian Gray* and *Billy Budd* by one another's light, but that can only be a testimony to the power of accepted English and American literary canons to insulate and deform the reading of politically important texts.
>
> (Sedgwick 1990: 48–49)

That is a wonderful moment of modern (comparative) criticism and Sedgwick goes on to show how in 'the deftly magisterial recounting that finally frames, preserves, exploits, and de-sublimates the male bodily image: *Dorian Gray* and *Billy Budd* are both that book', how 1891 is crucial to the discourses of modern sexuality, 'in medicine and psychiatry, in language and law, in the crisis of female status, in the career of imperialism', and how the way the traditional academy teaches these two canonized texts 'comes so close to disciplining the reading permitted of each that even [their] contemporaneity ... may startle'. In relation to that point about teaching, Sedgwick later in her book tells of how she once taught *Dorian Gray* to undergraduates, more than half of whom had met it in classes before.

> But not one had ever discussed the book in term of any homosexual content: all of them knew it could be explained in terms of either the Theme of the Double – 'The Divided Self' – or else the Problem of Mimesis – 'Life and Art'
>
> (161)

Her own reading of *Dorian Gray* may be sampled here to develop from what I said earlier about the picture displacing the triangular desire between the three men.

> The plot of the novel facilitates the translation back and forth between 'men's desire for men' and ... 'narcissism'. The novel takes a plot that is ... the competition between Basil and Lord Henry for Dorian's love, and condenses it into the plot of the mysterious bond of figural likeness and figural expiation between Dorian and his own portrait.
>
> (160)

Billy Budd, **Herman Melville'**s last and for many readers (including Thomas Mann whose *Death in Venice* has many parallels) his most perfected achievement, is, like his earlier 'Bartleby' (which we met in the last chapter), a woman-free zone but there is an unspoken femininity that haunts the text as an absent presence that hovers between the three protagonists – in effect, queering them. Billy's feminine beauty is unmanning for both the brute masculinity of Claggart and the patriarchal and paternal authority of Vere, who loves Billy in no less a repressed way than does Claggart. (The lawyer was unmanned by Bartleby.) Sedgwick puts the distinction between Claggart's and Vere's desire for Billy like this, after (to paraphrase) arguing that Vere desires Billy as displayed object (until literally closeted with him to pass on his death sentence, in a scene ritually excluded from the realm of narrative itself, let alone from display), while Claggart wants to provoke him as subject-in-action (in effect, to be raped by Billy).

> Vere's supposedly impartial motivations towards Billy ... are founded on a Claggart-like partiality as against which, however, they as well are imperiously counterposed ... Claggart's impotent constricted desire gnawing at his own viscera, Vere's potent systemic desire outspread through all the veins and fault lines of naval regulation.
>
> (109)

Billy's threat is one that might feminize the law of force and the force of law, dissolving their rigidities, even democratizing them in a time of French revolutionary war. Of course, mutinous political sympathies are part of the fictions in the charge sheet that need to be mobilised against Billy's unerring, uncanny beauty, its eloquent unmanly refusal (as Bartleby's was) to signify according to the conventions of power and gender – and language. In that sense, Bill's 'flaw', his stutter, takes us back to Hawthorne's 'The Birthmark' which, very remarkably, is explicitly evoked early in the novel when Melville compares the stutter to the 'blemish' on the cheek of 'the beautiful woman in one of Hawthorne's minor tales' (Ch. 2). Billy's flaw is Georgiana's flaw, feminized and unmanning sexuality. They threaten the vulnerabilities of masculinity and must be expunged, from the body and from the body politic.

I would connect this to the way the text, even more so than 'Bartleby', finds it so difficult to end, to come to the kind of traditional (male) satisfaction of fulfilled closure. In a celebrated and challenging deconstructive reading Barbara Johnson, in her 1980 book *The Critical Difference*, elaborates on the multiple endings. Critics agree that the short novel is Melville's 'last word', as if his 'will' of final intentions, conferring an intelligible disposition of literary property, but the text's proliferation of endings undermines that process.

The story, says Melville, 'properly' ends with Billy's death, at which, as many critics have noted, an extraordinary transference or mobility of erect and orgasmic bodies occur between Billy and Vere (but pointedly excluding the usual involuntary orgasm of the hanged man), then flowing through the assembled crew. But by adding 'three brief chapters' Melville actually provides four endings: adding to the 'proper' end, the death of Vere in naval battle (with Billy's name mysteriously on his lips); a naval publication where the Budd–Claggart story is (for political reasons) reversed, with Claggart as heroic victim; and an account of what Johnson calls the 'posthumous mythification' of Billy by sailors and the inclusion of a ballad in the form of a monologue spoken by Billy on the eve of his execution.

> Billy Budd's last words, like Melville's own, are thus spoken posthumously – indeed the final line of the story is uttered from the bottom of the sea ... Melville's last words are an affirmation of the necessity of 'ragged edges' ... The story ends by fearlessly fraying its own symmetry ... Far from totalising itself into intentional finality, the story in fact begins to repeat itself – retelling itself first in reverse, and then in verse. The ending not only lacks special authority, it problematizes the very idea of authority ... The sense of Melville's ending is to empty the ending of any privileged control over sense.
>
> (Johnson 1985: 80–81)

Johnson says this, about the crucial judgement exercised by Vere.

> The function of judgment is to convert an ambiguous situation into a decidable one. But it does so by converting a difference *within* (Billy as divided between conscious submission and unconscious hostility, Vere as divided between understanding father and military authority) into a difference *between* (between Claggart and Billy, between Nature and the King, between authority and criminality) ... Melville's story situates *its* critical difference neither within or between, but in *the relation between the two* as the fundamental question of all human politics.
>
> (105–06)

As the unstable centre between Billy and Claggart, Vere has polarized critical opinion, one relevant point about this being that he may be partly modelled on Melville's father-in-law, Lemuel Shaw, who found himself obliged to uphold the cruelty of the Fugitive Slaves Act despite his own well-attested hatred of slavery. Billy, as an impressed possession of the Crown, is in effect a slave and the war conditions operating, as well as fears of mutiny, may be seen to be relevant to Vere's judgement. Here I want to return to Eve Sedgwick who argues sharply that the discourses of mutiny and of homosexuality are coded together.

> Not an alternative to the plot of male-male desire and its prohibition ... the mutiny plot is the form it takes at the (inseparable) level of the collective ... [There is an] ineradicable double entendre between the mutiny question and the homosexuality question.
>
> (Sedgwick 1990: 101–03)

This, as we saw, is what Sedgwick also showed about the picture-plot in *Dorian Gray* taking on the silenced form of the male–male desire plot. I'd add that the discourse of Christian archetypes in *Billy Budd* (obvious at the surface level of the story) is, similarly, another 'allowed' form for the 'disallowed' plot of male–male desire. (And this connects with what I claimed above about Mira's narrative in relation to Gwendolen's 'disallowed' narrative of her child abuse in *Daniel Deronda*.)

In terms of the ambivalences that make up the presentation of Vere, the analogic iconic figure of Nelson is regularly mentioned in the novel but this is also an unstable element in the mix, as Robert Martin – referring to Melville's earlier (and part-autobiographical) *Redburn* – pointed out in 1986. He says that whether Vere measures up to Nelson is irrelevant.

> One would be surprised if it were otherwise: a loss of faith in Nelson is one of the most important of Redburn's deceptions in Liverpool. At the base of the statue of Nelson he sees 'four naked figures in chains' which he could never look at 'without being involuntarily reminded of four African slaves in the market-place'. Nelson is thus identified as a hero of the imperial venture, and that venture is one of the enslavement of the non-white world. Slavery is at the heart of *Billy Budd*.
>
> (In McCall ed. 2002: 365)

This is another cue for me to turn to the last text in these two connected chapters, one first published just a few years after *Gray* and *Budd* in 1902. Here slavery, and more largely race, are not just overtly foregrounded but are treated in a way that has elicited some famously aggressive criticism, as when its author was labelled 'a bloody racist'. Of course, I mean **Joseph Conrad**'s *Heart of Darkness*, a text that more than others in this chapter has best claim to be ushering in the modernist age. You'll also recall that Conrad was the third novelist allowed, with George Eliot and James, into Leavis's great tradition. Here's the novelist Chinua Achebe in 1977, after (rather selectively) quoting from passages about the African natives whom Marlow encounters in the Belgian Congo.

> The point of my observations should be quite clear by now, namely, that Conrad was a bloody racist. That this simple truth is glossed over in criticism of his work is due to the fact that white racism against Africa is such a

> normal way of thinking that its manifestations go completely undetected ... A Conrad student told me in Scotland last year that Africa is merely a setting for the disintegration of the mind of Mr Kurtz. Which is partly the point: Africa as setting and backdrop which eliminates the African as human factor ... The real question is the dehumanisation of Africa and Africans which this age-long attitude has fostered and continues to foster in the world.
>
> (In Richter ed. 2007: 1787)

David Richter relates Achebe's argument here to Edward Said's Orientalism and Toni Morrison's Africanism (more on Morrison in Chapter 9), adding that Morrison sees American literature generally, and its major works, as consciously or otherwise marked by the presence in the free republic of a completely subjected minority population. Achebe, says Richter, is expressing a very understandable bitterness.

> [This is] the bitterness with which the African views the white liberal position on British imperialism, which allowed England to deprive hundreds of millions of darker-skinned men and women of their political and economic freedom so long as that imperial rule was just and humane by European standards.
>
> (Richter 2007: 1766)

But another novelist, Wilson Harris, suggests that Conrad may be doing something more despairing in *Heart of Darkness* than Achebe thinks, writing, says Richter, 'not out of Enlightenment optimism, as Achebe suggested, but out of a profound despair' with how (in Harris's words) the 'sacred human' order may 'shelter the greatest evil'. Richter adds that writers like Harris have actively used Conrad to generate 'a fertile postcolonial literature' while Achebe may feel the need to 'misread' Conrad to create 'a site of resistance from which he can speak' (1766).

Edward Said himself, in a 2005 interview, described the novel like this.

> [It is] a kind of relentlessly open-ended, aggressively critical enquiry into the mechanisms and presuppositions and situatedness and abuses of imperialism ... [that] has obviously compelled many, many other writers to write in its wake.
>
> (In Shiach ed. 2007: 91)

Laura Marcus adds that Said, in the interview, noted that the legacy of the novel includes not only works by Achebe ('he can't stop talking about it, and he can't stop writing about it ... *Things Fall Apart* is unintelligible without it') but also novels like Graham Greene's *The Heart of the Matter* (1948), Ngugi wa Thiong'o's *A Grain of Wheat* (1967) and Tayeb Salih's *Season of Migration to the North* (1970), which Said describes as 'all rewritings of *Heart of Darkness*, in one way or another' (91).

Patrick Brantlinger, in a judicious 1985 response to Achebe and to those who have defended Conrad against him, developed the argument more broadly, rather than on the way the novel, in Achebe's words, 'eliminates the African as human factor'. Brantlinger admits that the voices that come from the 'heart of darkness' are almost exclusively white and male, and he has an apt joke about Kurtz's black mistress doubtless knowing everything, so it's 'unfortunate that Marlow did not ask her for an interview', but he adds crucially about the novel's voices that Kurtz's voice and his eloquence are positioned not as the source of presence and of knowledge, even of the dark knowledge of imperialism, but as a hollow absence.

> As a nearly disembodied 'pure' voice emanating from the very centre of the story, Kurtz is a figure for the novelist … The 'voice' that speaks out of the 'heart of darkness' is a hollow one … Through [his voice] Kurtz 'could get himself to believe anything – anything'. Is Conrad questioning or mocking his own 'voice' … point[ing] towards the production of novels that are hollow at the core … that contain, perhaps, only an abyss, a Kurtz?
>
> (In Murfin ed. 1996: 294)

I'd add that Kurtz's electrifying effect on audiences as an orator makes him akin to a particular kind of novelist, Dickens as an actor. Kurtz's voice is the embodiment of the performative principle, mouth as compulsive performance. He is pointedly described as 'essentially a great musician' (Ch. 3), music (as Walter Pater, whose views are extensively reproduced in *Dorian Gray*, suggested) being the art to which other arts aspire precisely because meaningless.

Brantlinger quotes the notorious scrawled footnote to Kurtz's impeccably liberal pamphlet about suppressing 'savage customs', in which, to use Marlow's words, 'at the end of that moving appeal to every altruistic sentiment it blazed at you … "Exterminate all the brutes!"' (Ch. 2).

> Viewed one way, Conrad's anti-imperialist story condemns the murderous racism of Kurtz's imperative. Viewed another way, Conrad's … story voices that very imperative, and Conrad knows it. At the hollow centre of *Heart of Darkness* … Conrad inscribes a text that, like the novel itself, cancels out its own best intentions.
>
> (295)

If Douglas at the opening of *Turn of the Screw* suggested that the story to be told won't tell about the governess's love in any usual or direct (or vulgar) way, he at least was operating within the conventions whereby truths will be told, or voiced, somehow or somewhere, even if otherwise ('aslant' to use Emily Dickinson's word). And if Vere and Billy's closeted exchange at the silenced heart of *Billy Budd* is in a narratively forbidden space, we're clearly meant to feel that the content of what was spoken matters. What makes Conrad's story a more purely modernist enterprise is that what exactly Kurtz's voice says – to anyone and in any context – literally doesn't matter, is meaningless. And what the novel's voice, or its voices – Kurtz's own, those of the narrators – will 'tell', and voice is, exactly, nothing and of nothing, of failures to narrate and communicate (Marlow's narrative breaks down more than once but not in order to provide illumination but only to gesture at more darkness) or, at best, of the enormous lie at the very end of the novel which, in effect, seeps back into the novel, undoing it.

I turn again to Peter Brooks's great book *Reading for the Plot*. (He uses the word 'taint', which I used about *Turn of the Screw*, in terms both of its own narrative being passed on and Miles's secret passed on to other boys.)

> One finally needs to read *Heart of Darkness* as act of narration even more than as narrative or as story. It shows this act to be far from innocent, indeed as based most of all on the need and the desire to implicate one's listeners in a taint one can't live with alone … Why are you telling me this? the interlocutor may want to ask – but by the time he comes to make such a response, it is already too late: like the Ancient Mariner's Wedding Guest, he has been made to hear … Another characteristic peculiar to late 19th and early 20th century narrative – that which we characterise as modernist – appears to emerge … This is the implication that all stories are in a state of being retold … There seems to be a need for protagonists and storytellers, and particularly protagonists *as* storytellers, to attach their narratives to someone else's, to be ever the belated followers of the track of another … Marlow, thinking to tell us of Kurtz's victory wrested from innumerable defeats, himself wrests a kind of defeat from the postulated victory.
>
> But to state the outcome of *Heart of Darkness* as either victory or defeat is to posit for it a finality which its very form subverts.
>
> (Brooks 1992: 261–62)

Works cited

Rosemary Ashton, 'George Eliot, *Middlemarch*, and The Lancet', *The Lancet* Vol. 394: November 2019.

Peter G. Beidler ed., *Henry James: The Turn of the Screw* (Bedford/St. Martin's: 1995)

Peter Brooks, *Reading for the Plot* (Harvard U.P.: 1992)

Peter Buitenhuis ed., *The Portrait of a Lady: Twentieth Century Interpretations* (Prentice Hall: 1968)

A.S. Byatt intro., *George Eliot: Middlemarch* (Random House: 1980)

Deborah Esch and Jonathan Warren edd., *Henry James: The Turn of the Screw* (Norton: 1999)

Michael Gillespie ed., *Oscar Wilde: The Picture of Dorian Gray* (Norton: 2007)

Michael Gorra ed., *Henry James: The Portrait of a Lady* (Norton: 2018)

Barbara Hardy ed., *Middlemarch: Critical Approaches to the Novel* (Bloomsbury: 2013)

Barbara Johnson, *The Critical Difference* (Johns Hopkins U.P.: 1985) [originally published 1980]

Peggy Johnstone, *The Transformation of Rage* (New York U.P.: 1994)
F.R. Leavis, *The Great Tradition* (Chatto and Windus: 1948)
Dan McCall ed., *Melville's Short Novels* (Norton: 2002)
Ross C. Murfin ed., *Joseph Conrad: Heart of Darkness* (Bedford/St. Martin's: 1996)
K.M. Newton intro., *George Eliot: Daniel Deronda* (Oxford: 2014)
Peter Raby ed., *The Cambridge Companion to Oscar Wilde* (Cambridge U.P.: 1997)
Margaret Loewen Reimer, 'The Spoiled Child: What Happened to Gwendolen Harleth?', *The Cambridge Quarterly* Vol. 36, Issue 1: 2007
David H. Richter ed., *The Critical Tradition* (Bedford/St. Martin's: 2007)
Eve Sedgwick, *Epistemology of the Closet* (California U.P.: 1990)
Morag Shiach ed., *The Cambridge Companion to the Modernist Novel* (Cambridge U.P.: 2007)
Tony Tanner, *Adultery and the Novel* (John Hopkins U.P.: 1979)

8 Modernisms

British, Irish and American literature 1890–1970

Emily Dickinson, Kate Chopin, Charlotte Perkins Gilman, William Carlos Williams, T.S. Eliot, James Joyce, Virginia Woolf, Samuel Beckett, Vladimir Nabokov, Sylvia Plath, Geoffrey Hill, Wallace Stevens

In early January 2020 boxes of letters were ceremoniously opened at Princeton University Library. It was a key moment in modernist history or perhaps, rather, in sexual politics. (I'll offer some thoughts on how to think about the term modernism shortly.) The boxes had been sealed since 1956. They contained more than a thousand letters from T.S. Eliot to Emily Hale. He had fallen in love with her before leaving for England in 1914 and had told her of his love. She didn't reciprocate – then – but came to cherish him later over their nearly thirty years of correspondence and occasional meetings, including the period when Eliot was very unhappily married to Vivienne and, because of his strict faith, when he couldn't bring himself to divorce her and marry Emily, which Emily wanted. But he seems to have, at least, given her strong grounds for hope in the event of Vivienne's death, which, after her confinement to a mental home, happened in 1947.

But Eliot didn't then marry Emily, to her bewilderment. Instead, nearly ten years later, at the age of 68, he married his 30-year-old secretary Valerie. One charitable way of reading this story is that Eliot (a devotee of Dante) was determined to keep Emily as his (mystified) Beatrice.

During the correspondence he had intimated he'd leave her letters to the Bodleain Library at Oxford, to be sealed for 50 or 60 years after their deaths. She left his to Princeton, with the fifty-year condition, and an accompanying note about their relationship. Stung by this news, he burned hers to him (or rather got a colleague to burn them) and wrote a 'Statement' to be opened (at Harvard) at the same time as his letters (at Princeton). Eliot may have feared that leaked letters might have upset his new young wife.

Emily Hale was a modest drama schoolteacher. She says, touchingly and generously, in her note to the letters in March 1957, that she was the confidante of what was pent up in a personality she knew was not only gifted and emotional but also 'groping'; she realized that there were obscurely personal

DOI: 10.4324/9781003127567-9

reasons against Eliot marrying again, reasons that she didn't understand, though she was gratified to think that their friendship perhaps helped to stabilize him. She also knew that she was the emotional source of some of Eliot's most celebrated poems, including 'Burnt Norton', the first of the *Four Quartets*.

Eliot's statement became available to scholars just before they turned to his letters to Emily. These letters were the subject of a long and elegantly written article in the *London Review of Books* by Paul Keegan, I think the first considered critical response, with authorized quotations. (I read this when drafting the current chapter.) Keegan's quotations from the letters make it absolutely clear that Eliot's love was deep, intense, unwavering and very needy. Her letters, and affections, were indispensable to him, as if literal lifelines. (The relationship seems to have been sexually unconsummated, at least in the Bill Clinton sense.) The neediness is quite startling, including his need to reprimand her for aspects of her religious practices. Keegan says this.

> Hale was the listener, and the talking cure was Eliot's own. The surprise is that what was released by her mild listening should be so vehement. His calm manner ... suggests composed fury ... He leaves behind the strangled idiom of devotion and soon becomes ... querulously intent on his own meanings ... These letters ride to hounds over Hale's feelings. He goads and scandalises her, in the hope that she will show another side rather than turn the other cheek.
>
> (Keegan 2020: 10, 12)

Eliot's Statement says (I'll paraphrase here) that marriage with Vivienne produced *The Waste Land* and saved him from a marriage to Emily who would have had the effect of killing him as a poet. Vivienne's death brought the sudden realization that he didn't, after all, love Emily who had already appeared to him as not very interested in poetry (certainly his) and worryingly possessed of a lack of both sensitivity and taste. His letters to her he now saw as those of a man suffering from hallucinations.

Michael Wood told the *New York Times* that the Statement showed Eliot rewriting a story that he feared the letters would tell on their own. Put another way, Eliot is trying to prove that he was never as vulnerable (or vulnerably in love) as the letters say. I find myself reminded of Hamlet's repudiation of Ophelia – 'I never gave you aught ... I loved you not' (3.1). Eliot (as we saw in Chapter 1) famously called that play an artistic failure, lacking the apparently necessary objective correlative. Perhaps there's some over-correlating in the Statement. More on Eliot below.

Let's go (in some relief after that) to three writers, all women and all American, one of whom I'm discussing here because, though writing (most actively) in the 1860s, she was neither read nor even published until the second half of the 20th century, which was also the case with the other two who wrote in the 1890s but were scarcely read until much later. We can think of them as modern, if only as that is how they seem to readers today. In Helen

McNeil's words about the poems of one of them, it 'seems to write itself before our eyes as work of the present' (McNeil ed. 1997: xviii). They are early modernist or (in the first case) proto-modernist writers and, in their various ways and especially in relation to gender, their work is deeply subversive (which connects with work about women by Hawthorne, which we looked at in Chapter 6).

I mean the poems of **Emily Dickinson, Kate Chopin**'s short novel *The Awakening* and **Charlotte Perkins Gilman**'s short story 'The Yellow Wallpaper'. To start our discussion of modernism here is to emphasize that, despite the text-book prominence of men (led and promoted by Ezra Pound, an advocate of a 'tough' masculinity of technique: he cut and shaped Eliot's *The Waste Land* manuscript to make it less tentative, less hesitant and more end-stopped; in effect, more masculine), there's a case to make for some of the most telling aspects of modernist language, style and method to be 'feminine', in the sense as defined by Helene Cixous as *écriture feminine*, a style marked by disruptions and sub-versions of the logical rules of 'male' language and originating in the realm of the pre-linguistic mother–child relationship.

That's one aspect of modernism, its tendency to what is fragmentary rather than whole, disrupted rather than uniform, subversive rather than acquiescent. It posits the author, and more generally authority, as marked more by ignor-ance than knowledge, and uncertainties rather than certainty. Its narratives are intended at least as much to disenchant than to enchant and its allegiances are to what is provisional and contingent (and arbitrary) rather than to the stabilities of 'common knowledge'.

Modernism is routinely distinguished, especially in discussions of the novel, from realism because of their sharply divergent notions of coherence, wholeness, plausibility, dimensionality and hierarchies of discourse. Again routinely, though rather too simply (as we noted with romanticism's time span), it is located in the period roughly between 1890 and 1950 and is associated closely with the wide-ranging effects of the First World War (as romanticism was with the French Revolution). But many critics argue that it is not just a matter of a strict chron-ological demarcation and at least as much a matter of a tension or dialogue between what we now call realist and modernist impulses (or those between enchantment and disenchantment or indeed, as we saw in Chapter 1, between what Roland Barthes called 'readerly' and 'writerly') that has operated within texts and within culture more generally from at least as long ago as the Protestant Reformation. Gabriel Josipovici quite recently wrote a bracing and combative book called *What Ever Happened to Modernism?* (2010) which I strongly recom-mend. In it he quotes the art critic Clement Greenberg. His definition of mod-ernism from the 1950s was very influential, though you'll see he downplays its subversiveness.

> I identify modernism with the intensification, almost the exacerbation, of the self-critical tendency … The essence of modernism lies, as I see it, in the use of the characteristic methods of the discipline to criticise the

discipline itself – not in order to subvert it, but to entrench it more firmly in its area of competence.

(In Josipovici 2010: 179)

Let's return to the three subversive proto-modernist or modernist women writers. Dickinson has more in common with Blake (whom we met in Chapter 4) than with the poets of her own period and in both cases their poetry connects with childhood rhymes, hymns as popularized by pious Victorians (and wickedly parodied in the *Alice* books), riddles and folk poetry, rather than 'high' art. Again in both cases, they started as complete outsiders, unread and isolated from the mainstream but, eventually, came to enlarge and redefine how that poetic mainstream can be understood and read – in the case of Dickinson, whose poems at first glance (the dashes, the lack of titles, and stripped of decorative adjectives and adverbs) seem to break all poetic norms and conventions, in effect redefining what a poem is. The influence, in turn, they exercised over later poets is of a quite different kind of influence than exercised by, say, Wordsworth or Keats over, say, Tennyson. It's more like a spiritual necessity that finds Sylvia Plath openly acknowledging how in thrall she was to Dickinson (more on Plath below).

Helen McNeil (quoted above) is a particularly acute guide to Dickinson, and she sees Dickinson's 'uncanny resemblance' to Blake, tracing it to their 'shared inheritance of radical Protestantism', though where Blake felt impelled to create a wildly alternative mythology Dickinson remains grounded in how our experiences create meanings from internal differences. And that crucially includes differences in ourselves. The 'self', for Dickinson, is always in question, as is her sceptical deployment of the word 'I', the most used word in her poems, says McNeil, after 'a' and 'the', and used 'to avoid the author-reader intimacy of Romanticism … [in] an almost modernist distancing of her speaker'.

When we find ourselves attributing the feelings of an 'I' in a Dickinson poem to a real person, I suspect this is not so much Dickinson herself as ourselves, her readers … The 'I' of Dickinson's emotive poems is the agency not so much of a self as mere agency itself – the force driving the act of the poem, and then driven by the agency it has established … Dickinson knew, however, that in a patriarchal culture a poetics of pure agency had a price: agency for whom?

(McNeil 1997: xxi–xxv)

There's a danger with reading Dickinson to focus on her immediacy of modernity and dislocate her from her own cultural and contextual moment, her being not just in the body but in history. Shira Wolosky addresses this well.

It is as if Dickinson wants both to find a linguistic body for her poetry and yet also not to limit it; just as, in her white dress, she wants both to be in the body and to be bodiless; to be gendered and yet to be genderless; to be

> in the world and yet to be in the spirit ... [These] often painful conflicts ... also broadly reflect her culture. Dickinson's texts are scenes of cultural crossroads, situated within the many and profound transitions taking place around her. These include the changing, indeed the tremendously dynamic, status of women in 19th century America ... and emerging re-definitions of selfhood, both in art and society ... [Dickinson's poems] textually enact a kind of cultural slippage in which a female gender complicates or contradicts assertions of an American or Romantic selfhood ... [and] self-fulfilment contests self-denial.
>
> (In Martin ed. 2002: 137–39)

And Wendy Baker situates Dickinson in even more localized contexts when she reminds us of her household work, her days and hours, her sense of the sun's enervating power – and of Sue, the love of her life.

> The words 'sun' and 'day' are the most frequently used nouns in the poems ... Over and over in her poems, the sun is the antithesis of nurturing ... Perhaps the most extreme example of the poet's fear of the sun's force ... appears in a letter to her dearest friend, Susan Gilbert, about to become the bride of the poet's brother ... [which suggests that] marrying meant becoming dependent upon a husband who, as a 'mighty sun', would ... 'scorch' or 'scathe' his bride with his culturally approved, even culturally decreed, dominance.
>
> (81–82)

There's little doubt that loving Sue was at the emotional centre of Dickinson's life. Sue, I feel sure, is behind the poem that ends 'Parting is all we know of heaven / And all we need of hell'. (Somewhere behind this is Satan in *Paradise Lost* Book 1: 'The mind is its own place and in itself / Can make a heaven of hell, a hell of heaven'.) There's no sign of any guilt or difficulty about it, either in the letters that survive or the poems that suggest, not just lesbian desire and practice, but also a kind of polymorphous sexuality, with her body a hyper-sensitized instrument, imaged in the poems as flowers, jewels, volcanoes. The sea offers 'exultation' and 'divine intoxication' and in another poem it threatens to 'eat me up / As wholly as a dew / Upon a dandelion's sleeve – '.

A crucial stage in Edna's awakening to her body in Chopin's *The Awakening* has her suddenly being able to swim in the sea, with 'a feeling of exultation' and 'intoxicated with her newly conquered power': identical words to Dickinson's (whom Chopin couldn't have read). As with Dickinson's consuming sea, Edna's sea is an image of a female lover, inviting her to 'swim far out, where no woman had swum before', with the water 'meeting and melting' with her 'excited fancy', with Edna 'reaching out for the unlimited in which to lose herself' (Ch. 10).

At the end of an earlier chapter in Chopin's novel, the narrative slips (quite unannounced) into the language of trance-like poetry to say this.

> The voice of the sea is seductive; never ceasing, whispering, clamouring, murmuring, inviting the soul to wander for a spell in abysses of solitude; to lose itself in mazes of inward contemplation.
>
> The voice of the sea speaks to the soul. The touch of the sea is sensuous, enfolding the body in its soft, close embrace.
>
> (Ch. 6)

And that passage is reprised on the novel's last page, when Edna returns to the sea.

In a particularly ecstatic-orgasmic poem Dickinson (I'm sure addressing Sue) longs for the 'luxury' of 'wild nights … with thee', calling that luxury 'rowing in Eden! / Ah! the sea! / Might I but moor / Tonight in thee!' where it's wonderfully unclear if that last 'thee' is the sea or Sue's body. Dickinson's eroticized body is part, though a crucial part, of her strategic transgressiveness, part of her way of refusing the predictable gender and social roles expected of her, intentionally courting the role of the 'myth' of Amherst in order to be her own myth, her own strategic self.

Indeed, everything she did or wrote was strategic or performative – as if anticipating Judith Butler's famous notion of sexuality as performative. She played up to the role of the whimsical and childish woman, a nobody, the smallest in the house, shut up in prose, for whom any poem she happened to write (there are about 1,800 of them) was 'my letter to the world / That never wrote to me', including poems coolly and calmly anatomizing her pain, which has 'no future but itself' and just strengthens over time, 'as sinews do with age'. She understood that it 'might be lonelier' without 'the loneliness' to which she felt 'so accustomed', and that hope might be an intrusion for someone not being 'used to hope'. (Weirdly, that reminds me of Bartleby at the end of Melville's astonishing story, which we looked at in Chapter 6. Offered food in prison, he calmly refuses, saying 'I am unused to dinners'.)

Dickinson's clear-headed and strategic choice to refuse and transgress are richly echoed in Kate Chopin's *The Awakening*. This only returned to print (appropriately in French) in the 1950s, just when Dickinson's poems were at last published in the form in which she left them. And it wasn't until the early 1970s when Gilman's astonishing 'The Yellow Wallpaper' was restored to a wide readership through the Feminist Press. These two texts dramatize young women almost literally struggling to own and express their own bodies against the proprietorial control of men, which we saw Dickinson warning Sue about on the verge of marriage.

Chopin's and Gilman's strategic choices in writing as they did, at the level of form and language, also echo with Dickinson. Gilman's breathless, miniature paragraphs wittily play up to the 'nervous' or 'hysterical' woman as labelled by her husband/doctor who not only medicalizes her but also infantilizes her, like Dickinson playing up to the role of the smallest child, shut up and silenced.

Chopin goes further, openly flaunting not only her very obvious debt to Flaubert's *Madame Bovary* but later 'packaging' the novel with what seem like postmodern and para-textually subversive ways of 'answering back' to the hostile (and misreading) critics that she anticipated. These are her 'Retraction' and two clearly fictitious letters which, taken together, function as deeply ironic commentaries on her own novel's radical notions and representations of female autonomous sexuality (see Jacobs in Aughterson and Philips edd. 2021: 119–22). Her novel, though on the surface following the hetero-normative plot of adultery and the fallen woman (as in Flaubert), is actually about a more literally bodily 'awakening', Edna's to her own sexualized body, 'for the first time' (a repeated phrase, used like a refrain), achieved without men, but an awakening also – and very achingly by the end – to the solitude of being even without desire: 'there was no one thing in the world that she desired' (Ch. 39).

The narrator in 'The Yellow Wallpaper' feels the need to release other (all) trapped women from the imprisoning bars of patriarchal power identified in the wallpaper (Dickinson says 'I tug childish at my bars'), and she ends the story in a bodily demonstration of her own caged imprisonment, tied to the bed, bleeding, and crawling or creeping (probably) naked. The story clearly has an intense muted relationship with the almost silenced story of Bronte's Bertha Mason. But she has also developed agency and autonomy, of a kind, one that allows her, at least symbolically, to pleasure herself and her body in her '*smooch*, as if it had been rubbed over and over' – with the effect of making her husband/doctor faint (as if feminized and un-doctored) at the sight. The hysteria he diagnosed in her is actually his. As Mary Jacobus and others have argued (Jacobus 1986: 229–48), the paper's colour, shape and smell evoke the female body as seen, imagined and feared by men. She has internalized male-hysterical fear of her own body and then enacts (in defiance and triumph – of a kind) the ultimate male terror of the sexually self-satisfying woman, without a man, or in this case stepping over him.

Here it may be useful to bring Dickinson, Chopin and Gilman together through Bonnie Zimmerman's 1992 discussion of the 'metaphorical lesbian'.

> The lesbian-as-sign … is a disruptor of heterosexuality … a hole in the fabric of gender dualism. She cannot be contained within these institutions; she exposes their gaps and contradictions; she signifies a radical absence. Her desire functions as excess within the heterosexual economy … She also creates a narrative or textual space in which she interrogates accepted norms of textuality and sexuality, and constitutes herself as subject.
>
> (In Walker ed. 2000: 238)

All three of these subversive women writers enact this process of re-constituting the objectified figure trapped in heteronormative subservience, defined as culturally subsidiary, into a newly empowered subjectivity and agency. They do so through the body, which for all three becomes the source of a sexuality that is no longer defined as uni-dimensional but in effect everywhere. What Luce Irigaray wrote in 1985 about woman, sex and language is powerfully relevant here.

> She finds pleasure almost anywhere … The geography of her pleasure is far more diversified, more multiple in its differences, more complex, more subtle than is imagined – in an imaginary system rather too focussed on sameness. 'She' is definitely 'other' in herself … Hers are contradictory words, somewhat mad from the standpoint of reason, inaudible for whoever listens to them with ready-made grids, with a fully elaborated code in hand. For in what she says too – at least when she dares to speak out – woman retouches herself constantly. She steps ever so slightly away from herself with a murmur, an exclamation, a whisper, a sentence left unfinished.
>
> (Irigaray 1985: 28–29)

We saw above Kate Chopin on the voice of the sea, 'whispering, clamouring, murmuring'.

We could now approach the 'high' modernist period of the 1920s with its iconic male figures like T.S. Eliot and James Joyce by one of two routes. One would connect Dickinson to the American modernist poet **William Carlos Williams**, who was determined to create a defiantly and localized (New Jersey) American modernist poetry and who is in sharpest distinction from his much more celebrated contemporary and ex-compatriot Eliot, who turned his back on America in favour of a European culture (to join what he called the mind of Europe), with new roots in a kind of mystified, royalist and high Anglican classicism. Williams called *The Waste Land* 'the great catastrophe to our letters … Our work staggered to a halt … under the blast of Eliot's genius which gave the poem back to the academics' (in Kermode 1989: 97). Or we could connect the proto-modernist women we've just looked at with Virginia Woolf and her wonderful *A Room of One's Own* (1929) which we looked at in relation to Charlotte Bronte in Chapter 6, and which is as much a novel as an essay.

A compromise would be to notice, as Charles Tomlinson (himself a fine poet) has noticed, the tendency in Williams's best early poems (his first book came out in 1917, the year of Eliot's landmark *Prufrock* volume) to locate language in the motions of the body, which is characteristic of the three women above. Here's Tomlinson on Williams (in his fine edition of 1976). Williams's war cry was 'no idea but in things'.

> In the imaginative play of Williams's poems, where the attention is frequently turned upon outward things, the sound-structure of the poems which embody that attention is an expression of strains, breath pauses, bodily constrictions and releases. Thus Williams's 'locality' begins with a somatic awareness, a physiological presence in time and space … [There's also a] predilection for the open-ended and assymetrical [which] leaves Williams free to accept the suggestion of his surroundings with their evidence of overlap and relativity … [This is expressed in] a form fully responsive to the waywardness and inconclusiveness of daily realities … Williams hears in all this, and in the profusion of natural fact, a kind of music – 'a vague melody / of harsh threads', as he says in 'Trees' [1917].
>
> (In Tomlinson ed. 1976: 12–13)

Tomlinson quotes Kenneth Roxroth who argues that Williams's poems show allegiances with Cubism (I've long thought the same about Dickinson), rather than the associative or free verse of an Eliot. (Williams always denied he practised free verse.) A 'melody of harsh threads' is a nice instance of what Roxroth calls here 'dissociation' and 'rearrangement'. About the poem 'Trees' Tomlinson, equivalently, says it offers 'no romantic fusion of subject and object' (13).

> Williams could be said to belong to the Cubist tradition … the dissociation and rearrangement of the elements of concrete reality, rather than rhetoric or free association … Williams has confined himself in a single strictness to the life before his eyes … [in] his long quest for a completely defenceless simplicity of personal speech.
>
> (15)

Williams's most famous poem is from 1923 and is his shortest, conventionally known as 'The Red Wheelbarrow' but originally untitled, starting 'So much depends' (and widely available online).

There could be so much to say about this miraculous poem, or precious object. For me I'm drawn to the fact that there's only one word – 'glazed' – that has to be figurative among all the other defencelessly literal signifiers. Hugh Kenner said this in 1975. (He quotes the great American poet Wallace Stevens, to whom I'll return in this chapter.)

> Not what the poet says, insisted Williams: what he makes … 'Mobile-like arrangement', said Wallace Stevens. Yes. The lines, the words, dangle in equidependency, attracting the attention, isolating it, so that the sentence in which they are arrayed comes to seem like a suspension system. This was one thing Williams meant by 'making' not 'saying'. Yet you do say, you do go through the motions of saying. But art lifts the saying out of the zone of things said … [into] a zone remote from the world of sayers and sayings. / That zone is what Williams in the 1920s started calling 'the imagination'.
>
> (Kenner 1975: 59–60)

Tomlinson says this.

> What depends on the red wheelbarrow for Williams is the fact that its presence can be rendered over into words, that the perception can be slowed down and meditated on by regulating, line by line, the gradual appearance of these words. The imagination accurately accompanies the wheelbarrow, or whatever facets of reality attract Williams, by not permitting too ready and emotional a fusion with them.
>
> (In Tomlinson ed. 1976: 17)

Chapter 2 of Woolf's *A Room of One's Own* tells a lovely story of how Woolf went to the British Library to try and find out what (male) scholars have thought about women. Scribbling down material furiously, she found herself with one page of notes headed 'women and poverty' which looked like this.

> Condition in Middle Ages of,
> Habits in the Fiji islands of,
> Worshipped as goddesses by,
> Weaker in moral sense than,
> Idealism of,
> Greater conscientiousness of,
> South Sea Islanders, age of puberty among,
> Attractiveness of,
> Offered as sacrifice to,
> Small size of brain of,
> Profounder sub-consciousness of,
> Less hair on the body of,
> Mental, moral and physical inferiority of,
> Love of children of,
> Greater length of life of,
> Weaker muscles of,
> Strength of affections of,
> Vanity of,
> Higher education of,
> Shakespeare's opinion of,
> Lord Birkenhead's opinion of,
> Dean Inge's opinion of,
> La Bruyere's opinion of,
> Dr Johnson's opinion of,
> Mr Oscar Browning's opinion of,
>
> (Woolf 1929: 24–25)

I think of this as a modernist, 'concrete', 'found' poem (or a Cubist painting, a Marcel Duchamp Dadaist 'sculpture', a happening, an event). Women: as database, or as deranged index, as in Nabokov's incomparable *Pale Fire*. You might also like to look again at the equivalently deranged Chinese encyclopaedia entry quoted by Michel Foucault in the Introduction.

I'll return to Woolf and her novels later. I'll turn to **T.S. Eliot** now with both Williams and that amazing moment in Woolf fresh in our minds. 'Prufrock' (1911) is clearly the best of the early (pre-*Waste Land*) poems and Michael Roberts in 1936 put it in his usual blunt way.

> It may happen that in some future state of society there will be no people in the position of Mr Eliot's Prufrock, and therefore no people for whom the poem is actual. But the rhetorical merit of the poem remains: it has

> said something which could not be said in ordinary speech, and said it exactly, and people who are interested in effective expression will read it.
> (In Roberts ed. 1965: 5)

But what strikes some readers (myself included) about Eliot is two things. First, his later poetry, after *The Waste Land* (1922), stages what seems to have been a deliberated retreat into more and more mystified and Christianized incantation or spell-making (a pertinent critical response to his 'Ash Wednesday' is Nabokov's hilarious parody of it toward the end of *Lolita*); and, second, the barely disguised sexual nervousness and fearful distaste for women in even these early poems where Eliot is at his best. There's also anti-Semitism. Frank Kermode noted that 'the word "Jew" remained in lower-case through all the editions of the poems until the last of his lifetime' (Kermode 1967: 112).

The prose-poem 'Hysteria' in the 1917 *Prufrock* volume has the poet drawn into and then lost in the throat of the woman who is laughing hysterically; he decides that the only hope of recovery for the rest of his day lies in this woman's breasts ceasing to shake. As in 'The Yellow Wallpaper' the hysteria is his, in the face of her sexuality.

There's no doubting that Eliot's early work displays the most prodigiously, almost preternaturally poetic gifts. (When he wrote 'Prufrock' he was 23.) What leaps off the pages of the best poems in the 1917 volume and then *The Waste Land* is the extraordinarily tuned ear, the uncanny use of rhyme to generate larger rhythmic structures, the unerring sense of the most apt word and phrase, seemingly unfolding automatically, the poet – quite unlike in Williams who is sleeplessly present in every moment and every word, alive to its potential, lifting it into music and meaning – effacing himself in the grand pursuit of impersonality.

Grand is the word that occurs to the reader of Eliot's 1919 essay 'Tradition and the Individual Talent' when he says 'but, of course, only those who have personality and emotions know what it is to want to escape from these things' (in Kermode ed. 1975: 43). Grand, if perhaps rather oddly imperious. And the expulsion or effacement of the person of the poet is more apparent than real. In one of the 'Preludes' in the *Prufrock* volume, for instance, among the impeccably impersonal evocations of the desolated and fragmented items that make up the urban landscape, we suddenly get this: 'One thinks' of the hands raising 'dingy' shades in the thousand furnished rooms of the atomized city (in which, though this is not said, poorer people live).

To which I want to say: 'Oh, one does, does one?' I want to resist that co-option, the assumption that I will collude in that attitude towards what the same poem diagnoses in a rather lordly way as 'masquerades', which these 'Preludes' (the word is rather self-consciously about music, as in the later *Four Quartets*), suggest are the masquerades of women, one of whom is addressed as 'you' and informed that she has a soul 'constituted' of a thousand (again) 'sordid' images, as well as 'yellow' soled feet. And when we eventually get an 'I' in 'Preludes' it is one moved by fancies 'curled' in those images, manipulatively echoing the woman (whose soul the poem finds sordid), who 'curled' papers from her hair. An 'I' in 'Morning at the Window' in the same 1917 volume seems unembarrassed to share his awareness of housemaids whose 'damp' souls are sprouting in despondency. Raymond Williams noted the sourness of the 'social contempt' there (Williams 1973: 288). In *The Waste Land* it's a corpse that may or may not be beginning to 'sprout', in a worrying correspondence of ideas (the embodied sexuality of young, unhappy and poor women; corpses).

In a very fair assessment of what happens in 'Prufrock' and *The Waste Land*, Martin Dodsworth put it like this.

> Prufrock puts himself in the margins of life and, since the poem centres on him, it has, as it were, no centre, just margins ... As *The Waste Land* floats its voice or voices into the void of post-war Europe, so Prufrock's floats off into a fog that symbolises his void, an insinuating barrier between him and the 'real' world he fears and hesitates to enter.
>
> (In Dodsworth ed. 1994: 198–99)

I'd add this. The 'I' in Dickinson, as we saw, is a performative necessity, a strategic move against the enclosures of feminine identities; the 'I' in Williams is a vulnerable presence ('defenceless' was Roxroth's very good word), aware of his potential intrusion on what he sees so intently, as when he ends the early poem 'Pastoral', which sees an old man who 'walks in the gutter / without looking up' with 'These things / astonish me beyond words' (the refusal to merge subject and object); while the 'I' of early Eliot (with the possible exception of the more deftly personified Prufrock) is an evasion, an effect of presence where he is actually blankly absent, and an attempt to enlist the reader in that process of distance, even of disdain – and theorized in the creed of impersonality which sometimes looks more like a kind of disgust.

It's at least possible to find a fastidiousness of disgust at the centre of Eliot's early poetry, which may or may not plausibly be traced to a generalized post-First World War futility, as often claimed about *The Waste Land*, or to Eliot more personally (who described the poem as his rhythmical grumbling and later blamed, as we saw in his Statement, his first and unhappy marriage for its state of mind). Elizabeth Bishop, a wonderful poet, was I'm sure not alone in suspecting that the poem's concern with impotence and sterility was not only symbolic or cultural but real and specific to Eliot. On a more general point about the association between high modernism and sterility, Edward Said very pertinently said this in 1983.

> In a large group of late nineteenth- and early twentieth-century writers ... the failure of the capacity to produce or generate children is portrayed in such a way as to stand for a general condition afflicting society and culture together ... *Ulysses* and *The Waste Land* are two especially well-known instances, but there is similar evidence to be found [widely elsewhere].
>
> (Said 1983: 16)

Said instances Mann's *Death in Venice*, Hardy's *Jude the Obscure*, Conrad's *Nostromo*, and texts by Proust, Mallarme, Hopkins and others.

Even Edmund Wilson, an early champion of Eliot, felt obliged to say this, in his *Axel's Castle* (1931).

> [Eliot is distinguished by] an excessive fastidiousness and scrupulousness ... regret at situations unexplored, that dark rankling of passions inhibited ... We recognise ... the peculiar conflicts of the Puritan turned artist: the horror of vulgarity ... the ascetic shrinking from sexual experience and the distress at the drying up of the springs of sexual emotion, with the straining after a religious experience which may be made to take its place.
>
> (Wilson 1931: 102–05)

Frank Kermode pointed to the crucial role, in Eliot's impulse to write, of the poet needing to surrender to and in 'the bewildering minute', a phrase from *The Revenger's Tragedy* that Eliot quotes (twice) in essays and that he plays variations on in his poems. Kermode calls the passage a 'blend of fascination and disgust ... [a] simultaneous enchantment and loss, the sexual surrender' and he connects it with what Eliot said about love's 'terrible aspect' in Dante: in 'our intenser experiences of other human beings there is a first, or an early moment which is unique, of shock and surprise, even of terror' (in Kermode ed. 1975: 13–14). Kermode later put it like this, about Eliot. 'In *The Revenger's Tragedy* that expression refers with excitement and disgust to the sexual act: its transfer to the impact of poetry is presumably not insignificant' (Kermode 1991: 290–91).

Here's a fine account of *The Waste Land* by Louis Menand from his 1987 classic *Discovering Modernism*.

> *The Waste Land* is presented as a contemporary reading of the Western tradition, which ... is treated as a sequence of gestures whose original meaning is unknown, but which every new text that is added to it makes a bad guess at ... The author of the poem classes himself with the diseased characters of his own work ... He cannot distinguish what he intends to reveal about himself from what he cannot help revealing: he would like to believe that his poem is expressive of some general reality, but he fears that it is only the symptom of a private disorder. For when he looks to the culture around him, everything appears only as a reflection of his own breakdown ... The poem itself, as a literary object, seems an imitation of [a] vision of degeneration: nothing in it can be said to point to the poet, since none of its stylistic features is continuous, and it has no phrases or images that cannot be suspected of – where they are not in fact identified as – belonging to someone else ... If the poem was indeed intended as a kind of deliberate dead end, an explosion of the 19th century metaphysics of style, leaving nothing in its place, this ambition was perhaps one of the things Eliot learned from Joyce. *Ulysses*,

> Eliot told Virginia Woolf ... 'destroyed the whole of the 19th century ... It showed up the futility of all the English styles'.
>
> (Menand 2007: 89–91)

Eliot called **James Joyce**'s method, and by implication his own, mythic rather than narrative. Here's the opening of *Ulysses* (1922), as quoted and discussed by Christopher Butler.

> Stately, plump Buck Mulligan came from the stairhead, bearing a bowl of lather on which a mirror and a razor lay crossed. A yellow dressing gown, ungirdled, was sustained behind him by the mild morning air. He held the bowl aloft and intoned:
>
> Introibo ad altare Dei.
>
> (Ch. 1)

Butler gives a clear account of the allusive method (common to both Joyce and Eliot).

> The primary modernist technique here lies in Joyce's making of allusions, which lead us to feel the presence of underlying conceptual or formal structures. And so, as Hugh Kenner notes in his brilliant guide, in this book, whose narrative will parallel that of Homer's *Odyssey*, the first nine words mimic the rhythms of a Homeric hexameter, and the bowl Mulligan bears is also ... a sacrificial chalice on which his shaving gear lies 'crossed'. His yellow dressing gown echoes a priest's vestments ... [while] 'ungirdled' (the cincture not tied as it would be for the priest's affirmation of chastity), it leaves him frontally naked, his private parts on display for mild air to caress ... And 'intoned' is deliberate; preparing to shave, he is also playing at the Black Mass with its naked priest. The words he speaks, which belong to the ... Catholic Mass, come from St Jerome's Latin version of Hebrew words ascribed to a Psalmist in exile: 'I will go up to the altar of God'. It is therefore a quotation of a quotation of a quotation, and originally a Hebrew cry for help amid persecution.
>
> (Butler 2010: 3–4)

Butler here adds Kenner's comment.

> We may also remark the appropriateness for the book of Bloom – its Jewish hero: the modern Ulysses – of an initial statement in disguised Hebrew, and note that as the Roman priest adopts the role of the Psalmist, so Irish political consciousness in those years was playing the role of the captive Chosen People, with Great Britain for its Babylon or its Egypt.
>
> (Kenner 1982: 34–35)

What Joyce gains for his novel from this richly allusive texture, says Butler, is 'a mythical as well as a historical organisation of narrative', as well as to suggest interconnected ideas such as the Irish being a persecuted Chosen People (Butler 2010: 4).

One way to distinguish between Eliot and Joyce is to say that if Eliot famously admitted in *The Waste Land* to shoring fragments against his own (highly personalized, as if privatized) ruin, Joyce wanted synthesis, from the human level outwards. So he knits together, through combining his own and Homer's outer narratives, the inner narratives of three forms of consciousnesses, Stephen's, Bloom's, Molly's, variously bereft and, in Raymond Williams's words, 'a family but not a family, out of touch and searching for each other through a myth and a history' (Williams 1973: 293–94). Eliot may have been right to identify a mythic method in *Ulysses* and, in effect, in his own early work. But the myth in Joyce serves the larger purpose of his deep interest in (and attachment to) the three protagonists; Eliot in *The Waste Land* mythologizes to make up for his indifference to the people who speak the poem.

I'll add that I re-read the poem after many years for this book: though as ever dazzled by the technique I felt bullied by its ideological rhetoric. About Eliot's later and more mystified and Christian poems, Geoffrey Hill in 1984 said that 'though Eliot advocates humility and surrender, I do not think that he ever consciously surrenders rhetorical mastery' (Hill 1984: 3).

In 1948 Harry Levin wrote movingly about Joyce and synthesis.

> Synthesis is Joyce's final intention … By proceeding through what William James termed 'the stream of consciousness' to what Jung terms 'the racial unconsciousness', beyond individual dream to collective myth … Joyce learned how to reconcile the principles of unity and diversity: 'the same anew' … The central human relationships, for him as for Proust, were warmly and tenderly domestic … His work, though far from didactic, is full of moral implications; his example of aesthetic idealism, set by abnegation and artistry, is a standing rebuke to facility and venality, callousness and obtuseness.
>
> (In Levin ed. 1963: 16–17)

Frank Kermode put it very well in 1967, arguing that *Ulysses* is as much about the refusal to mythologize as the opposite, despite Eliot's approval of Joyce for having modernized myth.

> *Ulysses* alone of these great works [of modernism] studies and develops the tension between paradigm and reality, asserts the resistance of fact to fiction, human freedom and unpredictability against plot … We might ask whether one of the merits of the book is not its *lack* of mythologising … And Joyce, who probably knew more about it than any of the others, was not attracted by the intellectual opportunities or the formal elegance of fascism.
>
> (Kermode 1967: 113–14)

Joyce's earlier 'The Dead', the concluding story in his *Dubliners*, has a claim to be his other indisputable masterpiece. Its principal modernist strategy is to prise apart the two halves of the realist cliché 'falling in love', in a sustained lyric and critical meditation on the relations between the two components. But it's also a text that must qualify as an elaborate blind on willing readers. We're fooled until the last pages into thinking that we're reading a kind of story that 'The Dead' pretends to be but isn't. The desolation that Gabriel experiences at the close is mirrored in our sense of exclusion, not only from his and Gretta's separate and private griefs but also from the story we thought we were reading.

As we negotiate the story's opening, we're invited to anticipate a death at the party. The second paragraph pointedly observes that the annual party had 'never once ... fallen flat', and what with a 'wheezy' hall door bell, a suddenly disastrous exchange between Gabriel and the girl Lily (about men these days) and his subsequent doubts about his speech falling flat – all this suggests an impending disaster. The story's opening dead cliché is again a deliberate misleading, suggesting that a tired and fallen language ('Lily ... was literally run off her feet') is going to convey the disaster in an appropriately ironic way.

So when Gabriel starts his speech with the cliché 'it has fallen to my lot ...', and then, halfway through its vacuities, lets 'his voice fall ... into a softer inflexion', we feel we're nearing the decisive fall, the story's event, its climax, especially as there's then mention of someone being in danger of catching 'her death of cold' and a song is then sung in which 'my babe lies cold ...'.

But it's all a blind and we fall into the misreadings, a process that continues even more painfully when the story opens out after the party and, like Gabriel, we fall into misreading the apparent signs of a renewed sexual passion between husband and wife. On the way to their hotel bedroom their feet are 'falling in soft thuds' and 'Gabriel could hear the falling of the molten wax into the tray'. The misreading (specifically of Gretta's mood) is most ironically pointed when Gabriel, 'trembling with delight at her sudden kiss' considers that now 'she had fallen to him so easily he wondered why he had been so diffident'. But then the story turns and opens again, this time properly, to disclose its real concern, the closing of a life and a love that Gabriel knew nothing about.

In the last pages 'fall' becomes a desolate refrain. Gabriel, 'shy of intruding on her grief, let [Gretta's hand] fall gently'. Her boot has its 'limp upper fallen down'. With 'a few light taps upon the pane', the seven-times repeated 'falling' snow chimes in the lyric that is the last paragraph with the swoon-death into which his soul is falling.

The trigger that impels these last notions of fall is a series of connected recognitions: that an Irish boy died of love for Gretta, that those two had been 'great with' each other in their young loves, that Gabriel had played so 'poor a part ... in her life', and that (in the story's saddest sentence) 'he had never felt like that himself towards any woman but he knew that such a feeling must be love'. This is a moving and subtle variation on the notion that we met with René Girard on the triangulation of desire (and Eve Sedgwick on Dickens's *Our Mutual Friend*), the triggering of love through the agency of a perceived rival – with the painful difference that this is a discovery, through the rival, of not loving, of not having loved, and of not being able to love.

The preoccupations and radical techniques of **Virginia Woolf**'s novels have been well summarized by Marianne Dekoven.

> Woolf's female and gender-ambiguous protagonists try to reform (literally, re-form) their worlds according to their enlightened ideas, their fidelity to the complex truths of their perceptions, and their connectedness to the culturally alternative truths of the psyche. At the same time Woolf pushed fiction as far formally as any of the other major Modernists, using fragmentation; collage-like juxtaposition; densely poetic language … narrative multiplicity and indeterminacy; temporal dislocations … fluidity and de-definition of characterization; and an utterly destabilising, pervasive irony.
>
> (In Levenson ed. 2011: 225–26)

Three years after *Ulysses*, Woolf (who in a moment of snobbishness dismissed the novel) described what she, and Joyce, wanted 'modern fiction' to do.

> Let us examine for a moment an ordinary mind on an ordinary day … Let us record the atoms as they fall upon the mind in the order in which they fall, let us trace the pattern, however disconnected or incoherent in appearance, which each sight or incident scores on the consciousness.
>
> (In Butler 2010: 50)

Woolf does that most radically in her novels *To the Lighthouse* (1927) and *The Waves* (1931), in both of which consciousness is dispersed and multiplied more elaborately than in any novelist before her. In a particularly close reading of *Lighthouse* John Mepham shows this at work in the simultaneities between sections of the novel in two parallel and strikingly symmetrical places (sections 5, 6, 7 and 8, 9, 10). Section 5 ends with Lily Briscoe painting and crying. '"Mrs Ramsay!" she said aloud. "Mrs Ramsay!" The tears ran down her face.'

> 6
>
> [Macalister's boy took one of the fish and cut a square out of its side to bait his hook with. The mutilated body (it was alive still) was thrown back into the sea.]

Then section 7 starts '"Mrs Ramsay!" Lily cried, "Mrs Ramsay!" But nothing happened. The pain increased … She remained a skimpy old maid, holding a paint-brush on the lawn.' Mepham says this.

> These two moments of the narration are the same moment of the fiction. But a gap has opened up, a gap with a particular shape (the square brackets / the square wound) … The story of Macalister's boy fishing … has the least significant relationship to any of the other stories being told … It is

> there so that it is available, when the moment comes, so that the narration can fly across space and find prepared just what it needs – a mutilated body thrown into the sea.
>
> (In Josipovici ed. 1976: 182)

In the other symmetrically arranged triad of sections (8, 9, 10), the outer sections are at sea (and include a moment where 'the relief was extraordinary') and the central section 9, also square-bracketed, starts with this: 'The sea without a stain on it, thought Lily Briscoe, still standing and looking out over the bay. The sea is stretched like silk across the bay.' Mepham adds this about pain and narrative texture.

> In the second case the pain is in the boat. But it is relieved there … The fabric remains 'stretched like silk' … Within the narrative order there is, in such passages, a movement towards intense concentration on individual pain and grief, but at the same time a vivid reminder of the larger impersonal order within which these subjective feelings are so small and insignificant. The narration holds together a vision of individual desire and its context of space and sea, of impersonal time and natural process.
>
> (184)

The radical deployment of the brackets in those sections remind me of an equivalently radical use of brackets, apparently illogical and impossible, at the start of *The Waste Land* where the poem mentions the 'shadow' under a 'red rock', adds '(Come in under the shadow of this red rock)', and then: 'And I will show you something different …'.

Rather than Joyce's synthesis or Eliot's fragments, Woolf's refusal to resolve contradictions is a gendered affirmation of difference. Dekoven says this about the end of *Lighthouse*.

> Lily Briscoe finishes her painting with a 'line there, in the centre'. The closing 'line' of Lily's, and the novel's, final 'vision' is a line of simultaneous separation and union … The text represents more clearly perhaps than any other the Modernist moment of unresolved contradiction, unsynthesized dialectic: of dualism that seeks neither unitary resolution in the dominance of one term over the other or in … synthesis, but rather the two-way passage, difference without hierarchy
>
> (In Levenson ed. 2011: 229–30)

In *The Waves*, consciousness is dispersed among six characters (who speak of a seventh) and an unnamed narrative voice whose intrusions become more and more infrequent. The effect has been very well described by Thomas Docherty in 1983. As we read on, the outline between the characters become less and less distinct.

> The attribution of phrases to names, and even the names themselves, become less and less important; indeed, as the novel progresses, the intrusive voice which attributes speeches to names intrudes less and less, speeches get longer and longer, until the final uninterrupted passage of Bernard's monologue. Edges blur between characters, and the spatial discontinuity of the six voices begin to dissipate ... We see that we do not have six characters in the conventional sense at all but rather that we have one source-voice for the text ... Here, then, is the essence of impersonality of modernist novelists: it lies in impersonation ... [Each character] is fragmented and dispersed and used as a series of metaphorical manifestations of the self whose voice attributes attitudes and images to her name.
>
> (Docherty 1983: 161–62)

Docherty aptly refers to W.J. Harvey's influential 1965 study *Character and the Novel.*

> This process, wherein our sense of duality between Self and World is diminished and in which discrete identities merge into the unity of a larger spiritual continuum, we may call psychic decomposition.
>
> (Harvey 1965: 124)

This process is most persistently and most disconcertingly elaborated in the great post-war novels and stories of **Samuel Beckett**, heir in this sense to Woolf as he is more famously to Joyce, once his mentor. (Beckett distinguished between himself and Joyce by saying that the more Joyce knew the more capable he became, whereas he, Beckett, was working more and more with ignorance.) I very much hope you read his great trilogy, *Molloy, Malone Dies* and *The Unnamable*, the last of which is the most radical in 'psychic decomposition'. It was, like the other two volumes, first published in French. Maurice Blanchot reviewed it on release in 1953.

> Who is doing the talking in Samuel Beckett's novels, who is this tireless 'I' constantly repeating what seems to be always the same thing? ... Is he merely going round in circles, obscurely revolving, carried along by the momentum of a wandering voice, lacking not so much sense as centre, producing an utterance without proper beginning and end, yet greedy, exacting, a language that will never stop, that finds it intolerable to stop, for then would come the moment of the terrible discovery: when the talking stops, there is still talking; when the language pauses it perseveres; there is no silence, for within that voice the silence eternally speaks.
>
> (In Graver and Federman edd. 1979: 116–17)

'Going round in circles.' The narrated figure (or one of them) in *The Unnamable* imagines spiralling himself convulsively home until, in a final spasm, he is catapulted out backwards 'without having said good evening'. Molloy (in

Part 1 of the first volume of the trilogy), having heard that someone lost in a forest who thinks he's walking in a straight line is actually going in a circle, does his best to go in a circle 'hoping in this way to go in a straight line'.

Directors of Beckett's wonderful play *Waiting for Godot* (also first published in French), to which I turn now, face a related puzzle. Does Act 2 see Pozzo and Lucky enter from the same side of the stage as they used to enter in Act 1, or the opposite? The former suggests that they are caught on a vast and inwardly spiralling structure (the rope connecting them is much shorter in Act 2); the latter suggests that they are swinging to and fro, on a pendulum that's slowing down.

Godot, as if at a stroke (or over the course of one evening), returned Western theatre to its roots, in ritual and its cyclical rhythms, after the long dominance of traditional realist-naturalistic drama with its linear narratives. To its roots: and also to the most ritualized scenes in late Shakespeare, as in the meta-theatrical rituals of the disguised Edgar, the mad Lear and the blind Gloucester at Dover (4.6) that we saw Jan Kott write about in his account of *King Lear* in Chapter 2. We can recapture the moment when theatre changed through the moving account of Alan Schneider, who later became the director of American productions of Beckett. In 1954 he'd heard rumours of the play quietly being acted in a tiny Paris theatre. He went with his wife.

> There were nine people in the audience ... Through the entire performance I sat alternately spellbound and mystified, knowing that something terribly moving was taking place on that stage. When the highly stylized 'moon' suddenly rose and night 'fell' at the end of that first act, I didn't have to understand French in order to react. And when, at the beginning of the second act, the once-bare tree reappeared with little green ribbons for leaves, that simple representation of rebirth affected me beyond all reason. Without knowing exactly what, I knew that I had experienced something unique and significant in modern theatre.
>
> (In Cohn ed. 1967: 52)

As early as 1961 Hugh Kenner, best – and funniest – of Beckett's critics (and best partly as he always insisted on how Beckett is above all a richly comic writer, in the tradition of Flaubert's last and absurdly proto-modernist novel *Bouvard and Pecuchet*, a comedian of the impeccably shaped and self-emptying sentence), wrote what has still a claim to be the definitive book on its author. (For Eliot, rhyme shapes everything; Kenner shows that, for Joyce, it's the phrase, and for Beckett – as for Flaubert – it's the sentence.) Kenner makes this fine point about Beckett's world. 'The Beckett universe, wherever we encounter it, consists of a shambles of phenomena within which certain symmetries and recurrences are observable, like the physical world as interpreted by early man.'

Here he is on *Godot*, and theatre as ritual.

> The drama is a ritual enacted in an enclosed space into which fifty or more people are staring. They are all more or less patiently waiting for

> something: the Reversal, the Discovery, the *deus ex machina*, or even the final curtain. Settled numbly for the evening, they accept whatever interim diversions the stage can provide: tramps in bowler hats, for instance ... 'The theatrical character', remarked Alain Robbe-Grillet ... '*is on stage*, this is his primary quality – he is there'. Hence, 'the essential function of the theatrical performance: to show what this fact of *being there* consists of' ... What [Vladimir and Estragon] talk about first is the fact they were both there, the one fact that is demonstrably true not only in art's agreed world but before our eyes. It is even the one certainty that survives an evening's waiting ... If the seeming improvisation of the tramps denies theatricality, it affirms at the same time quintessential theatre, postulating nothing but what we can see on stage: a place, and men present in it, doing what they are doing.
>
> (Kenner 1968: 133–38)

Doing what they are doing – in order to do rather than to know, or to feel, as well as doing in order to fill the pauses that, in Act 2, become silences. At the end of Act 1 Estragon, in a fury with the Boy, has a face 'convulsed' with sudden anguish at having to remember what he and the play had 'forgotten', to remember what the two of them have been doing and saying in order not to feel and to know: that they've been through all this with the Boy before and will again, that Godot – and salvation – will never come. Vladimir and the Boy look at Estragon uncomprehendingly. It's as if we're being invited not to comprehend either, to continue going round the circle of the dialogue, the play, the days.

But History has suddenly, irrevocably intruded, the history that is already driving Pozzo and Lucky down a slope towards their ruin (blinded, numbed: Lear and Gloucester at Dover cliffs), a history that Estragon and Vladimir have only the most precarious grip over not succumbing to themselves. Estragon's convulsed face and inability to explain are what the narrator in Beckett's best last short novel *Company* (1980) fears as the urge to have to own the personal weight of history, to 'have a past and acknowledge it', or what Mouth in his best last short play *Not I* (1973) tries to retain as her 'refusal to relinquish third-person'.

I want to turn, in the final phase of this chapter, to history and its complex place in the modernist project.

Beckett left Ireland for Paris in 1937 and played a role in the Resistance, preferring (like Joyce) an externalized exile in Europe to an internalized exile in Ireland. It's easy to read the sudden flow of masterpieces following the war – *Watt*, the trilogy, *Godot* and shorter works – as marked by the tensed strangenesses of occupied and unoccupied territories, minds, bodies, languages: the figurations of the defamiliarized; refracted history.

Vladimir Nabokov is a novelist who, on the face of it, could hardly be more different, though also writing in a second language (Beckett re-created his English, purified of Irish-ness, by translating from his own French) and also exiled from a richly complicated homeland, and though also a wonderfully comic stylist. Also like Beckett, he has been located as both a late modernist and early postmodernist. His *Lolita* is, among other things (and as he said himself), a love letter to his adopted language, in loss of his beloved Russian. It is also a magnetically sustained, rhetorically powerful attraction of the reader's complicity in crime, drawing on an array of more or less persuasive strategies (such as Humbert claiming to be helplessly suffering from pseudo-medical 'nympholepsy'). Lionel Trilling, in an early response of 1958, said this. (The word 'seduced' in the opening sentence below was later changed to 'subdued'. This is still a very male reading as 'our' in the same sentence suggests.)

> We have been seduced into conniving in the violation, because we have permitted our fantasies to accept what we know to be revolting ... leading us to become quite at ease with a sexual situation that should outrage us and then facing us with our facilely-given acquiescence.
>
> (In Page ed. 1982: 94–95)

But *Lolita* is also, as argued in a recent and excellent 2012 book by Will Norman – *Nabokov, History and the Texture of Time* – a strategic response to, and dialogue with, immediate post-war history in the forms of American psychoanalysis and, even more startlingly, of America's dealings with the Holocaust.

Nabokov famously resisted historical readings of his work and ran a running battle with Freud and the Freudians. Norman shows that a more complicated picture emerges through careful attention paid to the intricacies of the novelist's strategic deployment of some of the discourses and pressures of his time. He notices that one place visited by Humbert and Lolita on their travels in America was ('for the heck of it') the Menninger Foundation (Part 2, Ch. 2). Menninger was an American neo-Freudian of the most distortingly simplifying kind and argued that, despite Freud's insights into evil, his message was that 'man can be transformed with the nurture and dispersion of love'. Norman comments brilliantly on this.

> What better summary could there be of the reading of *Lolita* that ultimately places faith in Humbert's claims at the end of the novel to have truly realised his love for Dolores, to have regretted his theft of her childhood, to have reformed himself? This 'moral apotheosis' as John Ray, Jr. calls it [in his grotesque 'Foreword'], has been taken seriously by a significant number of *Lolita's* critics. My own argument is that it is Humbert's last, sick joke on the reader, and that the structure of moral regeneration through narration, the 'talking cure', forms Nabokov's response to a corrupt psychoanalytic practice as popularised in the United States after the war.
>
> (Norman 2012: 109)

There are a number of passages in *Lolita* (as in other Nabokov novels, but here, says Norman, both more covertly and more pervasively, as well as in details of Nabokov's own life) that inescapably evoke the Holocaust, as when

Humbert's dreams, after Quilty abducts Lolita from his own more apparently normalized abduction, feature 'the brown wigs of tragic old women who had just been gassed' (Part 2, Ch. 25). Norman follows other critics who argue for the 'Holocaust subtext' of the novel (119), noticing details like 'the ashes of our predecessors still linger[ing] in the ashtrays' of motels where Humbert and Lo stay, or the trains they hear crying in the night 'mingling power and hysteria in one desperate scream' (Part 2, Ch. 16). Norman also points to larger questions of post-war American guilt in its widespread complicity over the Holocaust, to connections between the German leaders' performances at the Nuremberg trials and Humbert's defence-narrative, and to the 'vigorous' and 'heated' debate in *Partisan Review* in 1949 over Ezra Pound being awarded the Bollingen Prize despite his public anti-Semitism (the prize committee included Eliot). One critic of the award asked how it can be possible 'for technical embellishments to transform vicious and ugly subject matter into beautiful poetry?' Norman adds this.

> This is of course the provocation to which Nabokov responds in *Lolita*, where calculated rape and child abuse are transformed into brilliant, often ecstatic prose, and where the shadow of the Holocaust falls over the attempt to extricate oneself, untainted, from the reading experience.
> (127–28)

Norman shows that the interweaving of psychoanalytic and Holocaust materials in *Lolita* constitute a powerful but submerged force over the reader. The father–daughter dynamic is, of course, particularly fraught in that context. The same is the case in a text – or a text at the centre of a group of texts, or what has become a case study or crisis of reading and control – with **Sylvia Plath**'s 1962 poem 'Daddy', first published, just after her suicide, in *Encounter* in 1963 and then in the 1965 volume *Ariel*, over the contents of which Ted Hughes exercised what we might call a very masculine control. (He clearly would rather have excluded 'Daddy' as he actually excluded other poems which implicated himself.) It is now in the 1981 *Collected Poems* (where it is excluded from the Index).

'Daddy' notoriously evokes and expresses the need to kill (or kill again as he was dead) Plath's father, in terms that fantasize Plath herself as a Jewish victim of the Holocaust and the father as a Nazi and fascist. Jacqueline Rose in her indispensable and powerful book on Plath (*The Haunting of Sylvia Plath*), a book that faced a series of obstructionist demands from Hughes and the family for control over not only the poems discussed but the manner in which Rose discussed them, shows how the poem outraged the critical establishment. Plath was accused of aggrandizing herself, not earning the right to make connections between her personal life and the Holocaust, leading Irvine Howe (for instance) to call the connection 'monstrous, utterly disproportionate' (in Rose 1991: 206). Rose puts the argument in a wider context of the relations between psyche and history.

> Psychic life in itself will not be relegated to the private, it will not stay in its proper place. It shows up on the side of the historical reality to which it is often opposed … Plath has been criticised for the way she weaves her personal mythology into historical moments and events, notably fascism and the Holocaust … I see the presence of these images in her writing as revealing something of the way fantasy operates inside historical process … In fascism, the realm of politics reveals itself as massively invested with the most primitive and intimate images of our fantasy life. Plath's writing presents us with those images at work … In doing so, she provides an extraordinary instance of the inseparability of history and subjectivity … There is no history outside its subjective realisation, its being-for-the-subject, just as there is no subjectivity uncoloured by the history to which it belongs.
>
> (7–8)

Two years after *Ariel* brought 'Daddy' to its shocked readers, **Geoffrey Hill** published what is certainly now his best-known poem, 'September Song' (1967: the year of the 'Six Day War'), about the death of a little Jewish girl in a Nazi concentration camp. Hill then included the poem in his second collection *King Log* (1968). That volume was included in a landmark collection of Hill's first three volumes in the US in 1975 with an influential Introduction by Harold Bloom pointedly (provocatively in terms of the Holocaust) called 'The Survival of Strong Poetry'. (Bloom's 'anxiety of influence' theory – strong (male) poets in psychic conflict, the later poet 'strongly misreading' the earlier – we met in Chapter 3.)

'Daddy' and 'September Song' could hardly be more different, as Holocaust poems. Where 'Daddy' is long, openly fantasizing, and vulnerably bitter and combative (and clearly coming out of deep personal unhappiness), 'September Song' is compacted, sealed in on its series of cruel puns, self-knowing and self-ironizing to the point of implicitly doubting its right to exist, to speak for this child's death – the self-scrutinizing and self-doubting that is precisely what Plath was accused of not even being able to feel the need to do. Unsurprisingly, the Hill poem has been praised for that very reason, for – in Gabriel Pearson's more sceptical account – 'how it escapes the charge of condoning by profiting (for its subject matter) from the atrocity it "sings"' (in Robinson ed. 1985: 43). That Hill was male and increasingly a favoured subject of the high academy (that is, the opposite of Plath) is presumably not irrelevant. Pearson puts it like this (in a way that I'd add matches my experience over decades of teaching this poem where, in seminars, 'having his cake and eating it' is something often voiced).

> I read 'September Song' as itself enacting an inevitable callousness, or at best intermittency, of moral imagination; we live in a universe where knowledge of atrocity and the blitheness of song go on co-existing … The essence of the atrocity is that the victim has been erased … and no form of commemoration of that erasure can serve to render it less complete,

> though it may momentarily assuage our sense of helplessness. For that, again, is what atrocity is and does to its victims, and to us.
>
> (43)

But we can still say that no recent poet writing in English has sounded and felt history as Hill has. What Hill, at least in part consciously, is doing in his best poems is engaging critically with the example of Eliot (particularly his *Four Quartets*), in restoring poetry to the history or histories that Eliot's mystifications had marginalized and dissolved. Pearson says this of Eliot's *Four Quartets*, in relation to Hill's magnificent 'Funeral Music' sequence about the Wars of the Roses in *King Log*.

> In the timeless image, the tough contradictions of history are reconciled ... the antinomies of experience resolved and transcended ... [In 'Funeral Music'] there is a discrete and regretful repudiation of Eliot's aesthetic sacramentalism, that consoling dissolution of historical contraries into a figuration on the ground of the redemptive scheme.
>
> (34–35)

For Hill history, including his own, is only recoverable through acts of mediation, as when his extremely beautiful sequence of love poems (poems of loss) in *King Log*, 'The Songbook of Sebastian Arrurruz', can only find its (Hill's) voice by claiming to be translations of a fictional Spanish poet (who 'died' in the year of *The Waste Land*) and as when his quite unexpectedly humorous third book, *Mercian Hymns*, a sequence of thirty prose poems, interlaces scenes and moments from the reign of the 8th century King Offa with glimpses of his own coming of age as a working-class adult and as a poet. The effect in all of Hill's poetic engagements with history is a kind of framed distancing, a means of recognizing and attempting a reconciliation with loss, something lost, what Hugh Haughton in a very fine essay calls Hill's 'fraught anachronism'.

> It can be argued that the fraught anachronism of Hill's poetry represents the imaginative pull of the past for a poet obsessed above all by the persistence of what has been lost, and the impossibility or reappropriating it: the idea of continuity – and the stark fact of distance ... [The anachronism is] a resistance to the specious glamour of the 'timeless moment' (to which ... Eliot succumbed), and the inertia of 'traditional appeal' – indeed the appeal of tradition.
>
> (131)

What makes Hill such a distinctive poet, and such an antidote to the later Eliot, is on the one hand his principled determination to attend to, and to trace back to, the roots of language, what Hill said in an interview about etymology being history; and on the other what Haughton calls his 'search for propriety of utterance in a world of excruciating improprieties and historical extremity'.

> Hill's is undoubtedly an extreme historical imagination, drawn to situations of maximum moral and civil conflict – the fate of the Jews in Europe, the armies of the Plantagenet kings … the endurance of poets, prisoners and martyrs … Yet he is also as a poet committed to an extreme formality, the idea of [poetry] as … an act of 'witness' … in which the authority of poetry, of Hill's own art is itself tested.
>
> (131)

I want to end this look at modernism with the late poems of **Wallace Stevens** from the 1950s. I mentioned him earlier in relation to William Carlos Williams and the localized American, rather than Eliot's European, poetic modernism that both poets were wanting to mark out. These late poems, in the opinion of many (including myself), are the most distinguished and moving poems of the post-war period written anywhere in English (if Hill takes on that distinction for the 1960s and 1970s).

These poems explore the transfiguring powers of the imagination. (Keats said that the imagination was like Adam's dream in *Paradise Lost*: he awoke and found it true.) A 'scrawny cry' that is heard or imagined in 'Not Ideas about the Thing but the Thing Itself' (placed at the end of the *Collected Poems* of 1954) yields 'A new knowledge of reality'. A painfully moving section of his 'Auroras of Autumn' about his mother's death ends with the imagined and re-created scene forty years earlier where upstairs 'The windows will be lighted, not the rooms'. (Dickinson, imagining her own death, has the windows failing.)

In a lecture of 2000, Helen Vendler describes the differences between earlier and later Stevens as an increasing resistance to a rhetoric of speculation (his earlier addiction to words like 'if', 'or' and 'but'): moving from the search for 'the' truth or arguing for dialectical 'truths' to, in the late work, aiming to approach 'a' truth 'plausible to his exacting mind' (Vendler 2001: 226). Vendler draws attention to a moment near the end of Stevens's 'An Ordinary Evening in New Haven' where reality 'may be a shade that traverses / A dust, a force that traverses a shade' and says this.

> We scarcely have words for these elusive and delicate traversings, but … Stevens's language makes us aware that – as the title of a late poem asserts – 'Reality Is an Activity of the Most August Imagination'.
>
> (241)

And Vendler looks finally at 'The Region November', a poem dated November 1954, at the end of Stevens's last full year of life. This poem evokes the north wind, deep and loud in the swaying treetops: 'Deeplier, deeplier, loudlier, loudlier'. (Perhaps this distantly evokes the very English 'Adlestrop' by Edward Thomas – whom Stevens's friend and rival Robert Frost knew well – which has birds singing 'mistier / Farther and farther'.) Vendler calls the Stevens poem 'a waste land of spiritual entropy' (243), by which she may be intending to evoke Eliot. But Stevens is re-creating language, inventing words, and the 'swaying,

swaying, swaying' trees of the last line are alive. Vendler says this about Stevens's 'fertility' of 'verbal invention'.

> [It is] a mental landscape anything but bleak, one that matches the distributed richness of the material world with its own unfailing engendering of emotional, intellectual, and linguistic forms.
>
> (244)

This late poetry makes a grounded accommodation with the real. These are poems (as Frank Kermode puts it) 'of death, or of the achievement of a posture in which to meet it correctly' (Kermode 1989: 79). Hill in his 'Songbook' says 'the metaphor holds; is a snug house'. Stevens evokes the search for the 'real' in a language without metaphor. The search is bound to fail but (in Beckett's words) the effort persists, to 'fail better'. Stevens wrote in a collection of axioms that 'the real is only the base. But it is the base.'

Kermode wrote movingly about Stevens's very beautiful late poem 'The Plain Sense of Things'. This wonderful poem says how difficult it is to find the right word or words for 'this blank cold, this sadness without cause' which, in another guess, I'd say may evoke William Empson's 1930s poem 'Let it go', which (with touching awkwardness) starts 'It is this deep blankness is the real thing strange'. Both poems also make me think of Emily Dickinson and what she called the hour of lead. (Dickinson is Stevens's spiritual ancestor as she is Plath's.) But unlike the Empson poem, Stevens's poem paradoxically builds an ornate array of objects (house, chimney, greenhouse, pond, leaves, mud, lilies – even a turban without apparently anyone wearing it) to be imagined as both in the poem and outside of it ('no turban ...'), as emblems of the failure of imagination – although 'the absence of imagination had / Itself to be imagined'. (Beckett has 'imagination dead imagine'.)

Kermode says this (referring to an earlier poem called 'The Snow Man') about the effort required to imagine a plain language, without metaphor and to 'hold the language there for the briefest moment'.

> Worth trying, he seems to say, but impossible, this attempt to behold 'the nothing that is not there and the nothing that is'. To make the attempt ... is 'to have a mind of winter'. Only such a mind, a snowman's mind, could attend to the frozen trees without adding to them some increment of language, of humanity, even if that increment is misery ... One tries to find an adjective for blankness, a tropeless cold. But to say 'no turban' is to introduce a turban, something exotic, a gift of imagination ... The pond has reflections, leaves, mud, as real a pond as imagination at the best of times could imagine. All these things have to be added to the plain sense if we want it; it is not to be had without comment, without poetry.
>
> (Kermode 1989: 173–74)

Works cited

Kate Aughterson and Deborah Philips edd., *Women Writers and Experimental Narratives* (Palgrave: 2021)
Christopher Butler, *Modernism* (Oxford U.P.: 2010)
Ruby Cohn, *Casebook on 'Waiting for Godot'* (Grove Press: 1967)
Thomas Docherty, *Reading (Absent) Character* (Oxford U.P.: 1983)
Martin Dodsworth ed., *The Twentieth Century* (Penguin: 1994)
Lawrence Graver and Raymond Federman edd., *Samuel Beckett: The Critical Heritage* trs. Richard Howard (Routledge: 1979)
W.J. Harvey, *Character and the Novel* (Chatto and Windus: 1965)
Geoffrey Hill, *The Lords of Limit* (Oxford U.P.: 1984)
Luce Irigaray, *This Sex Which Is Not One* trs. Catherine Porter (Cornell U.P.: 1985)
Mary Jacobus, *Reading Woman* (Columbia U.P.: 1986)
Gabriel Josipovici ed., *The Modern English Novel* (Open Books: 1976)
Gabriel Josipovici, *What Ever Happened to Modernism?* (Yale U.P.: 2010)
Paul Keegan, 'Emily of Fire and Violence', *London Review of Books* Vol. 42 Issue 20: October 2020
Hugh Kenner, *Samuel Beckett: A Critical Study* (California U.P.: 1968)
Hugh Kenner, *A Homemade World: The American Modernist Writers* (Alfred A. Knopf: 1975)
Hugh Kenner, *Ulysses* (George Allen and Unwin: 1982)
Frank Kermode, *The Sense of an Ending* (Oxford U.P.: 1967)
Frank Kermode ed., *T.S. Eliot: Selected Prose* (Faber: 1975)
Frank Kermode, *An Appetite for Poetry* (HarperCollins: 1989)
Frank Kermode, *The Uses of Error* (HarperCollins: 1991)
Michael Levenson ed., *The Cambridge Companion to Modernism* (Cambridge U.P.: 2011)
Harry Levin ed., *The Essential James Joyce* (Penguin: 1963)
Wendy Martin ed., *The Cambridge Companion to Emily Dickinson* (Cambridge U.P.: 2002)
Helen McNeil ed., *Emily Dickinson: Selected Poems* (Everyman: 1997)
Louis Menand, *Discovering Modernism* (Oxford U.P.: 2007)
Will Norman, *Nabokov, History and the Texture of Time* (Routledge: 2012)
Norman Page ed., *Vladimir Nabokov: The Critical Heritage* (Routledge: 1982)
Michael Roberts ed., *The Faber Book of Modern Verse*, revised ed. Donald Hall (Faber: 1965)
Ian Robinson ed., *Geoffrey Hill: Essays on His Work* (Open U.P.: 1985)
Jacqueline Rose, *The Haunting of Sylvia Plath* (Virago: 1991)
Edward Said, *The World, the Text, and the Critic* (Harvard U.P.: 1983)
Charles Tomlinson ed., *William Carlos Williams: Selected Poems* (Penguin: 1976)
Helen Vendler, 'Wallace Stevens: Hypotheses and Contradictions', *Proceedings of the British Academy* Vol. 111: 2001
Nancy Walker ed., *Kate Chopin: The Awakening* (Bedford/St. Martin's: 2000)
Raymond Williams, *The Country and the City* (Chatto and Windus: 1973)
Edmund Wilson, *Axel's Castle* (Charles Scribner's Sons: 1931)
Virginia Woolf, *A Room of One's Own* (Hogarth Press: 1929)

9 Postmodernity and the contemporary novel 1970–2020

with Sam Cutting and Joel Roberts

Jeanette Winterson, Ali Smith, Sara Paretsky, Attica Locke, Thomas Pynchon, John Barth, Robert Coover, Kathy Acker, William Gibson, Octavia Butler, Russell Hoban, Toni Morrison, Ishmael Reed, Lauren Oyler

At the end of Chapter 7, we saw how Conrad's *Heart of Darkness* was crucial to the development of many postcolonial novels. One way of approaching the postmodern moment and the contemporary novel is to trace out, as Laura Marcus does, the impact more broadly of the landmark novelists of high modernism on the novels that follow in their wake ('wake' being the obvious word in the case of Joyce whose *Finnegan's Wake* exhausted the modernist novel). Marcus argues that the 'legacies of modernism [are] a matter of direct, rather than diffuse influences' (in Shiach ed. 2007: 82) and she shows how, in particular, Conrad, Joyce and Woolf lead directly to work by novelists as varied as B.S. Johnson, Doris Lessing, Paul Auster, Don DeLillo, Jeanette Winterson and Zadie Smith.

For instance, Marcus invokes both Angela Carter and Salman Rushdie on Joyce.

> Carter celebrated the legacies of Joyce in her *Expletives Deleted* (1993), writing that *Ulysses*, whose 'magisterial project: that of buggering the English language, the ultimate revenge of the colonialized' had set Carter herself free to 'treat the Word not as if it were holy but in the knowledge that is always profane' … *Ulysses* and [Rushdie's] *The Satanic Verses* have also opened up, at different ends of the century, the cultural meanings of 'obscenity' and 'blasphemy' respectively. For Homi Bhabha, 'blasphemy goes beyond the severance of tradition and replaces its claim to a purity of origins with a poetics of relocation and reinscription'. In an interview … [on] the day in which the fatwa against Rushdie was declared … Rushdie spoke of his fascination with the conflict between 'the sacred text and the profane text, between revealed literature and imagined literature'. He also explored the significance of the notion of 'doubt' as a defining aspect of cultural modernism.
>
> (89–90)

DOI: 10.4324/9781003127567-10

Rushdie, whose *The Satanic Verses* explicitly draws on *Ulysses*, put it like this.

> One of the things that happened to us in the twentieth century ... is to learn how certainty crumples in your hand ... Everything we know is pervaded by doubt and not by certainty. And that is the basis of the great artistic movement known as modernism.
>
> (90)

Emily Dickinson, as so often, said it well in the 1860s: 'a doubt if it be us / Assists the staggering mind'.

Jeanette Winterson's reflections (in 1996) on modernism's continuing relevance and impact come with her expression of debt to Woolf (and Gertrude Stein).

> The nineteenth-century novel, and I include in there 95 per cent of English novels written now ... is a loose overflowing slack-sided bag ... To assume that modernism has no relevance to the way that we need to be developing fiction now, is to condemn writers and readers to a dingy Victorian twilight.
>
> (92)

Marcus notes that Woolf's *Orlando* and Stein's *The Autobiography of Alice B. Toklas* are crucial to Winterson as they are fiction pretending to be memoir and autobiography as performance. Marcus quotes Winterson.

> I prefer myself as a character in my own fiction ... It may be that to understand ourselves as fictions, is to understand ourselves as fully as we can.
>
> (92)

Jeanette Winterson's first novel *Oranges Are Not the Only Fruit* and her recent memoir *Why Be Happy When You Could Be Normal?* form together a troubled (or indeed postmodern) intervention into notions of 'truth' and fiction. The novel, Winterson admitted, was a 'cover story' with inventions that 'cover with planks the deep drops I needed to pass off as solid ground' (in Allen and Simmons edd. 2014: 262), and the memoir, rather than simply instating the 'real' story, reinforces the compulsion to repeat of the traumatized, returning to the absent mother not as autobiographical 'explanation' but as what Sonya Andermahr calls the obsessive 'preoccupation with m/other love ... as a structuring principal of her writing, polymorphous and polyvalent'. Andermahr connects this with the findings of Julia Kristeva and Geoffrey Hartman.

> Kristeva discusses ... what she calls the loss of the archaic mother. This goes ... [back] to a loss suffered before entry into the symbolic order ... pointing towards a primitive self – wounded, incomplete and empty. According to Kristeva, this melancholy is beyond signification ... 'an

> unsymbolizable, unnameable narcissistic wound'. Winterson's sense of loss is of this kind: 'This is the old present, the old loss still wounding each day' … As a trauma narrative *Why Be Happy* explores what … Geoffrey Hartman has called 'the relation between psychic wounds and signification' … Winterson [powerfully] figures her sense of loss as a wound.
>
> (In Aughterson and Philips edd. 2021: 199–200)

Ali Smith's recent novel, *How to Be Both* (2014), her best to date, can be read as a postmodern re-engagement with a modernist classic. The novel presents two apparently quite separate narratives and stories, one set in Italy in the 1460s, the other in a contemporary England, both titled 'One', and which – at least on a second reading – unfold together an extraordinarily crafted and movingly interlineated story. In a marketing stroke of genius, Smith or her publishers distributed copies to bookshops with a randomized order of the two narratives, thereby destabilizing the linear traditions of reading itself. There is no 'right' order in which to read the two parts, though both ways will clearly offer different experiences, and complicate the demands of re-reading to 'get the plot' as well as that of the unfolding of time. Vladimir Nabokov's 1962 modernist masterpiece *Pale Fire* – notionally an edition of a poem with an unusually extended commentary – seems to be a consciously echoed antecedent with its two main sections in a deliberately uncertain relation with usual linear reading. Indeed, the 'editor' sternly advises us to read the book in the 'wrong' order: commentary first, then poem, then (!) commentary again.

One can move sideways here and think about recent examples of crime fiction in relation to the hard-boiled (quasi-modernist) tradition of Raymond Chandler. (We'll see below that, for Brian McHale, crime fiction is definitively modernist where science fiction is postmodernist.) Will Norman gives a vivid analysis of **Sara Paretsky**'s 1988 *Toxic Shock* (US title *Blood Shot*) and **Attica Locke**'s 2008 *Black Water Rising*. Both are set in large cities in the US in the 1980s and share a focus on 'corporate corruption and its responsibility for social inequalities, and the use of environmental pollution as a … figure for wider social harms'. Norman contrasts these eco-crime novels with the crime novel tradition as most clearly typified by Raymond Chandler.

> The most important ground they share is a rejection of classic hardboiled fiction's insistence on the violent autonomy of the white male protagonist. Rather, their female (Paretsky) and black (Locke) protagonists are shown to be deeply embedded in their respective communities, and indeed find in those communities reserves upon which they draw in order to fight corporate criminality.
>
> (In Jacobs ed. 2018: 96)

That stress on the collective community as the source for empowered political action is something this chapter will return to in a later section on the black postmodern novel.

Paretsky's *Toxic Shock* actually draws on Chandler's classic *The Big Sleep* but in a much more pointed political way. Humbolt Chemical has poisoned its employees with chemical by-products and created Chicago's polluted marsh, Dead Stick Pond (where a body is discovered).

> This location serves as the double of the Sternwood's oil sump in *The Big Sleep*, but in this case the space is a public one, and … as a toxic wasteland at the topographical heart of the South Side [it] takes the effects of crime into the realm of public health. In this way, by dragging the traditionally private crimes of the hardboiled novel into the public and making them visible, Paretsky is able to channel the impulses of social-democratic protest into the genre.
>
> (98)

In *Black Water Rising* oil, secretly stockpiled to manipulate its price, has disastrously seeped into the local community, but the title also refers to the repressed histories of black struggle re-emerging into the present. Norman shows how the connections between race, oil and capital are echoed in a powerful 2015 essay by Ta Nehisi Coates on racist policing and its roots in slavery.

> [The enslaved] were not bricks in your road, and their lives were not chapters in your redemptive history. They were people turned to fuel for the American machine.
>
> (Quoted in Jacobs ed. 2018: 100)

The oil in the novel is loose but thick and clings like a parasite. Norman says this, noting that Locke added a note to the paperback edition saying that in the 1980s (with the advent of neoliberal economics of Ronald Reagan in the US and Margaret Thatcher in the UK) the country was gripped in a 'collective fit of amnesia' over the 'wounds and hurt feelings of the 1960s and 70s'.

> For Locke, race and capital are fluid, unwelcome entities that can be made visible but remain ungraspable. They are external to the human but colour it. They remind us of the repressed stories we have been trying to forget, but which remain untellable … Why might it be in the interests of government and corporations for us to forget about the forms of collectivity, community and solidarity that structured the protests of the late 1960s and early 1970s?
>
> (100–01)

What is identifiable here, in tracing the influence of modernism on the postmodern moment, is a sense of questioning or challenging the very issue of representation itself. Whether Bhabha's description of Rushdie's poetics as one of 'relocation and reinscription', Carter's desire to write the 'profane', Winterson's sense of writing as a kind of wound, Smith's destabilized and anti-linear narratives, or Paretsky and Locke's stories of protest and the repressed, what broadly characterizes such writing is a challenge to the assumed validity of previous forms of literary representation.

Let's turn to **Thomas Pynchon**'s *Gravity's Rainbow*, which will help focus our discussion of postmodern literature and of the work of leading critics in the field.

At the beginning of this freewheeling 1973 novel about the end of the Second World War, the beginning of the Cold War and the commencement of the 'American century', Captain Geoffrey 'Pirate' Prentice dreams that he is being evacuated from London, as war planes scream across the sky above him. It is night-time as Prentice dutifully boards the evacuation train, surrounded by a cast of unnamed others 'pressed in around' him – 'feeble ones, second sheep, all out of luck and time: drunks, old veterans still in shock'. Here, Prentice and the other passengers are in the 'total blackout' of the war, undertaking an evacuation that is represented as at once monotonous ('they pass in line, out of the main station, out of downtown') and traumatic ('there is nothing to compare it to now').

Gravity's Rainbow begins, then, with strangers crammed together on a train experiencing an event both familiar and unknown. Yet Pynchon's representation of this event is not an unproblematically realist, or even modernist, one. The evacuation 'proceeds', but this procedure is 'all theatre', a 'spectacle'. As the train leaves the station, the narrator wonders, 'is this the way out?', and the question is answered shortly after: 'No, this is not a disentanglement from, but a progressive *knotting into*'. The evacuees soon realize that they are not being led away at all: 'The caravan has halted. It is the end of the line. All the evacuees are ordered out … There is no way out.' Prentice then wakes up and prepares his breakfast (1975, Picador edition: 3–4).

What we are given in the opening pages of *Gravity's Rainbow* is a disorienting array of images that raise a number of important questions about modern fiction. There is the question of the legacy of the Second World War, of how the events of 1939–45 shaped the world that was formed in its wake. Related to this is the question of history. The images of evacuation spliced together with provocative allusions to Nazi concentration camps are coupled both with the 'theatre' of the scene and the fact that it is a dream by a character who has a unique ability to experience the fantasies of others and then wake abruptly to prepare breakfast. There is a sense here that life is staged in some way, scripted, that our experiences are not really our own. Instead of the multiple, proliferating perspectives of a modernist such as Woolf or Joyce, in Pynchon we find a questioning of the very idea of perspective – of where it comes from and how it is constructed.

The introduction to *Gravity's Rainbow* condenses some key issues of the post-war period. The 'screaming across the sky' could easily be the sound of nuclear war, which seemed a real and present danger after the war, exemplified by events such as nuclear testing and the Cuban Missile Crisis of 1962. *Gravity's Rainbow* is set in Europe, as the war draws to a close, with its protagonist, the US Army lieutenant Tyrone Slothrop, under investigation for his unique ability to predict the site of Nazi rocket attacks with his sexual activity. As the novel progresses, we follow Slothrop as he traverses, as Steven Weisenberger notes, 'a Europe with no clear boundaries', with his exploits at one point taking him to the Potsdam Conference of 1945, in search of illicit substances (Weisenburger 2009: 100). Indeed, it is instructive that Slothrop stumbles into Potsdam, which was a conference between the USSR, the UK and the USA to decide what should happen to Germany and its surrounding nations following the surrender of German armed forces in early May. Three years later, Congress passed the Marshall Plan, which provided $13 billion toward the reconstruction and reshaping of Europe in the aftermath of the war. This is the Europe of *Gravity's Rainbow*; it is a place with 'no clear boundaries', a place that is being remade, and it is being done so by American forces, preparing the way for the 'American century'. *Gravity's Rainbow* also raises the issue of what Fredric Jameson called consumer society. In his assertion that the evacuation is 'all theatre', Pynchon evokes a sense of an engulfing, calculated performance – that we may well be trapped in an endless string of adverts, of performances calculated to stimulate our consumption of mass-produced goods.

All of this can be seen as involving urgent questions about representation and, more specifically, about writing. How does one write the possibility of nuclear annihilation, which is by definition unrepresentable? How does one write the history of industrialized slaughter? And how does one represent a society wherein everything seems to be a representation; that is, wherein everything seems so *mediated*, so calculated for our consumption? How does one write when everything around you appears to be a sign, a symbol laden with meaning, with an 'intent to communicate' as Pynchon puts it in his 1965 novella, *The Crying of Lot 49*?

Pynchon was not alone in facing these questions. Novels by **John Barth**, **Robert Coover** and **Kathy Acker** are other examples. Coover's 1977 *The Public Burning* fictionally re-creates the events leading up to the execution of Julius and Ethel Rosenburg, convicted of espionage in 1951. Coover's reimagining raises questions about the writing of history, suggesting that what we understand as 'reality' may itself be made up of narratives, tropes and motifs more commonly associated with 'fiction'. This is a concern explored by leading critics like the historian Hayden White in his 1973 *Metahistory*.

Barth's 1966 *Giles Goat-Boy* is an absurdist allegory of the Cold War, where the protagonist George Giles, raised by goats on a university farm after being found inside a giant supercomputer, must lead the West Campus in their struggle against their Eastern counterpart. Like Pynchon, Barth's displacement of the Cold War into an outlandish allegory raises the question of how – and whether – it can be represented at all. And Acker's 1984 *Blood and Guts in High School* challenges the representation of desire in capitalist culture through a parodic narrative that follows the teenage Janey as she engages in a sexual relationship with her father, has two abortions, joins a gang, is kidnapped, and eventually dies of cancer. Acker's novel is characteristically postmodern in its foregrounding of its own artifice and it challenges the sanitized images of people, places, and things that are so often used to encourage the consumption of commodities in capitalist society.

The work of each of these writers is often described as 'postmodern'. While the word simply gestures towards its place after the modern, its descriptive function is more nuanced and often ambivalent. Sometimes used derogatorily to indicate that a text is too playful, cynical or stylized, the most coherent thread through 'postmodern' literature is helpfully suggested by Maxine Greene's 1994 essay 'Postmodernism and the Crisis of Representation'. As Greene says, and as Pynchon shows in the opening pages of *Gravity's Rainbow*, it is a *crisis* of representation that postmodern literature interrogates, and, provocatively, represents.

Many critics have sought to untangle what Pynchon describes as the 'progressive knotting into' of postmodern literature. In his very influential 1984 article *Postmodernism, or, the Cultural Logic of Late Capitalism*, Fredric Jameson included Pynchon as an example of the cultural commodities produced by late capitalism. Jameson explores a question we touched on briefly earlier: that of the representation of history in Pynchon's writing. For Jameson, the structure of the global political economy went through a series of changes at the end of the Second World War. This is the world of 'consumer society' where life's daily necessities, problems and challenges can be resolved only by the purchase of commodities and which is the primary means by which people relate to one another. Jameson, elsewhere, says this.

> Following World War II a new kind of society began to emerge (variously described as postindustrial society, multinational capitalism, consumer society, media society and so forth). New types of consumption planned obsolescence: an ever more rapid rhythm of fashion and styling changes the penetration of advertising, television and the media generally to a hitherto unparalleled degree throughout society.
>
> (Jameson 1998: 19)

For Jameson, as 'advertising, television and the media' penetrate into society to an unprecedented degree, it becomes harder to imagine life differently. This poses particular problems for our collective understanding of history, which, Jameson argues, itself becomes a commodity, something that is stylized and aestheticized, manufactured and given an impressive sheen, but where all depth is lost. Jameson characterizes this loss of depth as the 'transformation of reality into images' and 'the fragmentation of "me" into a series of perpetual presents' (20). History, Jameson suggests, has 'become a vast collection of images', in a process he describes as 'the remarkable ... intensification of an addiction to the photographic image' (Jameson 1984: 66). Advertising turns history into an image.

Here's a clear and very sinister example of Jameson's point: in his celebrated 1964 poem 'For the Union Dead' (which we met in Chapter 1), Robert Lowell sees an advert for a commercial safe called 'Rock of Ages' that shows an image of Hiroshima 'boiling' after the nuclear blast – in which one of those safes survived.

What does it mean for history to be an image? Beginning with the rise of Hollywood in the 1920s, Jameson understands 'the image as commodity' (69). When people buy things, they are not buying the object itself as much as they are buying the image of the object and the feelings that image evokes. Often, the feeling is nostalgia; that it was better back then, that it was a simpler time, a less conflicted one. With the intense circulation of such images, our collective ability to learn from the past about how we might act in the present – and for Jameson, to act in the present is to seek to bring about a socialist alternative to capitalist exploitation – is diminished. We experience 'the waning … of our lived possibility of experiencing history in some active way' (68). This is 'the fragmentation of "me" into a series of perpetual presents': instead of being people who learn from the past how to act in the present, the culture of postmodernism only ever allows us to experience the present as a series of romanticized memories of the past, used to sell the products of consumer society.

For Jameson, works of postmodern fiction such as Pynchon's are symptomatic of this culture of the image. Pynchon's novels draw attention to this culture, emphasizing the characters' experiences as 'all theatre' and highlighting the commodities of everyday life circulating in the novel, as when a seltzer bottle is incredulously described as an 'interesting prop' that 'They' have planted (1975: 197). The ubiquity of these products means that their images pop up, seemingly unannounced, in the book itself.

The culture of the image is also present in the 'cinematic' plots of postmodern fiction, which draw together disparate events in imagistic and intensely visual terms that are 'cut into' and 'cut away' from in an aestheticized process. The opening scene of *Gravity's Rainbow* that we looked at earlier cuts from Prentice's dream into his awakening, a transition reminiscent of a cinematic dissolve. This cutting between scenes characterizes the novel's movement through its four parts as it takes in experiments in behavioural science, the development of rocket technology and weaponry, the Civil Rights Movement, German colonization of West Africa and the conclusion of the Second World War, all the while telling the story of Slothrop's attempts to understand who may be exercising control over his life. Significantly, *Gravity's Rainbow* concludes in the cinema. Is the book we have just read what is projected on the screen? Perhaps this is the theatre we are told of in the novel's opening. As Scott Simmon puts it, in *Gravity's Rainbow*, 'the reader has become [the] audience, the novel [has] become [the] film' (Simmon 1978: 347).

At a séance, early in the novel, the medium observes that 'a market needed no longer be run by the Invisible Hand, but now could *create itself* – its own logic, momentum, style, from *inside*. Putting the control inside was ratifying what de facto had happened – that you had dispensed with God. But you had taken on a greater, and more harmful, illusion. The illusion of control' (30). The market has become so all-consuming and powerful that it no longer even needs God; it controls itself, and draws everything outside into it, creating the 'illusion of control'. All of the novel's organizations are embroiled in the exploitation of the earth and its populations in a way that as readers we can never completely connect together; the entanglement is simply too much to unknot. History has become a series of images that diminish our capacity to act in the present. Pynchon's novel turns history into something fantastical, farcical and ultimately unknowable. Slothrop cannot conclusively decipher who has control over him and how. By the end of the novel, there are only a 'few who can still see Slothrop as any sort of integral creature at all. Most … gave up long ago trying to hold him together' (1975: 740).

We are given a web of events so complicated and entangled that it is perhaps difficult to feel anything other than overwhelmed when reading them. This, for Jameson, is the feeling of the 'postmodern sublime' (1984: 79). There are a number of unanswered questions of *Gravity's Rainbow*, such as: what happens to the theatre at the end of the novel? Is it hit by a rocket? Which one? Who are 'They'? How exactly do they operate? Do we meet all of them in the novel? In Jameson's reading, this indeterminacy is indicative of the engulfment of life by the late capitalist economy, coupled to its culture of the image. We can only ever receive history as something too overwhelming for comprehension, which prohibits us from knowing how to act in the present.

Let's turn now to another leading critic and to postmodern science fiction.

Brian McHale's *Postmodernist Fiction* (1987) establishes a different position from which to engage with the problems posed by and in modern fiction. McHale's central aim is to articulate the concept of postmodern fiction through carefully relating the broad notions of modernism, postmodernism and genre fiction. This is to emphasize that postmodern fiction cannot be readily delineated by a set of isolated conventions or poetic features. Rather, McHale emphasizes, like Jameson, the way postmodern fiction is historically oriented, wishing to 'emphasize the element of logical and historical consequence' between modernism and postmodernism (McHale 1987: 5). The important difference in McHale's work is that he challenges Jameson's claim for a central cultural logic governing postmodern fiction. In an interview in 2006, McHale articulated this difference.

> Despite Fredric Jameson's very persuasive attempts to make all postmodernism responsive to a single cultural logic, it's hard to do, and that probably has to do with the interference between, indeed the intersection between, so to speak, exterior history and the interior histories of each of these disciplines or practices, which are being driven by their own internal dynamics, at the same time that they're all subject and responding to the cultural logic of late capitalism. And out of that come these different chronologies, these different sequences, and different strands of development.
>
> (McHale and Neagu 2006)

The literary critical tool that McHale uses to address the notion of these 'interior histories' is termed the 'dominant' (from Russian Formalism). It is the 'focusing component' or idea which seems to dominate the work. The dominant is a way of conceiving of plurality in literary texts, one which acknowledges the impact of different historical contexts: 'different dominants emerge depending upon which questions we ask of the text, and the position from which we interrogate it'. For McHale, asking ourselves 'what is the focusing component or dominant for this work of fiction?' is more useful than attempting to label texts through a catalogue of features or by seeing texts in this period as merely defined by the culture of the image. Beginning by asking what appears to focus or *dominate* the work of fiction allows us to differently address the sorts of questions we asked at the start of this chapter and also ask how 'in the course of literary history one system has given way to another'. McHale also emphasizes the idea of the world as a contested term. 'What is a world? What kinds of world are there, how are they constituted, and how do they differ? What happens when different kinds of world are placed in confrontation, or when boundaries between worlds are violated?' (McHale 1987: 6–11).

You can see that McHale's approach to the question of modern fiction is very differently situated to Jameson's. McHale allows us greater plurality in our interpretations of texts and more flexibility in thinking about their historical and political relations with the world. McHale applies the terms *epistemological* and *ontological* in relation to modernist and postmodernist texts respectively. For modernist texts, questions of epistemology are dominant, whereas for postmodern texts ontological questions are dominant. At the start of the chapter, we saw that Laura Marcus highlighted the way epistemological doubt (doubting knowledge of the world) was central to Rushdie's understanding as a writer. Linking back to our previous questions, for McHale what is dominant in postmodern fiction is not the problem of knowing about the world, but the problem of the world itself (ontology): how to represent a world which continually questions the centrality or stability of its existence. If the focusing aspects of modernist texts were questions about what can be known and how such limits are present in the world, the focusing aspects of postmodern texts concern the foundations of the world which is the basis for the interrogation of such knowledge.

What McHale's conception allows for is the 'intersection' and 'interior histories' of different texts and genres and one of the most important overlaps and intersections for McHale is the genre of science fiction. He draws this parallel between science fiction and detective fiction.

> Science fiction, we might say, is to postmodernism what detective fiction was to modernism: it is the ontological genre par excellence (as the detective story is the epistemological genre par excellence), and so serves as a source of materials and models for postmodernist writers.
>
> (16)

Science fiction, suggests McHale, challenges the basis of the world like postmodern fiction, either by transporting us to a different world, or staging an encounter between worlds in its pages. We can return to the 'crisis of representation' identified at the start of this chapter. How might science fiction novels relate to Pynchon's sense of a 'progressive knotting into' in post-war fiction? And in what sense can science fiction address those questions of 'unrepresentable' events, like the horrors of war and the threat of nuclear annihilation? A more general way of thinking about this would be to ask how modern fiction addresses the representation of technology in the spectacle of life in late capitalism. If the problem of representing history is what seeds postmodern fiction, the problem of representing the ever-evolving technological future is its continued outgrowth into the 1980s and 1990s, moving into the internet novel, which we will address at the end of this chapter.

Neuromancer (1984) by **William Gibson** is a cyberpunk novel, a type of science fiction text which makes personal digital technology integral to its plot, its characters, and its overall aesthetic. Often such technology is of a cyborg nature, combining the organic with the technological within the human body. In the text, the protagonist, a hacker named Case, constantly 'jacks in' to a digital plain, with his disembodied consciousness projected into the 'consensual hallucination', a technological virtual reality (1984, Berkley edition: 5). There is a link here between Pynchon's sense of 'progressive knotting into' and the difficulty of escape, as well as the theatricality of experience that post-war fiction attempts to address. The experience of cyberspace in *Neuromancer* is a willed, desired hallucination, a total performance that allows characters to transcend their bodies. We could suggest it presents a form of escape from this 'knotting into', while also asking whether such an escape is sustainable. The transcendence that cyberspace provides is in constant conflict with the physical. Case wants to escape the 'meat space' of his body, in order to leave behind both his surveillance by the state and his mental illness. The near-future corporate dystopia that Case inhabits stages an encounter between exploitative economic systems, the human body and digital technology. Drawing on elements of detective and noir genres, the novel follows Case and his cyborg compatriot Molly Millions through a plot involving state conspiracy, underworld trading of technologically augmented body parts and supercomputer AIs.

We can see in reading *Neuromancer* how Jameson and McHale's ideas suggest different ways of thinking about postmodern texts. Jameson describes the novel as one that looks to reinforce the consumerist power of later capitalism, providing readers with 'the free-market deliria of cyberpunk, which assumes that capitalism is itself a kind of utopia of difference and variety' (Jameson 2012: 125). Cyberpunk is the ultimate 'imaging' of reality, a vivid and electrifying experience of the world which is lived as an intense, perpetual present. Indeed, Jameson refers directly in *Postmodernism* to the way that cyberpunk's attempts to represent technology highlight the networked logistics of late capitalism, the sheer difficulty of understanding anything before or after the mesmerizing moment of networked connection.

> Our faulty representations of some immense communicational and computer network are themselves but a distorted figuration of something even deeper, namely, the whole world system of a present-day multinational

> capitalism. The technology of contemporary society is therefore mesmerizing and fascinating not so much in its own right but because it seems to offer some privileged representational shorthand for grasping a network of power and control even more difficult for our minds and imaginations to grasp: the whole new decentered global network of the third stage of capital itself.
>
> (Jameson 1984: 37–38)

Jameson reads cyberpunk as 'shorthand' for the unrepresentable, 'global network' of capital. The encounters between characters, systems and technology in the novel are shadowed by loss or absence when it comes to their own history, or even the possibility of their future.

McHale's sense of the dominant would direct attention to the language of technology in the novel. The social consequences of new technologies are constantly highlighted in terms of markets, trading, specialist knowledge and criminality. A key question asked is how developing technologies might challenge or alter our ideas of what we understand as the human being, or human subject. One way of answering lies in the novel's conclusion, when Case buys a 'new pancreas and liver' and a new console computer (Gibson 1984: 270). His body is seemingly made human again by becoming biologically, internally complete. At the same time, the Neuromancer AI leaves Earth, transcending human civilization as a perfected technology, like a deity. The epistemological boundaries of the human, the ability to know the self, are reinstated in the protagonist Case, and the ontological boundaries of Earth are transcended by the disembodied technology.

What remains is the question concerning the present day of the novel. While cutting-edge technological systems remain stubbornly on Earth, how do we understand the ways they alter the world? And how might we continue to try and represent them? McHale's notion of the dominant reorients the reading towards the relationship of ontological categories of the human and the technological, rather than Jameson's sense that we must accept 'the whole decentred global network' as a kind of god which cannot be resisted or understood.

Octavia Butler stages the encounter between worlds, and transport to another world, very differently. She confronts the problem of representing possible futures beyond late capitalism, and the haunting presence of the violence of the past. Her novel *Dawn* (1987) also demonstrates a different approach to the problem of 'progressive knotting into'. The novel stages an ontological intervention which is cosmic in scale and allows us to ask how technology as a broad frame for human progress is present in postmodern fiction.

Dawn explores the need to rebuild the human race in the wake of nuclear apocalypse. Its protagonist is one of the last humans alive, Lilith. She wakes on an alien ship, that of the Oankali. They had saved a number of humans from Earth in order to help restore their race, storing them in stasis and waking them hundreds of years later. Lilith is tasked with choosing which human beings are to be released from stasis, to help rebuild human society under the influence and guidance of the Oankali. The notions of hierarchy, dominance and control are things that the Oankali try to remove from human beings in order that they might rebuild a more sustainable future for their race. As Lilith is told, 'your Earth is still your Earth, but between the efforts of your people to destroy it and ours to restore it, it has changed' (Butler 2012, Open Road edition: 34). Lilith struggles to even look at the Oankali initially, experiencing 'a true xenophobia' and an 'overwhelming panic' (23). The difficulty Lilith has in looking at this alien race who wish to restore her world speaks to the crisis of representation in postmodern fiction.

As the novel progresses, so does Lilith's understanding of this alien race. They are beyond human beings in many ways: they can perceive DNA differently and alter it with their bodies; their understanding of gender and sexual pleasure is entirely plural rather than binary; and they can cure and simultaneously instrumentalize the disease of cancer to aid technological development. Cancer in the novel represents both the damaging presence of hierarchy in the human race and its limited understanding of how technology might progress. The novel works through an ontological problem about the confrontation of the human world with an imagined world of different social and political possibilities. In *Dawn*, technological progress is not the pursuit of godliness, or only a part of the unfathomable network of late capital, but can be used in a process of restoring social life. Butler's response to the crisis of representation is to shift our perspective off Earth and to ask McHale's question 'what is a world?'

Where Gibson's novel speaks to the problem of representing new technology on Earth, Butler's is concerned with the way technology is a part of conceiving new worlds and ways of living, viewing the world from outside itself on an alien ship. But this is just one set of 'intersections', to use McHale's word. What other approaches to the crisis of representation can be seen in postmodern literature? If science fiction orients readers towards the problems of representing the future, how might other forms of fiction in the modern period orient the reader differently to the past?

A novel in the dystopian tradition, a tradition closely related to science fiction, may answer that question in a particularly eloquent way. This dystopian novel, like Butler's *Dawn* a post-nuclear imagining, is one that perhaps most terrifyingly and most brilliantly engages with the crisis of representation, posed in this case by the disintegration and painful reconstitution of the known English language, and the near impossibility of reading the fragments of that language that still co-exist. This is **Russell Hoban**'s *Riddley Walker* (1980).

This is also a novel that dramatizes two opposing ways of conceptualizing time and history, a dialectic that has deep roots in our culture and that emerges whenever cultural anxiety is at its most pervasive. This is certainly the case in the post-apocalyptic England of *Riddley Walker* (and presumably even more so in the world that led up to that apocalyptic nuclear war) and perhaps also today when some Western governments, like that currently in the UK, are so determined to survive (just to survive rather than do good in the world) through propagating populist narratives of fear, hatred and antagonism towards others (especially those less fortunate), as well as myths of vainglorious isolationism, to blind their citizens to the collaboration needed in the face of worldwide climate and pandemic threats. One of these two ways of thinking about time explicitly involves the making and cultural diffusion of history-denying myths.

David Cowart has written very well about *Riddley Walker* in the light of these ideas and, particularly, in the way they have been illuminated by the work of Mercia Eliade. Cowart sees the novel in terms of the conflict between what has come to be known as 'linear' and 'mythic' (or cyclical) historical models, but he adds that both models, in the novel, have been subsumed in what Eliade called the 'terror of history'. (Walter Benjamin, whom we met in Chapter 1, distinguished between sacred time and empty time.) Eliade, as we'll see below, noted that the myth of 'eternal return' can be found in advanced societies as well as Riddley's: it is what religion and archetypal cultural patterns underpinning literary genres (as identified by Northrop Frye) depend on, all of which in turn emerge from daily, seasonal and annual rhythms. Such a myth of eternal return may also help us understand the myth of England's solitary imperial prowess, as in the at least partly fictionalized history of the Second World War currently deployed in the 'culture wars' in the UK. Cowart says this about *Riddley Walker.*

> Hoban conceives of history as something tragically lost in this blighted future … He imagines a primitive society surrounded by evidence of its more civilized origins. Thus two antithetical conceptions of past time – primitive and civilized – coexist within the novel and constitute a dialectic in terms of which Hoban examines 'the terror of history' – Mircea Eliade's phrase for the suspicion or conviction that history answers to no transcendent rationale … The characters know about the advanced civilization that preceded them and half-remember that civilization's idea of history as a [linear] sequence of discrete events, the etiology of the present. At the same time, however, they embrace a mythic model of history … which Eliade calls 'archaic' or 'primitive', [and which] involves the periodic repudiation or transcendence of … historical time … Eliade refers to this idea of periodic reversion to a timeless beginning as the myth of the eternal return [and] notes … that the myth of eternal return also finds expression in advanced societies … The distinction between circular and linear historical models matters less than the distinction between perceptions of history as the expression of some transcendent or divine will or as something essentially meaningless, however self-perpetuating. Unfortunately, says Hoban, echoing Eliade, humanity in its sophistication proves less and less able to interpret history – whether cyclical or linear – as the reflection of any vast but coherent purpose. As one contemplates the bloody ebb and flow of human events … one may begin to recognize intimations of a blind, oppressive, random-yet-deterministic mechanism. One experiences the terror of history.
>
> (Cowart 1989: 83–85)

The myth within the myth that Lorna tells Riddley – 'Why the dog won't show its eyes' (Ch. 3) – is a particularly deft and brilliant version of the Christian Fall, also deployed within this primitive society to 'explain' and, as all myths do, relieve anxiety about how the current new Stone Age came about. It has a powerful evocation of what current eco-critics like Jonathan Bate (see Chapter 1) have identified as the formative Golden Age myth, which our current ecological anxiety needs to remember: Lorna's story starts with the dog (and by implication nature generally) working in harmony with the first man and woman, a mutual nurturing that was 'the good time' before human greed and competition emerged, alienating ourselves from our natural home.

It is one of the most moving moments in modern fiction and typical of Hoban's audacious treatment of history. Within a few sentences it telescopes the story of our species from hunter-gathering, through settling and agriculture, to industrial capitalism (with 'boats in the air' and 'picters on the wind') up to the nuclear catastrophe. It has its echo (in terms of both understanding and not understanding) in the moment when Riddley and a friend find themselves inexplicably weeping as they stand next to the 'power-ring', the still humming nuclear reactor that presumably was crucial to the war that ended their (and potentially our) wars. The novel's great cry is Riddley's 'O, what we ben! And what we come to!' (Ch. 12). And the devastated landscape of the new Stone Age landscape of this futuristic novel is also, of course, an ecological as well as a political warning.

We'll turn now to the critical work of Linda Hutcheon and Daniel Grausam to help us think more about the postmodern novel.

McHale critiqued Jameson's formulation of postmodernism on the grounds that different arts have different internal logics, different ways of understanding themselves and of developing as disciplines, that cannot be reduced to a singular 'cultural logic'. This we can understand as a *formalist* reading of postmodern literature. But Jameson's approach to postmodernism has been critiqued in other ways. Linda Hutcheon, for example, has developed an alternative understanding of the relationship between history and postmodern literature. For Hutcheon, the trait most commonly associated with postmodern literature – that it is aware of its own artifice – is a quality that has been present in storytelling at least since Ancient Greece. Hutcheon reads the myth of Narcissus, fascinated by his own reflection, as allegorical of the process of narrative itself. For Hutcheon, this self-fascination is re-discovered by postmodern novelists after what she provocatively describes as the 'aberration' of 19th century realism. She argues that fiction has long been interested in its own artifice, as is evident in *Don Quixote* and *Tristram Shandy* (Hutcheon 1980: 40).

Nonetheless, postmodern fiction does have important consequences for our understanding of history. In her 1988 *A Poetics of Postmodernism*, Hutcheon contends that postmodern literature does more than mine the past to make it into a product to be sold in the face of late capitalism's complexity. Rather, the engagement of postmodern literature with the past asks critical questions like: who gets to write about the past? What language are we given to understand it? What makes the past 'past'? Who decides what matters about the past and what doesn't? Postmodern literature interrogates the way the past is *constructed* in the present, and the political questions that this construction raises. Hutcheon says this.

> It is true ... that postmodern art does not offer what Jameson desires, a 'genuine historicity' ... as 'ultimate objects'. But its deliberate refusal to do so is not a naïve one: what postmodernism does is to contest the very possibility of our ever being able to *know* the ultimate objects of the past. It teaches and enacts the recognition of the fact that the social, historical, and existential reality of the past is *discursive* reality when it is used as the referent of art, and so the only 'genuine historicity' becomes that which would openly acknowledge its own discursive, contingent identity.
>
> (Hutcheon 1988: 24)

If postmodern literature seems to lack a concrete comprehension of the past, as a series of well-understood events that can lead to action in the present, this is not because the past has simply become a product. Rather, it is because postmodern literature understands that the past is something that is consistently reconstructed in the present, that literature is an important site of this reconstruction, and that the present reconstruction of the past raises some questions that need answering before 'the past' can be spoken about with any kind of easy certainty.

For this self-conscious relationship to the past that Hutcheon finds in postmodern literature, she coined the term 'historiographic metafiction', by which she means the self-conscious writing of history. For Hutcheon, this is what postmodern literature does and this is how she reads Pynchon's fiction. She puts it like this.

> Pynchon's obsession with plots – narrative and conspiratorial – is an ideological one: his characters discover (or make) their own histories in an attempt to prevent themselves from being the passive victims of the commercial or political plots of others.
>
> (Hutcheon 1988: 120–21)

As Slothrop journeys through *Gravity's Rainbow*, he becomes increasingly aware of the shadowy institutions trying to impose themselves on him, with their murky, clandestine existence summed up through the ambiguous reference to them as the 'They-system'. For Hutcheon, Slothrop's paranoia is an attempt to exercise some control over his life by discerning the forces that have shaped it. This slant on the paranoid, conspiratorial thinking of postmodern literature is different from Jameson's. Rather than being a failure to adequately comprehend the capitalist dynamics shaping the world, it is instead an attempt to understand the historical memories shaping the present. Slothrop needs to understand his past, in order to understand his present, though doing the former is no easy task. Slothrop's story illustrates Hutcheon's point – that postmodern literature is about both the necessity and the difficulty of understanding history.

'History', as Pynchon reminds us, 'is not woven by innocent hands' (1975: 277). *Gravity's Rainbow* draws attention to the artifice of history, to its construction. It's not simply 'there' for us to uncover but rather woven, put together, constructed, and not 'by innocent hands'. For Hutcheon, Pynchon's novels present history in this contingent way, as something that flickers in and out of focus, in order to demonstrate that history is not fixed, that our collective understanding of what happened in the past is changeable and that how we understand it is a political act.

Pynchon offers an alternative memory of the Second World War to the popular perception of it in America at the time. For Pynchon, 'the mass nature of wartime death' is popularly remembered in a way that teaches children: 'History as sequences of violence, battle after battle, [in order to] be more prepared for the adult world' (1975: 105). Indeed, when *Gravity's Rainbow* was published, heroic narratives of American heroes in the Second World War were in effect the cultural arm of military recruitment for the Cold War. However, for Pynchon, World War Two need not be this tool for preparing children for the 'inevitability' of conflict. Instead, it could be remembered that 'the real business of the War is buying and selling' (105), as the narrator informs us and as is suggested by the profits accruing to weapons manufacturers in the novel. Perhaps one of the reasons Slothrop never conclusively discovers who 'They' are is because 'they' are nothing more than the profiteering arms manufacturers and resource companies he encounters on the way.

Hutcheon's central proposition, that the writing of history is a political act, one in which literature is implicated, and foregrounded by postmodern literature, is also explored in Daniel Grausam's 2011 *On Endings*. Surveying the critical landscape of postmodern fiction and its evident, if evidently complicated, relationship to history, Grausam says this.

> Somewhere behind Jameson's wholesale rejection of the idea that postmodern texts might be capable of representing history as anything other than depoliticized pastiche and Hutcheon's celebration of postmodernism's historiographic interests is a story waiting to be told about the historical pressures that led to this complicated relationship to history in the first place.
>
> (Intro. Grausam 2011: online ed.)

The question Grausam asks is: is there something historical about postmodern literature's attention to history? For answers to this question, Grausam turns to the Cold War. Here, Grausam reads another of Pynchon's novels, *The Crying of Lot 49*, published in 1965. This follows a woman named Oedipa Maas as she attempts to execute the will of her former lover, Pierce Inverarity. As in *Gravity's Rainbow*, Oedipa never completely gets to the bottom of the mystery she begins to unveil in the process, unsure whether the secret postal system she has discovered actually exists or is a trick played posthumously on her by Pierce, or simply the product of her overactive imagination.

Grausam links this lack of closure to the Cold War context in which the novel was published. Images of nuclear apocalypse abound in the novel but there is no actual apocalypse. Indeed, there is no satisfactory ending to the novel at all. For Grausam, this is a symptom of the novel's attempt to represent the unrepresentable possibility of nuclear war. This is because 'such revelation can never arrive; we can only wait for it in the knowledge that the end offered by total nuclear war will be one we can't even experience as an end' (Ch. 2). Like Hutcheon, Grausam finds a more ambiguous relationship between postmodern fiction and its social and economic contexts than Jameson does, suggesting that the often-incoherent endings of such novels are representative of the climate of potentially imminent apocalypse that characterized the Cold War. Grausam finds this narrative technique – of building toward a seemingly impossible resolution – to be evident not only in Pynchon but also in Coover's *The Public Burning,* with its sense that loss for the United States in the trial of Julius and Ethel Rosenburg would also represent the unthinkable loss of the Cold War, as well as in John Barth allegorizing the Cold War in *Giles Goat-Boy*. For Grausam, the prominence of metafictional techniques in post-war American literature is intimately related to the unrepresentability of the Cold War.

There is another history of the knowing, metafictional techniques of postmodern literature, which offers an alternative understanding to the ones we have explored so far. This other history is the deployment of metafictional, 'postmodern' techniques in black literature. This affinity is explored in Madelyn Jablon's 1997 *Black Metafiction* and was outlined earlier by Henry Louis Gates Jnr in his 1988 *The Signifying Monkey*. These critics note that whilst the techniques associated with postmodern fiction, as analysed above, are central to the black literary tradition, the relationship between them has remained little discussed. As Jablon puts it, 'Hutcheon … acknowledges the work of **Ishmael Reed** and Clarence Major as metafiction but omits discussion of the tradition of self-consciousness in African-American literature' (Jablon 1997: 5).

The practice of 'historiographic metafiction' is often a central concern in black literature. For example, Ishmael Reed's 1972 *Mumbo Jumbo* draws together multiple forms of writing, such as the filmic, the academic and the visual, as it reimagines the Harlem Renaissance through a detective story about the attempts of the elite 'Wallflower Order' to suppress 'Jes Grew', which represents the black culture of the Renaissance. In its narrative and presentation, *Mumbo Jumbo* draws attention to the written-ness of history, to its textual quality, as well as to its political implications, particularly in the attempts of the Wallflower Order to get Warren Harding elected as President, in the belief that he will help them to suppress Jes Grew. With a narrative as fantastical and eccentric as *Gravity's Rainbow* (which was published one year later), *Mumbo Jumbo* likewise emphasizes that history is constructed by the way it is told, by who gets to tell it, and by what is considered to be 'legitimate' historical knowledge. It diverges from *Gravity's Rainbow* by drawing attention to the artifice of the dominant, institutional histories of black people and black life. The Wallflower Order (which is a parody of the Ivy League) attempts to suppress alternative histories and modes of artistic creation in favour of those that are institutionally sanctioned and legitimated.

The work of **Toni Morrison** can also be productively read as historiographic metafiction. Her 1987 novel *Beloved* self-consciously rewrites the 19th century slave narrative. Drawing on the true story of a woman called Margaret Garner, who escaped from slavery in pre-Civil War America, the novel is centred on a woman called Sethe, who kills her child so that she is not returned to slavery when they are caught. *Beloved* rewrites the slave narrative by troubling the timeline of the move from slavery to freedom, telling the story through flashbacks and hauntings that work to undermine this distinction. The novel is also metafictive. María Lourdes López Ropero describes the novel in this way.

> [It is] intensely self-conscious about the way in which [its characters] toil to construct and come to terms with their past … [as in] Sethe's comparison of remembering to the daily activity of 'working dough'.
>
> (Ropero 1999: 175–76)

To remember is to work – to construct, to build, and to (re-)create in the present. Both Morrison's characters and the novel itself know that they are constructing the past in and through memory and in the awareness that memory is written, constructed in and through the texts that record it.

In addition to reflecting Hutcheon's historiographic metafiction, the black literary tradition is also concerned with issues raised by McHale's theory of the dominant. One way we can understand the history of this tradition is through the shift McHale identifies from questions of epistemology (modernism) to ontology (postmodernism). Henry Louis Gates Jnr notes that this is central to the relationship between *Mumbo Jumbo* and two earlier novels that it draws on. These are Richard Wright's *Native Son* (1940) and Ralph Ellison's *Invisible Man* (1952). Gates explores their intertextual lineage.

> Whereas Ellison tropes the myth of presence in Wright's title of *Native Son* and *Black Boy* through his title of *Invisible Man,* Reed parodies all three titles by employing as his title the English-language parody of black language itself.
>
> (Gates 1988: 221)

We can see again the process observed at the beginning of the chapter: from the realist depiction of African-American life in the industrial North in the early 20th century in *Native Son*, to the modernist reimagining of this experience in *Invisible Man*, to the postmodernist intensification of this modernist moment in *Mumbo Jumbo*. In each case we move, as Gates observes, one step further away from an easily graspable 'presence'. Each text moves further towards the acknowledgement of the role of literature in the constructedness of experience. The 'native son' becomes the 'invisible man' becomes 'mumbo jumbo' – becomes language, the product of representation rather than something that precedes it.

One key question that follows is whether the black literary tradition critiques, extends and perhaps even exceeds typical postmodern critical frameworks. For Gates, the aesthetic innovations of African-American literature cannot primarily be related to the overwhelming circulation of images in post-war consumer society (Jameson), to the evolution of the 'dominant' in the literary tradition (McHale), to the historiographic metafictive impulse of writing itself (Hutcheon) or to a critique of the nuclear threat underlying the Cold War (Grausam). For Gates, the 'postmodern' aesthetic of African-American literature is traceable to the signifying tradition of the 'trickster' figure of black mythology. This figure features 'prominently in the mythologies of Yoruba cultures found in Nigeria, Benin, Brazil, Cuba, and Haiti, among others' (Gates 1988: xxi), and is part of the cultural practices that survived the brutality of the Middle Passage.

Gates outlines two key qualities of the trickster found in the myths told about them. They 'privilege both the figurative and the ambiguous' and are indicative of 'the indeterminacy of interpretation' (22). It is this tradition on which Reed and Morrison draw, over and above any other historical or philosophical causality that might explain their work. Gates's understanding of the 'postmodern' qualities of African-American literature as part of the signifying tradition of the trickster of black mythology focuses on the literary history to which such literature belongs.

Another way of thinking about the postmodern aesthetic in black literature is presented in Fred Moten's analysis of the relationship between blackness and performance. His book *In the Break* (2003) analyses a range of black cultural and political performances in the light of two key issues: first, to explore the ways that they resist the violent conditions in which they take place, as in the violence of a slave master or the violence of an expectant white gaze; and second, to suggest that it is something about this resistance – namely, its collective, sensuous quality – that such violence seeks to eliminate. Moten is particularly interested in what can be learned about resistant black performance by *listening* to it, by focusing on the aural, and much of *In the Break* deals with 20th century black music. It is in this analysis that we can find another way of understanding black metafiction.

In a survey of the latter part of Marvin Gaye's career, Moten makes this observation.

> The call to sing that is song, that whole so-called postmodern, metafictional, improvisational arrangement, the internalization of call and response in the form of a deconstruction and reconstruction of the song and of the song form itself: this is an integral part of 1960s black popular music but goes all the way back to the complex and unavailable origins of black performance. Again, something like this self-reflexive [rearrangement] is often cited as a hallmark of so-called postmodern art, though its often more subtle and sophisticated parallel or antecedent is never thought within the context of investigations of postmodernism.
>
> (Moten 2003: 228)

For Moten, the metafictional qualities of postmodern art are inherent to black performance itself. Across *In the Break*, Moten explores the irreducibly collective nature of such performances; they desire and require others to participate in order to take shape. It is in this gesture toward the collective production of the performance that Moten locates the postmodern aesthetic of black art. The desire for the performance to be a collective one produces the kind of reflexivity we associate with postmodernism; the awareness of the artifice of what one is constructing signals a kind of checking or revision that is also an invitation to participate, to help with its construction. This is simultaneously a matter of survival, as with the cry for help in situations of extreme brutality, as well as a radical political act, as it calls for participation in the production of something common and shared, rather than private and individual.

Moten's analysis of the relationship between the postmodern aesthetic and black performance gives us another way of understanding black metafiction. If we read these texts as undertaking a kind of performance, and more specifically of performing certain *gestures*, then their postmodern features take on a different quality. Morrison's historiographic metafiction of plantation slavery and its aftermath becomes an invitation to understand history as something collective, as something made together in the present because of the memory of lives that were lived together in the past. Reed's focus on 'mumbo jumbo' – on the constituting powers of language in relation to identity – works as an invitation to the collective usage of language towards the production of new and alternative ways of relating to one another and the world around us. Moten explains what black performance does and doesn't contain.

> [Not] incredulity toward narratives of transcendence that is said by some to characterize canonical postmodernism, to accompany the fiction's ironic self-reflexiveness or self-*destruktive* inward turns, [but it rather contains] a vicious critique, but never an abandonment, of these narratives and their destinations – freedom and … pleasure.
>
> (228)

If *Mumbo Jumbo* parodies the authentic vernaculars of *Native Son* and *Invisible Man*, then this is 'critique' rather than 'abandonment' of the freedom and pleasure available through the collective shaping and reshaping of language in black performance.

For the final section of this final chapter, we look at the treatment of time in postmodernism, the new genre of the internet novel and how it brings fresh problems of representation.

The latest 'turn' in the relation between the novel and postmodernity is (with some predictability) the so-called internet novel. We'll explore this very soon but it may be helpful first to share with you what Mark Currie, a leading narrative theorist, has identified as the importance of three concepts in approaching the treatment of time in postmodern literary culture and theory. These three topics of what Currie calls 'epochal temporality' are: 'time-space compression' (following David Harvey's 1989 *The Condition of Postmodernity*), 'archive fever' (following Jacques Derrida's 1998 book of that name) and 'accelerated recontextualization' (in Jacobs ed. 2018: 24–26). The first of these derives from the simple historical observation that temporal experience is subject to the accelerated speed possible across the globe and the ensuing contraction of space, that contraction increasing with modernity. Archive fever for Derrida, says Currie, is 'a kind of psychic illness that frantically archives and preserves everything' but in the way opposite to what may have been assumed, in so far as postmodernity insists that 'the archive produces the event that it purports to record' (25). And 'recontextualization' is 'accelerated' in the sense that the gap between an original (as, for instance, in fashion) and its recycling in new contexts has drastically shrunk with the effect of making labels like retro or even irony unclear.

All three are of course intimately connected with new media and digital technologies and they share the anxiety consequent on the elimination of delay and the increased importance of the notion of uncertainty which Currie calls the 'core idea in our new epochal temporality'. Our modernity is a period convinced that the future is somehow blocked and felt as a kind of repetition in which 'the very concept of originality is under suspicion, where all that remains open to us is to endlessly repeat, recycle and reconstrue the cultural forms of the past' (36). This is Frederic Jameson's perpetual present. Whether events in the new millennium like the 9/11 terrorist attacks in New York in 2001 or the global financial crash of 2008 have – as has been argued – unblocked history remains in question. The ever more urgent climate crisis must also question any model of time based on uncertainty.

Ryan Ruby explored the development of the internet novel in a recent online article (also excerpted in Chapter 1 of this book) from *New Left Review* in which he reviewed *Fake Accounts*, the debut novel by the (reportedly very fierce) critic **Lauren Oyler**. Ruby says this.

> For over two hundred years, [the realist novel] has managed to adapt to the radical transformations of modernity: the nuclearization of the family, the entry of women into public life, the liberalization of sexual mores, industrialization and deindustrialization, urbanization and suburbanization, secularization, the life-worlds of dominated classes and colonized nations, war on a planetary scale, and new conceptions of cognition and identity formation … But over the last decade or so it has become clear that changes in the texture of the contemporary itself, due primarily to the diffusion of digital networked media, have begun to strain the capacity of the novel – as an institution, as a medium, as a form – to fulfil its traditional remit.
>
> (Ruby 2021: online)

Ruby says this partly explains the growth and prestige of genre fiction at the expense of the 'literary' (and realist) novel which is faced with additional new technical challenges, particularly what Ruby (following Fredric Jameson) calls 'the collective representation problem'.

> How can any of the narrative perspectives available to realist fiction function … for the perspectives of the hundreds of millions of users on a single social media platform? … The name [Internet novel] betrays … an uneasy recognition that the Internet is not merely an object, nor is being online simply an activity, but that taken together they [represent] a series of social relations so extensive and intensive that they have contaminated all the other objects of potential representation too.
>
> (Ruby 2021: online)

Ryan's identification of the internet as a contamination of the objects of representation brings us into a set of problems concerning representation that is similar to but different from those we've explored through Pynchon and other novelists in this chapter here. It is a Jamesonian observation, in the sense that the internet is 'so extensive and intensive' that it is difficult to comprehend or effectively represent. Conversely, a reading inspired by McHale might suggest that internet novels are presenting the very form of technology as the dominant concern. The internet novel poses a further set of ontological problems for the novel in the 21st century, but such problems can also be seen as yet another version of the 'knotting into' of writing, representation and history.

And that might be an appropriately open-ended way of finishing this chapter, and indeed this book.

Works cited

Nicola Allen and David Simmons edd., *Reassessing the Twentieth-Century Canon* (Palgrave: 2014)

Kate Aughterson and Deborah Philips edd., *Women Writers and Experimental Narratives* (Palgrave: 2021)

David Cowart, *History and the Contemporary Novel* (Southern Illinois U.P.: 1989)

Jacques Derrida, *Archive Fever* trs. Eric Prenowitz (Chicago U.P.: 1998)

Henry Louis Gates Jnr, *The Signifying Monkey: A Theory of African-American Literary Criticism* (Oxford U.P.: 1988)

Daniel Grausam, *On Endings: American Postmodern Fiction and the Cold War* (Virginia U.P.: 2011)

Maxine Greene, 'Postmodernism and the Crisis of Representation', *English Education* Vol. 26, Issue 4: December 1994

David Harvey, *The Condition of Postmodernity* (Blackwell: 1989)

Linda Hutcheon, *Narcissistic Narrative: The Metafictional Paradox* (Wilfrid Laurier U.P.: 1980)

Linda Hutcheon, *A Poetics of Postmodernism: History, Theory, Fiction* (Routledge: 1988)

Madelyn Jablon, *Black Metafiction: Self-Consciousness in African-American Literature* (Iowa U.P.: 1997)

Richard Jacobs ed., *Teaching Narrative* (Palgrave: 2018)

Fredric Jameson, 'Postmodernism, or, the Cultural Logic of Late Capitalism', *New Left Review* Vol. 146: July–August 1984
Fredric Jameson, *The Cultural Turn: Selected Writings on the Postmodern 1983–1998* (Verso: 1998)
Fredric Jameson, 'In Soviet Arcadia', *New Left Review*, Vol. 75: 2012
Brian McHale, *Postmodernist Fiction* (Routledge: 1987)
Brian McHale and Adriana Neagu, 'Literature and the Postmodern: A Conversation with Brian McHale', *Kritikos* Vol. 3: May 2006. Accessed 29 June 2021 <https://intertheory.org/neagu.htm>
Fred Moten, *In the Break: The Aesthetics of the Black Radical Tradition* (Minnesota U.P.: 2003)
María Lourdes López Ropero, 'Beating Back the Past: Toni Morrison's Beloved as Historiographic Metafiction', 1999. <http://institucional.us.es/revistas/philologia/13_2/art_19.pdf>
Ryan Ruby, 'Reading the Room', *New Left Review: Sidecar* 22 February 2021
Morag Shiach ed., *The Cambridge Companion to the Modernist Novel* (Cambridge U.P.: 2007)
Scott Simmon, 'Beyond the Theatre of War: Gravity's Rainbow as Film', *Literature/Film Quarterly* Vol. 6, Issue 4: Fall 1978
Steven Weisenburger, 'In the Zone: Sovereignty and Bare Life in Gravity's Rainbow', *Pynchon Notes* Issue 56–57: Spring–Fall 2009
Hayden White, *Metahistory: The Historical Imagination in Nineteenth Century Europe* (Johns Hopkins U.P.: 1973)

Index

Richard Jacobs Literature and the Critics